SF:UK

HOW BRITISH SCIENCE FICTION
CHANGED THE WORLD

SF:UK

HOW BRITISH SCIENCE FICTION CHANGED THE WORLD

DANIEL O'BRIEN

WITH AN INTRODUCTORY CHAPTER BY KIM NEWMAN

CONSULTING EDITOR: MAX CARLISH

Reynolds & Hearn Ltd
London

LATER

ACKNOWLEDGEMENTS

Grateful thanks to Charlie Baker, Alan Barnes, Max Carlish, Mark Gatiss, David Hanks, Marcus Hearn, John Herron, Felix Katz, Gary Kramer, Jules McNally, David Miller, Joe McIntyre, Simon Middleton, Kim Newman, David O'Leary, Richard Reynolds, Jonathan Rigby, Adrian Rigelsford and Stephen Richards.

Grateful thanks also to the interviewees for the television series SF:UK: Gerry Anderson, Steve Aylett, Roy Ward Baker, David Bishop, Anthony Daniels, Malcolm Edwards, Marcus Hearn, Stephen Jones, Nigel Kneale, Roger Levy, Kim Newman, Justina Robson and Joss Whedon. All opinions expressed in this book, except those quoted as direct speech, belong to the authors.

Frontispiece: *The first flying saucer? Gulliver encounters the Flying Island of Laputa. From T Morton's nineteenth century illustrated edition of* **Gulliver's Travels.**

First published in 2000 by
Reynolds & Hearn Ltd
61A Priory Road
Kew Gardens
Richmond
Surrey TW9 3DH

A CIP catalogue record for this book is available from the British Library.

ISBN 1-903111-16-1

Designed by Peri Godbold

Printed and bound in Great Britain by MPG Books Ltd, Bodmin, Cornwall.

CONTENTS

FOREWORD

We Brits have always been pretty morbid. For us the future is as full of demons as it is of angels. Perhaps that's why our stories of future of possibility – our science fiction – have captured the imagination of the world.

This nightmarish quality gave me the original idea for the series and the book SF:UK – an exploration of the genetic code of British SF from its conception and earliest moments to the most contemporary examples I could find.

Incredibly, it's the first ever history of its kind. But perhaps that's a feature of our modesty as Brits, or even our shame of a genre that has suffered its fair share of bullying in the cultural playground.

Whatever the reason, the opportunity to create such an ambitious project, albeit on scarce resources in the face of many obstacles, was irresistible.

It's a project that's been brewing for many years. I've been watching science fiction since I was a babe in arms. One of my earliest memories was falling asleep on my mother's lap during the millennial masterpiece 2001: A Space Odyssey. Mind you, I was four years old. And I know quite a few adults who have struggled to stay awake for the whole 160 minutes...

But just like Brave New World, where people are brainwashed in their sleep, 2001 made me want more stories about space, computers and aliens.

I'm sure I twigged quite early on that the stories made in Britain didn't often have happy endings. But that made them even better. Because becoming a teenager in the dying years of the Cold War meant that tales of global invasion and bleak Fascist states matched my mood of cynicism and sense of alienation.

Buck Rogers, The Bionic Man and the crew of Star Trek could do all they wanted to keep the future safe. But the darker cadences of Doctor Who, 2000 AD and V for Vendetta seemed far more scary and compelling.

SF:UK attempts to get to the roots of this philosophical pessimism. But at the same time it is a celebration of our very British obsession with progress and the future. It's an examination of the many wonderful books, TV shows, comics, movies and people who made British science fiction a global phenomenon.

In the television series, my presenter Matthew D'Abaitua has helped me to realise the vision on screen and I owe a large debt of gratitude to him. I am similarly grateful to the associate producer Jules McNally.

As for the book – the results speak for themselves, but I would like to thank Kim Newman and Daniel O'Brien for their superlative work on the text and especially Richard Reynolds and Marcus Hearn for their support and for the excellent job they have done on SF:UK – How British Science Fiction Changed the World.

Max Carlish
Producer and director, SF:UK
London, September 2000

INTRODUCTION

"No one would have believed in the last years of the nineteenth century that this world was being watched keenly and closely by intelligences greater than man's and yet as mortal as his own; that as men busied themselves about their various concerns they were scrutinised and studied, perhaps almost as narrowly as a man with a microscope might scrutinise the transient creatures that swarm and multiply in a drop of water. With infinite complacency men went to and fro over this globe about their little affairs, serene in their assurance of their empire over matter. It is possible that the infusoria under the microscope do the same. No one gave a thought to the older worlds of space as sources of human danger, or thought of them only to dismiss the idea of life upon them as impossible or improbable. It is curious to recall some of the mental habits of those departed days. At most terrestrial men fancied there might be other men upon Mars, perhaps inferior to themselves and ready to welcome a missionary enterprise. Yet across the gulf of space, minds that are to our minds as ours are to those of the beasts that perish, intellects vast and cool and unsympathetic, regarded this earth with envious eyes, and slowly and surely drew their plans against us. And early in the twentieth century came the great disillusionment."

H G Wells, *The War of the Worlds* (1898)

Herbert George Wells, *whose novels included* The Time Machine (1895), The Island of Doctor Moreau (1896) The Invisible Man (1897) *and* The War of the Worlds (1898).

Put it down to an insular, island mentality, the loss of the empire, dwindling global/economic significance, uncertain national identity, lingering resentment over the industrial revolution or race memories of long ago invasions (of the terrestrial variety). Whatever the reason, the British imagination tends to exhibit a peculiarly morbid streak, suggesting a fairly pessimistic nation. Even our legends undermine any hint of an idyllic golden age with a strong dose of disillusion.

Take the saga of King Arthur, probably the best known and certainly the most potent of British myths. Having drawn the sword Excalibur from the stone, founded the Camelot order of knights and brought peace to a war ravaged land, the Once and Future King might have expected to live happily ever after. Instead, he's betrayed by his wife and best friend, seduced by his evil half sister and finally killed by his incestuous bastard son. All this while his kingdom descends into famine and anarchy. Aside from a guest appearance in 2000 AD comic, we're still waiting for the big comeback.

Similarly, our visions of the future evoke disaster as often as triumph, the monstrous as much as the miraculous. As embodied in British science fiction, this distinctive national trait has gripped and inspired the imagination of the whole world for nearly two centuries. From Mary Shelley's 1818 novel *Frankenstein* onwards – through *Dr Jekyll and Mr Hyde*, *The War of the Worlds*, *The Quatermass Experiment* and *Doctor Who* – British science fiction poses the age-old question 'What if?' and answers with the stuff of nightmare. When Shelley's idealistic medical student embarks on the creation of an artificial lifeform, the outcome never looks good. Robert Louis Stevenson's Henry Jekyll succeeds in isolating the savage, bestial side of human nature, only to discover that it cannot be controlled.

H G Wells's chronicles of alien contact (*The War of the Worlds*), drug experimentation (*The Invisible Man*), time travel (*The Time Machine*) and pioneering plastic surgery (*The Island of Dr Moreau*) are similarly bleak and disturbing. It's typical of the genre that Aldous Huxley's seminal novel *Brave New World* possesses one of the most ironic titles of all time. The desire to explore the great unknown, whether the far reaches of outer space, or the secrets of life itself, is invariably countered by both fear of what will be discovered and a cynical lack of faith in frail human nature, arrogant and corruptible. When *The Quatermass Experiment* brings back an alien-infected astronaut from deep space, not only is the

unfortunate man doomed, but his fate ultimately becomes a matter of indifference, as Professor Quatermass eagerly launches his next rocket project. Even if the future offers peace, prosperity and technical marvels beyond the wildest imaginings, mankind will almost certainly screw it up. Just as the distant galaxies are filled with terrifying, malevolent creatures, so the human mind harbours monsters of its own. The drug that transforms Wells's Dr Griffin into *The Invisible Man* appears to have the unfortunate side effect of rampant megalomania – yet perhaps it merely stimulated a characteristic already latent within Griffin himself.

The British seem to have a deep-seated ambivalence towards almost any kind of scientific progress, reflected in the recent real-life controversy over genetically modified crops, rapidly dubbed 'Frankenstein food' by the popular press. This distrust of scientific tampering and its associated secrecy, whether on an individual, corporate or state level, often demonises the researchers along with the research. Hammer Film Productions' 1950s reinvention of Baron Frankenstein as a cool, rationalist, ruthlessly obsessive seeker of knowledge has a lot to answer for, aside from a motley collection of human body parts. Our greatest scientists may devise cures for all known diseases, and invent machines for space travel and the general conquest of the universe, yet the pessimistic nature of UK science fiction dictates that virtually every enlightened genius will prove to have an insane, megalomaniac villain lurking inside, with or without the benefit of Dr Jekyll's mystery potion.

Even the largely reassuring, feelgood James Bond film series occasionally throws up a seriously demented loon among the run-of-the-mill power crazed maniacs. *Moonraker*'s Hugo Drax is a man with a very bad plan, namely to wipe out the Earth's 'inferior' inhabitants with bacterial spores fired from space and repopulate the planet with genetically perfect beautiful people. Only a slightly tired-looking Roger Moore stands in his way, which would be pretty scary if the outcome hadn't been well-established in the previous ten Bond films. Incidentally, billionaire industrialist Drax is played by a French actor, Michel Lonsdale, another kind of 'alien' somewhat closer to British shores than the standard space bug.

This is not to say that Britain has any kind of a monopoly on dystopian visions. H P Lovecraft (1890-1937), probably the strangest ever inhabitant of Providence, Rhode Island, USA, devised an entire cosmology – the Cthulhu Mythos – centring on the

Great Old Ones, terrifying godlike creatures who once ruled the earth and still lurk in the dark corners of the universe. Compared to these horrors, the gene-splicing Martians of *Quatermass and the Pit* seem more or less harmless and the monolith-planting aliens of *2001: A Space Odyssey* positively saintly. During the Cold War era of superpower antagonism and nuclear anxiety, American authors such as Richard Matheson (*The Shrinking Man; I Am Legend*) and Jack Finney (*The Body Snatchers*) devised razor-sharp stories of mutation, apocalyptic plague and alien takeover, all of which seemed grimly plausible at the time. Joss Whedon, creator of the hit supernatural television series *Buffy the Vampire Slayer*, argues that the US has always turned out its share of disturbing fantasy, citing the science fiction-tinged *Twilight Zone* as a prime example: 'I think it's a misconception to say that all American stuff is sort of watered-down, happy feelgood.' Closer to home, French writer Pierre Boulle produced the similarly allegorical *La Planete des Singes* (1959, translated in 1963 as *Monkey Planet*), which gave mankind a malicious knock back down the evolutionary ladder in favour of chimpanzees but is now best known as the inspiration for Twentieth Century-Fox's *Planet of the Apes* series.

Hollywood has drawn on British science fiction for decades, often with spectacular results, yet US science fiction tends to deal with external menace, retaining a basic optimism in human – or at least American – nature. The Body Snatchers may look, act and sound exactly like us but they remain indisputably Other, whether taken at face(less) value, as seed pods from Outer Space, or as an insidious manifestation of the Red Menace (on the pool table, in the basement and quite possibly under the bed). As *Quatermass* creator Nigel Kneale points out, the American film industry, catering to a mass global audience, is not inclined to risk its profit margins by upsetting people. From this perspective, at least, British-made science fiction films have a little more freedom to explore dark and disturbing ideas, a good example being mankind's dormant but still dangerous Martian genes in *Quatermass and the Pit*. Kneale would be the first to admit that his own verdict on the human race, 'We're really not a very healthy species', is not a very Hollywood message. In any case, the genre's templates and ground rules were laid down on this side of the Atlantic, whether the starting point is taken as Prospero's staff, Victor Frankenstein's laboratory or the nameless Time Traveller's machine.

Something in the British character, as a nation, a tribe, gives us very mixed feelings about the future.

Any hope for the best of all possible worlds is tempered by an expectation of the worst. This has given the best of British science fiction a conviction that makes it compelling. It can be argued that these unrelentingly pessimistic visions of the future are really a healthy sign, an indication of ultimate optimism in mankind's destiny. Along with a lingering child-like impulse to destroy, there is a sense of wicked wish-fulfilment to imagined apocalypses. Ruins have a strange fascination and the more complicated someone's life is, the more interesting the wreckage will be. In the cinema, spectacular, often beautiful explosions are the pyrotechnic equivalent of a Busby Berkeley musical number. This is certainly true in the case of the Bond movies, where at the climax the villain's secret base is invariably blown to pieces and all the evil henchmen in blue boiler suits and orange hard hats get squashed. At the other end of the scale, the telepathic wrecking of London in *Quatermass and the Pit* carries no sense of elation, merely a grim realisation of man's innate capacity for self-destruction. Whatever the case, generations of British talent, working in virtually all media, have braved critical snobbery to pursue their visions in a genre still widely regarded – sometimes with justification – as juvenile and immature. SF:UK takes a look at the books, films, television shows, comics, music, special effects and, above all, the people from Britain who through science fiction have helped change the way we see the world, their ideas and visions eagerly adopted and adapted. While the quality and imagination of other nations' science fiction cannot be disputed, the darker imaginings of British-produced science fiction are somehow more cynical, more persuasive, more 'real'.

PROLOGUE
IN SEARCH OF SCIENTIFIC ROMANCE
KIM NEWMAN

As the century which named science fiction gives way to the century the genre has so often imagined, the dominant image of sf is inescapably American.

The very term 'science fiction' was coined in the United States in the mid-1920s, by (Luxembourg-born) immigrant publisher Hugo Gernsback, an evolution of his more unwieldy (but also wittier) 'scientifiction'. The label was soon required for the pulp magazine racks where Yank genres like the Western and the hard-boiled detective story were being born, and which had just begun to stretch to Gernsback's *Amazing Stories* and such rivals as *Astounding Science-Fiction* (later *Analog*), *The Magazine of Fantasy and Science Fiction* and the more supernaturally-inclined *Weird Tales* (all of which survive, in some mutant form or another). From crude but vigorous pages and colourful covers marched a parade of square-jawed space heroes with grit and know-how under their glass bowl helmets, brass-brassiered heroines with a tendency to become imperilled, tentacled or bug-eyed alien monsters, eccentric genius tinkerers, thrusting phallic rocketships, clanking rebel robots and planet-smashing wonder weaponry.

In this form, sf had already been perfected by American scribe Edgar Rice Burroughs (creator also of *Tarzan of the Apes*) in his Martian novels (from *A Princess of Mars*, 1912), but it was through the pulps and (later) comics that it truly entered the culture. Almost all American sf has roots in the pulps: the space operas of E E 'Doc' Smith, the comic strip (and movie serial) heroics of Flash Gordon and Buck Rogers, the comic book and radio feats of Superman (who arrived from Krypton or Cleveland in 1938), the more mature but still bombastic fictions of Isaac Asimov and Robert A Heinlein, the televised adventures of *Captain Video* (1949-55) and *Rocky Jones – Space Ranger* (1953-54), the mutants and invaders of 1950s drive-in movies, the feud between Bugs and Daffy and the Roman-helmeted Marvin the Martian, the space-faring organisation men of *This Island Earth*

(1955) and *Forbidden Planet* (1956), the *Right Stuff* of NASA, the neurotic but colourful Marvel Comics heroes of the 1960s (The Fantastic Four, Spider-Man), the voyages of Captain Kirk and his many successors, Charlton Heston's travails on the *Planet of the Apes* (1968), the high adventure of *Star Wars*, the mix of technophilia and technophobia of novelist and filmmaker Michael Crichton, the semi-mysticism of *Close Encounters of the Third Kind* (1977), the fairytale sentiment of *ET: The Extra-Terrestrial* (1982), the violence and messianic streak of James Cameron's films, the drop-out chic cyberpunk cowboys of William Gibson and many imitators, the paranoid yearnings of *The X-Files* (1993-). Even writers as sophisticated as Ray Bradbury, Fritz Leiber, Philip K Dick and Harlan Ellison began as penny-a-word page-fillers toiling in the depths of the pulp-mills.

American science fiction is a lot like American popular music (with a crossover in Sheb Woolley's 'Flying Purple People Eater' or Billy Riley's 'Flying Saucer Rock and Roll') or even American politics. Forms of extremes, they are: brash, loud, exciting, violent, childish, covertly sexual, reductive, money-grubbing, inventive, wholeheartedly optimistic (or equally wholeheartedly despairing), abuzz with effects, uncomfortable with real people, rarely cerebral, often astounding. And American sf is unashamedly chauvinist, theoretically open to all the wondrous possibilities of the future and the alien but actually closed to all but a few select voices from outside the States. In the consensus space opera of the pulps or *Star Trek*, the Earth stands for America and the aliens for foreigners, and matters of cosmic import often boil down to interpretations of the Constitution. Gene Roddenberry's epic creation is almost like an evolving report on American foreign policy, with new races of baddies coming along to represent each new enemy the White House needs to demonise. The Oscars of the sf field are named the Hugo, after the quixotic but untalented Hugo Gernsback – as if he were the inventor rather than the namer of the genre – rather than the Bertie, after the author who more than any other could truly claim to be the founder of science fiction.

But there is another story.

The purpose of this book, and the television series which it complements, is to remind you of that other story, a specifically British tapestry of achievement as multi-stranded, colourful, challenging and surprising as anything from America.

Our islands – this is not merely an English epic, but a saga out of Scotland (from Stevenson and Doyle to Iain M Banks and Ken MacLeod), Ireland (from Swift and Shaw to James White and Ian McDonald), Wales (from Terry Nation to Christopher Evans) and even the Isle of Man (Nigel Kneale) – boast heroes and monsters of different stripes. Our complex, intricate and endlessly fascinating landscape is crammed into a comparatively small space, and everywhere are echoes of empires lost and traditions in eclipse, but also of futures and alternatives, of possibilities and implausibilities. Before 'science fiction' was slapped on a cover let alone contracted to the moron chirrup of 'sci-fi', the favoured term was 'scientific romance' – a far more evocative apparent oxymoron. Scientific romance implies a conflict between scientific observer and romantic dreamer, but the central realisation of the British genre is that in the end both are necessary, and all the really interesting work has to take place in the cramped space the two can share. Throughout British sf, we find the figure of the scientific romantic – at once rigorous and eccentric, involved and detached, serious and ironic, important and trivial, whimsical and adult.

These are the worlds of Camelot and Utopia and Erewhon, Prospero and Gulliver, Christian and Crusoe, Buonaparte's Channel Tunnel and Bismarck's invasion of Dorking, Victor Frankenstein and his Monster, the paradox worlds of Wonderland and the Looking Glass, the life-essence Vril (commemorated to this day in the savory spread Bovril), the experiments of Dr Jekyll and Dr Moreau, the Time Traveller and the Morlocks and Eloi, Dr Nikola and Fu-Manchu, Cavorite and the Grand Lunar, the Anarchists of the Air and the Honeymoon in Space, the Invisible Man, the Napoleon of Notting Hill and When William Came, the Face at the Window, Martian cylinders and heat-rays, the *Riddle of the Sands*, Professor Challenger and his dinosaurs, *Ultus the Unknown* and Zenith the Albino, the decanted bottle babies of *Brave New World*, Biggles and 'Tiger' Clinton, Odd John and the *Last and First Men*, the Chief and Wings Over the World, *Garth* and *Jane*, the Blue Streak and the Bouncing Bomb, Winston Smith and Big Brother, the *Man in the White Suit*, Dan Dare:

Pilot of the Future, 007 and the Moonraker, Triffids and Cuckoos, Professor Quatermass and the British Rocket Group, Middle Earth and Narnia, the dreadful outpourings of Lionel Fanthorpe's fiction factory, little Alex and his droogs, the Loch Ness Monster and the Abominable Snowman, Doctor Who and the TARDIS, Jeff Hawke and Modesty Blaise, Daleks and Cybermen, Professor Branestawm and *Stig of the Dump*, WASP and International Rescue, *Bleep and Booster* and the War Game, the Nazi Occupation that Happened Here and the Pavane world where the Armada prevailed, Steed and Emma and the Cybernauts and the *Man-Eater of Surrey Green*, the Bonzos' 'Urban Spaceman' and the Kinks' 'Apeman', Number Six and the Rover Balloons, the Silicates and the Composites, Robot Archie and the Spider, a Yellow Submarine and a Scarlet Captain, Adam Adamant and Don Quick, HAL9000 and the monolith in Jupiter orbit, the Old Men at the Zoo and Scotch on the Rocks, Jerry Cornelius and the Dancers at the End of Time, the Clangers and the Trigan Empire, *New Worlds* and *Interzone*, Krapp's Tapes and *Prospero's Books*, Professor Quist and Toby Wren, Jim Ballard and his car crashes, Jim Herbert and his rats, the Standees on Zanzibar, Ziggy Stardust and Diamond Dogs, *Sapphire and Steel* and *Blake's 7*, the Jubilee cry of 'no future', Grimly Feendish and Judge Dredd, the Prime Ministerships of Francis Urquhart and Harry Perkins, the Guy Fawkes-masked terrorist V, bomb-blasted Sheffield, the spaceships and alien landscapes of Chris Foss and Jim Burns, Arthur C Clarke's *Mysterious World* and Stephen Hawking's *Brief History of Time*, the Violent Unknown Event and Friendship's Death, Witchwater Country and Mythago Wood, the *Singing Detective* and the *Edge of Darkness*, the London psychogeographics of *King Lud* and *Hawksmoor*, the post-Earth misadventures of Arthur Dent and the crew of the *Red Dwarf*, Helliconia and the Xeelee, continuum-hopping patriot Luther Arkwright, the Plenty and the Culture, Wallace and Grommit and the *Wrong Trousers*, Fairyland and ThiGMOO.

It is an untidy muddle, with few of the clear-cut divides found in American sf. In Britain, genres evolve in the way that our cities have – with ancient settlements or Roman snap decisions compounded by thousands of years of random, unplanned growth. America was able to create communities on neat grids and fill them in like diagrams, but Britain has had to adapt to the landscape or to structures that have been present so long they seem part of the landscape. (Stonehenge is a site in so much UK sf). Thus our science fiction community has to take account of standing stones like *The Tempest* (1611),

Robinson Crusoe (1719) or *Frankenstein: or The Modern Prometheus* (1818) that were there long before H G Wells started building, in a burst of unparalleled energy that may have come because he believed he only had a few years to live. The new genre of scientific romance had to wind carefully around these features, perhaps going so far as to incorporate Mary's monster-maker (whose very name became a synonym for several uses and misuses of science though his creator might as easily have made him a sorcerer) while never quite embracing Defoe's castaway (though the hot science of Crusoe's day was geography, and many an adventurous voyage into the unknowns of space is indebted to the Mariner of York).

A side-effect of this is that we in Britain tend to dismiss our bad science fiction (and there is reams of it, from vintage Badger Books to the wonky sets of *Blake's 7*, 1978-81) as pseudo-American, while treating Wells, Aldous Huxley, Olaf Stapledon, George Orwell, Anthony Burgess and J G Ballard like the major artists they are. When essaying their own challenging brand of sf, American writers like Kurt Vonnegut Jr or Gore Vidal can never quite shuck off the taint of pulp, and litter the likes of *The Sirens of Titan* (1959) or *Visit to a Small Planet* (1956) with half-embarrassed schlock devices to signpost that they don't take this sort of stuff entirely seriously. This is an attitude you'll rarely find in Big Brits, who (with the exception of Ballard, who fetishises his clichés) write as if they were unaware that there was such a thing as American pulp science fiction. Orwell clearly knew his Wells – and Eric Blair may have copped his writing name consciously or unconsciously from Herbert George Wells, whose vision of the future he moderated with a lunger's pessimism – and recognised Yevgeny Zamyatin's Russian *We* (1924) as a precedent for *Nineteen Eighty-Four* (1949), but you get a sense from his shuddering disgust at James Hadley Chase's mock-American thriller *No Orchids for Miss Blandish* (1939) that he probably never read a word of A E van Vogt or Lester Del Rey.

Among the major ur-texts of scientific romance are Thomas More's *Utopia* (1516), an account of an imaginary land where society is ordered as the author believes it should be, and lessons are to be drawn for the improvement of a world that would shortly be clamouring for More's head; and Jonathan Swift's *Travels into Several Remote Nations of the World in Four Parts … by Lemuel Gulliver* (1726), which voyages to imaginary lands where societies are disordered as the author believes they generally are but the follies of the age and the species are dressed up in fantastical,

satirical modes. (Gulliver's sojourn among intelligent horses and the human-shaped Yahoos is echoed in many a tale, from *The Island of Dr Moreau* to *Planet of the Apes*). It may be something deep-rooted in the British character, but the purposes of these vastly different works are surprisingly similar. The authors both set out to do more than entertain, to speculate on things as they are and things as they might be in order to prompt their readers to independent thought (or to blind agreement).

Whether dealing with a supposed past (as in the Arthur stories that make up the Matter of Britain), a distant land (like More's Utopia or Swift's Laputa), a world beyond our own (like Blake's 'Jerusalem' or Lewis Carroll's Wonderland), an alternate timeline (a theme introduced to fiction by Charles Dickens in the 'Yet to Come' section of *A Christmas Carol* (1843), which reveals to Scrooge a concrete future that his reformation wipes out) or the future (Lord Lytton's *The Coming Race*, 1871, which gave the world Vril, or General Sir George Tomkyns Chesney's gloomier *The Battle of Dorking*, 1871), British authors conjure up alternative Britains which readers might aspire to or be afraid of. Propagandist purpose or sheer didacticism on the model of *Pilgrim's Progress* (1678-84) is at the heart of the British scientific romance, but generations have read John Bunyan's tract as a magical adventure story, and it is striking

an imaginary land where society is ordered as the author believes it should be

how many of these attempts to educate or argue achieved their greatest success not because of their intellectual content but their emotional affect, with almost-unintended felicities making for literary works that have lasted well beyond their passing topicality.

The Battle of Dorking depicts a near future Britain overrun by frighteningly efficient Prussians. Written in the wake of the Franco-Prussian War by a Blimpish military man who was incensed by politicians who repeatedly cut the defence budget, this slim pamphlet, initially issued anonymously as by 'A Volunteer', was intended as propaganda for the modernisation of the armies of the Empire. It succeeded in its task to the point that its vision of affairs was discussed in Parliament: as with such later future wars as the films *The War Game* (1965) and *Dr Strangelove* (1964), the establishment's reaction was to pick holes in the plot in an attempt to reassure the public that these horrors could not come to pass. But the book was a runaway hit – model for literally hundreds of imitations and answer-back stories, and distant inspiration of all alien invasions from *War of the Worlds* (1898) to *Independence Day* (1996) – because of its terrifying vision of the home counties destroyed by modern warfare and the familiar made surreal by destruction. Chesney had set out to make people think, but with a surprising burst of skill managed instead to make them feel. This pattern has recurred again and again, often resulting in angry exchanges between artists like H G Wells or Stanley Kubrick (an American who worked in the genre only in Britain) and their audiences, with politicians, editorial writers, critics, clergymen and all manner of other experts getting in on the act. The signature tune of too many splenetic scientific romancers might well be 'that's not what I meant at all'.

Science fiction is only really possible in a society stable enough to allow people to think beyond the next meal, to give a sense of a future that extends as far as the past. The Ancient Greeks and Romans experimented with lunar voyages and imagined perfect societies (though 'utopia' is a coinage of More's), but Britain could not sustain such imaginings until the Tudors. Besides More, this age produced Shakespeare, whose fantasies on themes from the past (note the recurrence of murdered monarchs) were often intended as warnings about the dangers of the near future and whose *Tempest* stands as a template (for *Forbidden Planet*, among other things) for any number of stories about islands or empires or planets inhabited by powerful sorcerer-scientists, their beautiful daughters, spirits of Earth and Air and castaway adventurers. Shakespeare's

stories about islands or empires or planets inhabited by powerful sorcerer-scientists

Prospero is a magician, but he might also be classed as a proto-scientist alongside his real-life contemporary Doctor John Dee (a regular in fictions from Derek Jarman's *Jubilee*, 1978, through Michael Moorcock's *Gloriana, or: The Unfulfil'd Queen*, 1978, to Peter Ackroyd's *The House of Dr Dee*, 1993) or Christopher Marlowe's *Doctor Faustus*, a seeker after knowledge who uses necromancy but works out of a laboratory and a university rather than a wizard's cave. This clutch of characters forms a bridge between Merlin and Frankenstein, and then to researchers as varied as Jekyll, Moreau, Quatermass and Quist.

Since Gloriana's days, Britain has seen a succession of short-lived attempts at home-grown utopiae (often, as with Kennedy's administration, with evocations of Round Table and Camelot): the Interregnum with its Diggers, Levellers and Puritans, all under the Iron Will of Cromwell; the Restoration, with its explosion of frippery and wit; the Johnsonian Age of Reason, which produced Swift and Defoe; the idylls of Romanticism, as fired by the French Revolution and scientific discoveries as by landscape and love; the rise and plateau of the British Empire, expanding across the globe; the industrial revolution and the Great Exhibition of 1851, as railways and steamship lines spread across the world; the dignified widowhood and complacent Jubilees of Queen Victoria, the gaslight era of *The Strand* and 221B Baker Street; the activist demands of the Suffragettes, the National Strikers, the Jarrow Marchers and CND; Sir John Reith's notion of the British Broadcasting Corporation and J Arthur Rank's godly cinema; Churchill's vision of a resolute stand against Nazi tyranny and a perpetuated Empire; the post-War foundation of the welfare state; the Festival of Britain and the Festival of Light; Carnaby Street and Beatlemania; 'I'm backing Britain' and the 'white heat of technology'; the Commonwealth and the Common Market; Concorde and the Chunnel; Anarchy in the UK and Babylon's Burning; Thatcher's blue Britain of money and self-reliance; Tony Blair's Cool Britannia (a term coined by Vivian Stanshall 30 years earlier) and the Millennium Dome. All of these have had a nightmare underside, have included a dystopian yang to the utopian ying, but they were all genuine attempts to make real visions that sprang first from the imagination.

Throughout this history, science fiction/scientific romance has been there, pointing the way, issuing warnings, making suggestions, voicing complaints, passing comment and taking the piss.

The single greatest figure in the history of sf (British or otherwise) is H G Wells (1866-1946). At the time of his greatest output, he was often bracketed with the Frenchman Jules Verne, who had specialised in wonderful new means of transport like the submarine *Nautilus* and the *Clipper of the Clouds*, and he was certainly writing in a tradition of magazine fiction that included *The Battle of Dorking* and even the hoax-like scientific stories of Edgar Allan Poe. All Wells's great works have their precedents and inspirations (in scientific thought as well as literary effort), but he was nevertheless the man who got there first. With the possible exception of the 'alternate history', he essayed a seminal novel or story in every single sub-genre of sf – and given his concern with table-top war games that might give a different outcome to a historical battle, he might even lay claim to a significant contribution to AH. Wells has so much become a part of our mental landscape that it's too easy to forget that titles as deceptively familiar as *The Time Machine*, *The War of the Worlds* and *The Invisible Man* were once new-minted and fresh and irresistibly evocative of the new and the terrifying.

Consider this record: 1894: 'The Flowering of the Strange Orchid', first bud of Triffids and Little Shops of Horrors to come; 1895: *The Time Machine*, the first use of scientific time travel into the future, and also a vision of the far future development of humanity; 1896: *The Island of Dr Moreau*, another fable of evolution but also a lost island adventure, a brutal satire on the beasts in men, an essay about the ethics of vivisection and a development of the stories of Frankenstein and Gulliver; 1897: 'A Story of the Stone Age', one of the first attempts to imagine our prehistoric past and consider where humanity might have come from (a book-end, in effect, to *The Time Machine*); 1897: *The Invisible Man*, still the definitive version of the theme of scientifically-produced invisibility but also a dark comedy about experimentation and an impulse to megalomania; 1897: 'The Star', an early cosmic disaster tale in which the Earth is destroyed by a collision with a heavenly body; 1898: *The War of the Worlds*, the great novel of 'first contact' and alien invasion, populariser of the term 'Martian' and ultimate generic evolution of the 'England Invaded' theme; 1899: *When the Sleeper Wakes*, a utopian variant in which a man from our times is revived in a socialist future and given a tour of a world he proceeds to change; 1901: *The First Men in the Moon*, which stirs anti-gravity paint and an analysis of another evolved (insect-like) society into the lunar voyage tradition of Verne and Cyrano de Bergerac; 1903: 'The Land Ironclads', which imagines the motorised war vehicles that would become familiar as tanks; 1904: 'The Country of the Blind', a Swiftian 'lost race' parable in which an old saying is lived out and refuted by a remote people; 1905: 'The Empire of the Ants', which prophesies that intelligent insects will overwhelm humanity and is a dry run for all the attacks by bugs, birds, sharks and reptiles in nature-runs-amok horror stories to date (see also: the jellyfish of 'The Sea Raiders'); 1906: *In the Days of the Comet*, in which a near-miss with a comet transforms the manners and morals of all Earth; 1908: *The War in the Air*, a spirited satire on the 'future war' and 'wonderful weapon' genres of the nineteenth century that turns into a hideous draft of the post-holocaust world of Mad Max; 1914: *The World Set Free*, which

800,000 years in the future, Weena (Yvette Mimieux) is menaced by a Morlock in George Pal's production of The Time Machine (1960).

extrapolates from an abstruse scientific paper and imagines the use of atomic power in warfare and peace. Now try to find a work of science fiction that doesn't make use of any of the above themes.

And all this was the work of a man who was as concerned with writing non-fantastical social novels like *Kipps* (1905) and *The History of Mr Polly* (1910), which share many concerns with his scientific romances, with agitating for various political and scientific causes, with the pursuit of sexual adventures on a scale that would shame a modern rock star and with the composition of an enormous amount of journalism, propaganda and history. In later life, Wells tended to downplay his extraordinary output of the 1890s and 1900s and insist that this was less serious work than *The Outline of History* (1920) or the modestly-titled *The Work, Wealth and Happiness of Mankind* (1931). Wells lived through two world wars, the rise and fall of fascism as a political force (like a lot of odd sorts, he admired Mussolini at the start but came to loathe Hitler for his irrationality and philistinism), the congealing of the Russian Revolution into a Stalinist tyranny and the first use in anger of atomic weapons. He must have felt like a man who had stepped into a wonderland of his own making. He called his last published book *The Mind at the End of Its Tether* (1945) and, frankly, no wonder.

Again, the content of all the great science fiction – obsessively working over the theme of human evolution in all forms – is partially eclipsed by the fun stuff. *The Time Machine* or *The War of the Worlds* are magical, wonderful, terrifying books for readers who have no idea who Charles Darwin was, but who are swept away by Wells's confident story-telling (even in *The War of the Worlds*, which lacks anything like a conventional plot). We now find quaint the world of Wells, almost as cosy as the smoke-filled study of

a scientific elite imposes improvements on the mass of humanity

Sherlock Holmes, and we are struck by the period charm of the brassbound time machine or the tripodal Martian devices, and the adventure story aspects of *The Island of Dr Moreau*, which Wells presumably didn't care about at all, are as thrilling as anything in Haggard or Kipling. Wells wrote to warn and transform, and his spirit (evoked in such recursive fictions as Christopher Priest's *The Space Machine*, 1976, Michael Moorcock's *The War Lord of the Air*, 1971, and Stephen Baxter's *The Time Ships*, 1995) remains a discomfiting presence as much as an inspiring one. A key chapter in *War of the Worlds* has the narrator encounter a survivalist ex-soldier whose vision of how to get along in the ruins ('there won't be any poems published') is an exact prediction of the attitudes of many an American action hero to come, but is also condemned out of hand as utterly insane. Through his (then, and again now, freakish) commitment to socialism, he espoused attitudes that sit ill with the establishment-oriented patriotism of such contemporaries as Arthur Conan Doyle and William LeQueux (both influenced by him) and have filtered into the entire British sf genre, which has generally been oppositional to the state of things rather than a cheerleader for progress. Wells's own visions of utopia, as represented by the finale of the film *The Shape of Things to Come* (1933), strike us as chilling – a scientific elite imposes improvements on the mass of humanity – prompting Orwell and others to have second thoughts – but he saw all too clearly where we were going wrong.

Even now, Wells cannot safely be ignored.

It seems likely that the first British science fiction film was *Making Sausages* (1897, also known as *The End of All Things*), made in Brighton by the pioneering George Albert Smith, and a blatant imitation of an American mini-epic called *The Sausage Machine* (1897),

a comic vignette about automation that perhaps seems less funny now we are actually worried about what goes into our food. The film shows a machine that takes live pigs at one end and produces a string of link-sausages at the other, and the workers get laughs by stuffing it with cats and dogs, a duck and an old boot. Later versions of the theme, such as the American *The Corpse Grinders* (1971), would add human meat. Smith cashed in on another hot recent scientific discovery with *X-Rays* (1897, also known as *The X-Ray Fiend*), in which the first of the British sf cinema's many eccentric and/or cracked boffins – played by end-of-the-pier comic Tom Green – uses Roentgen's X-Ray machine to spy on a courting couple, and exposes their embracing skeletons. This would also serve as a recurrent plot, in the silent days and down to the nudie cuties of the 1960s.

One of Smith's rivals in the dawn of British cinema was Robert Paul, whose most interesting notion sadly never got beyond the stage of filing a patent. Impressed in 1895 by the publication of *The Time Machine*, Paul contacted H G Wells and proposed to build a working model of the device for travelling through time – which sounds like an exact precursor of the thrill rides of modern-day theme parks. The audience would enter a room and take their seats on a platform designed to resemble a charabanc version of Wells's time-cycle, whereupon motion pictures would be projected on the walls and the ceilings to give the impression of travelling swiftly through time as in the novel – which some have speculated was influenced by Wells's early exposure to motion picture trickery – and then, in the meat of the show, to view scenes that represent life in the ancient past or the far future. In its own way, the story of this patent – which is told by Terry Ramsaye in *A Million and One Nights* (1926), the first history of the technical development of the cinema – is among the most uncannily accurate prophecies that Wells, who lived to see as many of his guesses miss the mark as hit home, was ever involved in. Paul pressed on with more conventional cinema, and did turn out a few sf movies, mostly in imitation of the French conjurer Georges Méliès. These included *An Over-Incubated Baby* (1901), in which an incubation device is used to fast-forward through an entire life so that a new mother is presented with a doddering old man (a lot of trick films strike us now as horrific rather than funny, suggesting a callousness we don't associate with the Edwardian era); and *The Voyage of the Arctic* (1903), the first British sf film adapted from British sf literature, with Fred Farren repeating his stage role as Captain Kettle, the adventuring hero of a series of 'lost world'-type stories by the redoubtable C J Cutcliffe Hyne, published in *Pearson's Magazine*.

In the first years of the twentieth century, the imitators of Wells were pouring out stories of flying warships (George Griffith's *The Angel of the Revolution*, 1893), submersible dreadnoughts, humanity wiped out through new plagues (M P Shiel's *The Purple Cloud*, 1903), bizarre experiments, lady automata, ice ages descending upon London, lost races (Cutcliffe Hyne's first such story was the evocatively-titled *Beneath Your Very Feet*, 1898), voyages to the outer planets (Griffith's *Honeymoon in Space*, 1900), future societies where current trends had got out of hand (there were laboured anti-Suffragette satires about prissy matriarchies) and other wonders. Sir Arthur Conan Doyle turned out *The Lost World* (1912), an authentic masterpiece of 'scientific romance', tapping into a craze for paleontology 80 years before Michael Crichton, creating in the ape-like Professor Challenger an sf hero to match his detective Sherlock Holmes and imagining a remote plateau in South America where dinosaurs still survived. Merely the best of many such tales – and a variant on the 'lost race' fantasies of Sir Henry Rider Haggard – this was a story that caught the imagination, and eventually fed into the movies, providing the source for a 1925 American film that is crucial to the development of special effects. These effects were provided by model animator Willis O'Brien, and were the direct inspiration for *King Kong* (1933), another showcase for O'Brien's work, and a horde of monsters to come. Challenger returned, in the mock-apocalypse novella 'The Poison Belt' (1913) and in a few other strange stories. In 'When the World Screamed' (1929), he discovers that the planet is a living organism. *The Land of the Mist* (1926) is a propagandist novel about spiritualism. Though Cutcliffe Hyne, William LeQueux (who specialised in fiendish Hun invaders) and George Griffith were Wells's rivals, only Doyle matched his popular touch, just as only the visionary Olaf Stapledon – whose *Last and First Men* and *Star-Maker* remain among the most astonishing sf novels ever published – was his heir in the abstruse and intellectual field.

The cinema, which was evolving from gimmick pictures that ran less than five minutes into a sophisticated narrative form, was naturally delighted by new inventions and, like many writers of the period, was keen on seizing any new invention and imagining what it might be like when perfected. There were many British films about flying machines, ranging from the winged automobile of Robert Paul's *The '?' Motorist* (1906) through the ornithopter (an aeroplane with flapping wings) of *Rescued in Mid-Air* (1906) and the Cavorite-style paint of *The Professor's Anti-Gravitational Fluid* (1908) to the future wars of *The Airship Destroyer* (1909), *The Aerial Submarine* (1910), *The Aerial Anarchists* (1911) and *The Pirates of 1920* (1911). Many of these flying movies were also paranoid warnings of wars to come. The Battle of Dorking was refought in *England Invaded* (1909), an unusual multi-media event that tied in with an alarmist series of articles (and publicity stunts like dressing up local toughs as Huns and having them swan around provincial towns like occupation forces) sponsored by the Harmsworth press empire. This was so successful that imitations swiftly followed, *The Invaders* (1909), *Invasion: Its Possibilities* (1909), *England's Menace* (1914), *An Englishman's Home* (1914), *If England Were Invaded* (1914, aka *The Raid of 1915*) and *Wake Up!* (1914, aka *A Dream of Tomorrow*).

In the busy years before the First World War that so many of these films were predicting, there were several other British screen precedents: *When the Man in the Moon Seeks a Wife* (1909), our first alien visitor – his mission on Earth is a clear precedent for the girl-napping likes of *Mars Needs Women* (1966), *The Night Caller* (1965) and *Frankenstein Meets the Space Monster* (1965); *The Duality of Man* (1910), the first UK adaption of *Dr Jekyll and Mr Hyde* (1886), though the story had already been done several times in Denmark and America; and *A Message From Mars* (1913), adapted from an 1899 stage drama (the first sf play?), in which an angelic alien named Ramiel reforms a selfish Earthling on the Scrooge model and Martians are presented in a somewhat better light than the vampire squid *of War of the Worlds*. The Great War, a shattering experience for a generation, seems to have taken all the fun out of inventing things, and there were almost no British science fictions from 1914 to 1929, when another theatrical adaptation – *High Treason* – came along to depict the London of 1940, with aeroplanes everywhere, skyscrapers towering over St Paul's Cathedral, a Channel Tunnel to a United Europe (the jury's still out), women wearing silk pantaloons in public, a feminist pacifist lobby using assassinations to avert war and television and radio having driven print journalism out of business. A rough imitation of the German *Metropolis* (1926), *High Treason* was nevertheless the most important British sf film until Wells came back into the story with *Things to Come* (1936).

The story of British media sf still revolves around Wells in the early 1930s, but relocates from grey London to sunny California, where British filmmaker James Whale, whose *Frankenstein* (1931) may stand as

Frank Cellier
and Boris Karloff
in the 1936
brain-swapping
thriller The Man
Who Changed
His Mind.

the most influential science fiction (or anti-science) movie of all time, tackled a faithful film version of *The Invisible Man* (1933), with Claude Rains under the bandages as the velvet-voiced madman unseen until the final moments of the picture. As with Paul's patent, Whale's film shows how cutting edge Wells really was. Even 30 years after the novel's publication, *The Invisible Man* had to invent most of the techniques necessary to dramatise it, and images from the novel have entered the repertoire of the cinema as if they were coined for it. Wells admired Whale's film. He despised the lurid mish-mash of *Dr Moreau* Paramount unleashed in *Island of Lost Souls* (1932), with a leering Charles Laughton cracking the whip in a frenzy of perversity, cruelty, vivisection and bestiality that was banned by a horrified British censor. While Hollywood was making sf horror films with British-born Boris Karloff and based on British authors like Shelley, Stoker, Sax Rohmer and Wells, the best we could do was lure Karloff back for a spot of brain-swapping in the wittily-titled *The Man Who Changed His Mind* (1936). Otherwise, Maurice Elvey, of *High Treason*, remade a German film about digging under the Atlantic as *The Tunnel* (1935), an entry in a persistent strain of British sf about the construction of tunnels under the Channel or to America.

The summation of all this effort, and perhaps of the genre to date, came in 1936 with *Things to Come*, one of those ultra-British efforts that could only be

co-directed and designed by an American (William Cameron Menzies) and produced by a Hungarian (Alexander Korda), though it boasts impeccably West End acting tones from Raymond Massey and (as the first of the cinema's many post-holocaust tyrants) Ralph Richardson and a still-stirring score by Sir Arthur Bliss. An unwieldy, episodic mammoth of a picture, which combines the very good with the exceedingly bad, *Things to Come* is nothing if not ambitious, shaping Wells's 'history of the future' into a series of scenes showing how the London-like Everytown is changed by a future war that breaks out in 1940 (a chilling detail, now) and rages for decades, turning the modern city into a ruin where cars are pulled by horses (an image in many a Mad Max movie), diseased zombies stagger among barbed wire and a brutal warlord, the Chief (Richardson) rules through violence. From the sky descends a saviour, Cabal (Massey), a black-leather-clad airman in a domed helmet, a representative of a scientific elite who are rebuilding civilisation. Then, Everytown is rebuilt as a neo-Grecian city of glass and marvels, and a new Cabal considers that man must venture into space.

Things to Come is ultimately a utopian vision, but it shares some of its vision with works that Wells would have violently objected to, Aldous Huxley's *Brave New World* (1932), with its amoral society of gene engineered decadents, and Orwell's *Nineteen*

Eighty-Four (1949), an expose of the incipient fascism (or Stalinism) inherent in Wellsian utopiae. These two books and one film represent the souring of scientific romance, and perhaps also its extinction. 1936 was also the year Hollywood's biggest pure science fiction film to date came out, the comic strip serial Flash Gordon. Ever since, science fiction has been derided as 'that Buck Rogers stuff'. Whatever you thought of Huxley, Wells and Orwell – and all their visions produced as many virulent responses as nervous endorsements – they were worth arguing about, worth taking seriously. Their efforts were intended to add to debate (Brave New World was an 'answer' book for J B S Haldane's Daedalus, 1924). In a climate dominated by these thinkers, even E M Forster ('The Machine Stops', 1909), Joseph Conrad and Ford Maddox Ford (The Inheritors, 1901) or George Bernard Shaw (Back to Methuselah, 1921, The Apple Cart, 1930) weren't embarrassed to turn to sf. After Flash Gordon, that became much harder – and the likes of Anthony Burgess and Kingsley Amis tended to find their sf excursions less well-received than their 'mainstream' fiction.

This may have been the point when Britain lost control of scientific romance, when science fiction became the dominant form. The most significant British sf writers of the post-war era had at least one eye on America, and were (initially) as often published in US magazines as British periodicals. Minehead's own Arthur C Clarke was an early sf fan and chairman of the British Interplanetary Society, and sold his first story ('Loophole') to Astounding Science Fiction in 1946. An inheritor of the Wellsian tradition of prophecy (much has been made of his 'invention' of the communications satellite), Clarke was also inspired by the 'puzzle'-type sf story associated with the American Isaac Asimov and has, throughout his career, been distrustful of the American tendency to resolve plots (or real-life situations) through ultra-violence (it didn't occur to him that communications satellites would at least initially be used for military and espionage purposes). Clarke established himself as a novelist with The City and the Stars (1948-1956) and Childhood's End (1950-53), both evolving texts that began as pulp stories and became novels he has occasionally (and awkwardly) revised. Clarke secured his real place in the pantheon with 'The Sentinel', the story that was the seed of Stanley Kubrick's 2001: A Space Odyssey (1968), a film which probes Clarke's

technological utopia and finds the soul-freezing dystopia lurking within.

Clarke decamped to Sri Lanka in 1956, and though his prose remains English (rather than American), his homeland rarely impinges on his imagination. By contrast, John Wyndham, heir to another strain of Wellsian work, rarely left the home counties. His early, interplanetary work was imitative of American pulps, but mostly published in UK magazines, but after the War he turned out a series of novels that became minor classics and remain on the reading

the soul-freezing
dystopia lurking within

lists of people who would never consider cracking open a paperback by Clifford Simak or Bruce Sterling. The Day of the Triffids (1951) and The Midwich Cuckoos (1957) are his best-known works, essays in what Brian W Aldiss has called the 'cosy catastrophe', importing alien presences to the familiar English cityscapes and countrysides. The Day of the Triffids, in which most of humanity is blinded by a meteor display and the survivors are plagued by perambulating anthrophage plants, was followed by The Kraken Wakes (1953), in which underwater aliens raise the sea-level and drown London. These books pick up on the apocalypses of Shiel and Wells, and are precedents for imitations (John Christopher's Death of Grass, 1956, John Lymington's Night of the Big Heat, 1959 – note how many British apocalypses are about that national obsession, the weather) and surreal variants (the transforming disasters of J G Ballard's The Drowned World, 1962, or The Crystal World, 1966).

The Midwich Cuckoos, familiar from the film Village of the Damned (1960), is about subtle alien invasion, as the

Oswald Cabal (Raymond Massey) heralds a new age of technology in Things To Come (1936).

H G Wells wrote the screenplay for Alexander Korda's production of Things To Come (1936), based on his own novel The Shape of Things To Come.

women of a small English community wake from a mysterious sleep to find themselves pregnant with babies that grow to be a threatening hive-mind. More benign variants on this theme include the post-holocaust *The Chrysalids* (1955) and the domestic *Chocky* (1963). Wyndham's sf, which mixes wild ideas with familiar settings, was an influence on Nigel Kneale, who similarly took the stuff of despised US pulps and entered it into the mainstream of British culture with his *Quatermass* TV serials and such one-offs as the BBC-TV production of *Nineteen Eighty-Four* (1954) and the influential scientific ghost stories *The Road* (1963) and *The Stone Tape* (1972).

Kneale is also the last major writer to have made his first fiction appearance in *The Strand*, home of Sherlock Holmes and the *First Men in the Moon*; while Wyndham tended to sell his short fiction and even the first drafts of his novels to US science fiction or mainstream magazines like *Amazing* and *Collier's*. Neither paid much attention to *New Worlds*, the UK's homegrown sf magazine, which was founded in 1946

and trotted along in the tracks of the Americans for years. *New Worlds* became a forum for newer British writers like Aldiss, Ballard, John Brunner, Ken Bulmer, E C Tubb and James White – all of whom wrote work genuinely suspended between America and Britain – before Michael Moorcock took control in the mid-sixties and transformed the magazine into a venue for experimental sf that was as likely to come from American writers like Thomas M Disch, Harlan Ellison, Samuel R Delany and John Sladek as Brits like Ballard, M John Harrison, Ian Watson and Barrington J Bayley. Though it lurched from crisis to crisis, alienating a great many traditional sf fans while attracting Arts Council funding, *New Worlds* has had an enormous footprint in British literary sf, and certainly is responsible for the establishment of Aldiss, Moorcock, Harrison and Ballard as not merely major British sf writers, but major British novelists. Under Moorcock, *New Worlds* shifted its attention away from rockets and aliens, turning towards what Ballard termed 'inner space', a landscape as much of the mind as of the future. New Worlds writers were as likely to find their inspiration in fringe-science fields like media studies or sociology as in physics or speculative biology, and some readers who had grown up with the cosiness of Dan Dare or E.C. Tubb were as sniffy (or downright rude) about works as remarkable as Ballard's *Vermilion Sands* stories or Aldiss's *Barefoot in the Head* sequence as some old-fashioned university academics were about trendy-jumpered polytechnic lecturers whose fields weren't 'proper'.

When *New Worlds* transformed into a series of paperback anthologies and disappeared into several limbos – with the occasional reincarnation – a great hole was left in the field. The established names, and newcomers like Christopher Priest, Robert Holdstock, Keith Roberts, Garry Kilworth, Brian Stableford, Richard Cowper and Christopher Evans, maintained careers in the seventies and eighties primarily as novelists, each marking out distinctive, British territory. Like Wyndham and Kneale, and unlike Clarke (or Aldiss), all these writers ventured only sparingly, if at all, into interplanetary space opera, still the dominant mode of US sf. Their attention was on the landscape around us, whether it be physical or cultural, and they continued a program of British self-analysis that owes as much to Dickens, John Cowper Powys or Anthony Powell as to Wells.

With the establishment of *Interzone* in the eighties, *New Worlds* seemed reborn, and the magazine's first few issues were dominated by NW writers, though the mere existence of a market soon attracted new names, many of whom were equally influenced by the narrative verve and colour of American genre (though not exclusively sf) writing and the *New Worlds* school, yielding a school that has sometimes been tagged 'radical hard s-f'. Among the important writers to emerge in the eighties and nineties, mostly in or around *Interzone* (whose collective editorship devolved to the Stakhanovite David Pringle), are the Canadian UK resident Geoff Ryman, Colin Greenland (whose first book was a study of *New Worlds*), Paul J McAuley, Gwyneth Jones, Stephen M Baxter, Mary Gentle, Peter F Hamilton, Michael Marshall Smith, Jon Courtenay Grimwood, Jeff Noon, Iain M Banks, Alastair Reynolds, Justina Robson, Simon Ings and Eugene Byrne.

The 1950s were the founding decade of sf cinema in the US, with paranoia and wonder fuelling the likes of *The Thing From Another World* (1951), *The Day the Earth Stood Still* (1951), *War of the Worlds* (1953), *Them!* (1954), *The Creature from the Black Lagoon* (1954), *Forbidden Planet* (1956) and *Invasion of the Body Snatchers* (1956). These were major studio releases, though the

budgets usually went on effects rather than star names, and came out as a part of a balanced output of Westerns, crime movies, comedies, musicals and soap operas, intended for general cinema audiences. However, the sf movies really clicked with the kids of the early fifties (who also tuned in to the primitive space adventures of Captain Video, Rocky Jones and other TV heroes, including George Reeves as Superman), who grew into the rock 'n' rollers of the late fifties. So the great proliferation of the genre was in the teenage drive-in pictures made by Roger Corman and others for AIP, downgrading the superficial quality but upping the energy quotient, until the genre was capable of something as wild as Corman's original *The Little Shop of Horrors* (1961).

In Britain, sf cinema had a parallel evolution, but took a few odd country lanes along the path. *The Perfect Woman* (1949), with Patricia Roc in a leather corset impersonating a female robot, and *The Man in the White Suit* (1951), with Alec Guinness inventing a fabric that never gets dirty or wears out (and thus becoming a hate figure for the rag trade), are sf as knockabout satire, and it's hard to know what to make of *Mr Drake's Duck* (1950), scripted by Ian Messiter (of *Just a Minute* fame), in which Douglas Fairbanks Jr raises a duck which lays atomic bomb eggs. Comparatively few American films (Howard Hawks' *Monkey Business*, 1952, is one) take this approach to genre, but it is a strand that has proved especially persistent in the United Kingdom, popping up as late (and as low) as *Spanish Fly* (1975), *Percy* (1971) or *Percy's Progress* (1974) – in which sf contrivances affect sexual performance or desire with the expected oo-er results. This was also the era of Frank Hampson's Dan Dare, the Battle of Britain-style space pilot who made his debut in the *Eagle* in 1950 and spent two decades defying the Mekon and showing a lot less interest in space

a landscape as much of the mind as of the future

scientist Jocelyn than tubby Northern sidekick Digby (who was from Wigan), in the utter sexlessness typical of British comics. Following Dan was Jet Morgan, the wireless hero created by Charles Chilton for *Journey into Space* (1954) and sequels.

In 1953, the two forces which would shape British media sf for over a decade made their separate appearances. Hammer Film Productions, a B-picture grindhouse (which had experimented with a death ray in the wireless-derived *Dick Barton at Bay*, 1950), had staff director Terence Fisher turn out the first British sf films on the Yank pattern, albeit based on UK

Bernard Archard, Patrick Holt and Bernard Cribbins (seated) in the 1960 television adaptation of John Lymington's novel Night of the Big Heat.

sources. *Four-Sided Triangle*, from a novel by William F Temple, and *Spaceways*, from a radio play by Charles Eric Maine, are about cloning and space travel respectively, but also include drawing room adultery, pipe-smoking plods and other hold-overs from the stuffy British cinema of the period. The same is true, albeit with a lot more unusual material, of *The Quatermass Experiment*, the six-part BBC-TV serial that introduced Nigel Kneale's rocket boffin to the public, and rivetted the whole country with the story of a returned astronaut (Duncan Lamont) transforming into a giant half-cactus creature that could spore and destroy humanity. (There was only one TV station at the time, and the many people without TV sets did their best to visit more affluent neighbours when it was on.) In a significant moment, the monster staggers into a cinema where a standardised American sf film (in 3-D) is playing, and Kneale contrasts the agonies of this conflicted character with the certainties of B fiction. In fact, *The Quatermass Experiment*, and its follow-ups – *Quatermass II* (1955), *Quatermass and the Pit* (1959) and *Quatermass* (aka *The*

Quatermass Conclusion, 1979) – rely on conventional sf themes, but treat them with high seriousness, a commitment to realism and an engagement with the realities of the times that no American TV production would ever really manage.

Hammer bought the rights to *The Quatermass Experiment* and Val Guest filmed a slimmed-down version in 1955 (aka *The Creeping Unknown*, which must have given Kneale a bitter laugh). Hammer followed it up with *Quatermass 2* (aka *Enemy From Space*, 1957) – *Quatermass and the Pit* (aka *Five Million Years to Earth*) didn't arrive until 1967 – and Kneale's yeti story, *The Abominable Snowman* (1957). These are all interestingly grey, black-and-white movies, with the sort of understated commitment in performance and realist locations that was familiar from British war and crime films (in the 1950s, it was reckoned that Brits did these action genres in a less gung-ho, more convincing way than the Yanks). The first *Quatermass* even had Jack Warner, a police icon from *The Blue Lamp* (1949), as the befuddled copper who trots along after Brian Donlevy's bullish Quatermass, as well as strong little cameos from familiar actors as an array of scientists, civil servants, cops, soldiers, spivs, drunks, BBC personnel and shirty bystanders. Hammer continued with sf in the lurid *X the Unknown* (1956), originally planned as a Quatermass sequel until Kneale objected, and Joseph Losey's extraordinary *The Damned* (1963), about deliberately irradiated children being trained to survive a world war. The 'Quatermass' style recurs in a string of well-acted, alternately thoughtful and melodramatic, wildly-titled pictures: *Village of the Damned* (1960), Val Guest's *The Day the Earth Caught Fire* (1961), *Children of the Damned* (1964), *The Night Caller* (1965 – the one in which the alien comes to Earth in search of women advertised in *Bikini Girl* magazine), *Unearthly Stranger* (1963), *The Earth Dies Screaming* (1964), *Island of Terror* (1966), *Invasion* (1966), *Night of the Big Heat* (1967) and *The Body Stealers* (1969).

Alongside these pictures were a few movies that looked across the Atlantic for inspiration. They often took in lower-case Yank guest stars (Gene Evans in *Behemoth, the Sea Monster*, 1959), modelled themselves on specific American films (*The Projected Man*, 1966, is a scrambling of the atoms of *The Fly*, 1958) or even (as in *First Man into Space*, 1958, and *Fiend Without a Face*, 1958) pretended that home counties locations were New Mexico (though they rarely remembered which side of the road a borrowed jeep should be driven). First and most cherishable of these is *Devil Girl From Mars* (1954), with a PVC dominatrix (Patricia Laffan) and her walking fridge robot menacing a small Scots community in search of virile men, which is one of a series of 'aliens down the pub' pictures that revolve around drinking establishments. *Immediate Disaster* (aka *Stranger From Venus*, 1954) is another, taking star Patricia Neal from its inspiration (*The Day the Earth Stood Still*), as are *Strange World of Planet X* (1957) and *The Trollenberg Terror* (aka *The Crawling Eye*, 1958), both of which mix Forrest Tucker (imported by Hammer to replace TV's Stanley Baker in *The Abominable Snowman*) with plots taken from ITV serials put on air in an attempt to compete with the BBC's Quatermass franchise.

There were even British attempts at space opera, from the camp of *Fire Maidens From Outer Space* (1956), with spiv-types Harry Fowler and Sydney Tafler as chain-smoking astronauts discovering Atlantean babes dancing to Borodin on one of Jupiter's moons, to the pomp of *Satellite in the Sky* (also 1956), with Donald Wolfit and Kieron Moore clashing over the desirability of testing an A-bomb in low-Earth orbit. Connoisseurs of the bizarre are also recommended the contributions to mad science of distinguished

character actors George Couloris and Michael Gough. In *Man Without a Body* (1957) and *Womaneater* (1959), George Couloris revives the severed head of Nostradamus and feeds chunky tarts to a killer tree, while *Horrors of the Black Museum* (1959) and *Konga* (1960) find Gough dosing his assistant with Jekyll formula or enlarging an ape until it can rampage across a Godzilla-style London miniature (not to mention feeding a girl to another hungry plant). This underexplored arena of the strange also features *Gorgo* (1960), another Toho-style giant monster movie (whose mother-and-son plot has proved very influential, popping up in *Jaws 3-D*, 1983 and *The Lost World: Jurassic Park*, 1997).

Having made a mint with their sf ventures, Hammer were encouraged to branch out into colour and horror with Fisher's *The Curse of Frankenstein* (1957), casting Peter Cushing (a horror 'name' from the Kneale version of *Nineteen Eighty-Four*) as a dashing, rakish Baron Frankenstein and Christopher Lee as his stumbling, geek-look monster. At the time, the film was condemned for its sadism (dismembered body parts, bright red spurts of blood), but the real change it made on British science fiction was the yanking in of an almost-camp attitude previously hinted at in British cinema only in the wilder Gainsborough bodice-rippers or the more experimental weirdnesses of Powell and Pressburger.

chain-smoking astronauts discovering Atlantean babes dancing to Borodin

Cushing has a knack of making his lines seem wittier than they are, and Fisher cuts from a gruesome murder to Cushing at breakfast asking Hazel Court to pass the marmalade, segueing from a yuck to a laugh in a way that was jarringly unusual in 1957 (though a cinema staple ever since). The chocolate-box colours of the cinematography and the fussy detail of the laboratory sets are a real contrast with the grimy, sparse bomb sites and government offices of the Quatermass films. Hammer swiftly followed up with *Dracula* (1958) and a run of mostly supernatural horror films, but they imported a genre-bending tone to British sf, yoking in an Olde Junke Shoppe aesthetic, a very British cruelty and a commitment to the eccentric that informs contributions as far apart as *Doctor Who*, *The Avengers*, Michael Moorcock and the Bond movies.

Hammer kept coming back to sf, notably in Fisher's run of mostly extraordinary Frankenstein

Michael Carter (Hugh McDermott) defends Earthmen everywhere from Nyah (Patricia Laffan) and her robot Chani. Beware the Devil Girl From Mars (1954).

features with Cushing engaging in wilder and nastier experiments, but also in such sports as Michael Carreras's delirious *The Lost Continent* (1968), a ripping Dennis Wheatley yarn set in the Sargasso Sea, and *Moon Zero Two* (1969), a space Western with Warren Mitchell coveting a sapphire meteorite. By then, the field had escaped from them. The 1960s saw an explosion in British pop culture in everything from music to fashion, and cinema – which had the reaction time of an ocean liner compared to nippy little media like TV or pop records – lagged behind. The Bond movies, which began with *Dr. No* (1962), are Anglo-American product but in love with the idea of Britishness (and despising 'foreigners' of all sorts), and break with the realist tradition of *Saturday Night and Sunday Morning* (1960) much as the Hammer films did, with a similar enthusiasm for heaving bosoms and post-death wisecracks.

But the real pacesetters in mod sf were *New Worlds*, which was into wild experimentation, and from supposedly staid television, which launched series that became accepted national institutions but were (and are) deeply strange: *Doctor Who* (1963-1989, 1996), *The Avengers* (1961-69, 1976-77) and *The Prisoner*

(1967-68). Not to mention the succession of 'Supermarionation' shows produced by Gerry and Sylvia Anderson (*Supercar*, 1961-62, *Fireball XL5*, 1962-63, *Stingray*, 1964-65, *Thunderbirds*, 1965-66, *Captain Scarlet and the Mysterons*, 1967-68) or even the mutation of sketch comedy shows into the utter surreality of Spike Milligan's *Q* cycle, *Do Not Adjust Your Set* (1967-68) or *Monty Python's Flying Circus* (1969-74). Here is a post-Wells, post-Hammer world of casually-accepted mind-blowing concepts ('it's bigger on the inside than the outside'), overturned social conventions (Cathy and Emma in leathers, drop-kicking stuntmen, and the Angels flying against the Mysterons while posing as fashion models), hang-overs from a Victorian or a WWII past (note the many Blimp figures from *Who*'s Brigadier to the officer class loons of Python), sixties-style gadgets (a pop-up toaster in 1066, the interchangeable pods of Thunderbird 2) and pick 'n' mix dandyisms. The key was the collision of past and future, represented by Steed's bowler hat and Cathy's kinky boots, or the teaming of defrosted Edwardian Gerald Harper and with-it dolly bird Juliet Harmer in *Adam Adamant Lives!* (1966-67). Off television, similar end-of-the-pier kaleidoscopes can be found in the records of The Bonzo Dog Doo-Dah Band (or even the Beatles) and the Cornelius or Bastable books of Michael Moorcock.

All of this began on television, and spilled tentatively into the cinema with such artefacts as the colourful mid-sixties Dalek and *Thunderbirds* movies and the seventies run of Python shows. The end products of this culture are Douglas Adams's multimedia franchise *The Hitch-Hiker's Guide to the Galaxy* (still best in its original radio incarnation, 1978) and the sit-com *Red Dwarf* (1988-), though the style has diffused into the cinema via the work of American Python Terry Gilliam, whose *Time Bandits* (1981) is another scrambling of *Who* and *Python*. Though the prevailing tone is jovial, it can also be despairing – especially when Americans like Stanley Kubrick (*Dr Strangelove*, 2001, *A Clockwork Orange*), Richard Lester (*The Bed Sitting Room*, 1969), Cornel Wilde (*No Blade of Grass*, 1970) or Gilliam (*Brazil*, 1985) get in on the act. There are more apocalypses than utopiae in this vision of a future mired in the past. The Swinging London scene of the 1960s could throw out *Scream and Scream Again* (1969), with a government-sponsored Frankenstein (Vincent Price) letting a floppy-shirted vampire composite loose on the disco scene, and *War Game* auteur Peter Watkins's *Privilege* (1967) – with Paul Jones as a pop star manipulated by a repressive government into a propaganda tool.

2001: A Space Odyssey, impossible to define as British or American, remains the most important science fiction film of all time, though it was succeeded in influence by the trivial, annoying *Star Wars* and *Star Trek* franchises. One of the effects of *2001* was to turn the attention of British sf to global (ie: American matters), with British creators delivering amazingly strange visions of the alien world across the Atlantic in works as varied as Nicolas Roeg's *The Man Who Fell to Earth* (1976) and *2000AD*'s succession of Judge Dredd strips. Sadly, this also meant that properties like *Doctor Who*, *The Avengers* and *Judge Dredd* would wind up revived in malforms tailored to or masterminded by Americans who couldn't understand what the whole point was and sent these vital, intriguing franchises – which had hitherto thrived or self-destructed through change – into an ossified limbo from which they are unlikely to recover. A similar process can be observed in the *Alien* series, which began as an Anglo-American effort (behind and in front of the cameras) in 1979 and has become more and more a standard Hollywood franchise.

Attempts at making US-style sf in England have not prospered – whether cheap (*Inseminoid*, 1980, *Split Second*, 1992, *Death Machine*, 1992) or expensive (*Saturn 3*, 1980, *Life Force*, 1985, *Slipstream*, 1989). These productions invariably top-line US players and are made by directors who are either American or want to be. There remains a bubbling-under of vital activity in the despised area where the pretentious meets the profound, and it is here that the spirit of *New Worlds* survives: Derek Jarman's *Jubilee* (1978), Peter Greenaway's *The Falls* (1980), Peter Wollen's *Friendship's Death* (1987), Ngozi Onwurah's *Welcome II the Terrordome* (1994) and Chris Petit and Iain Sinclair's *Asylum: or The Last Commission* (2000). Even British television sf, which was once willing to look to Isaac Asimov (*The Caves of Steel*, 1964) when Hollywood wouldn't touch an adaptation of a major sf novel, has taken a turn for the worse, to the point when it's possible to consider even the ropey *Blake's 7* as of some interest in its jaded look at the underside of *Star Trek*. In the eighties, there were major sf (or sf-tinged) outings like *Threads* (1984) and *Edge of Darkness* (1985), but the last decade, despite a last hurrah from Dennis Potter (*Cold Lazarus*, 1996), has been marked by compromises like *Invasion: Earth* (1998), which seem only tangentially aware of the tradition they are stumbling into.

Nevertheless, as of 2000 AD, British sf has as much potential for the future as it has a tradition to build upon. British authors, illustrators, directors, comics writers, scientists, visionaries and critics remain at the forefront of a field that is much more integrated (everyone does two or three jobs) and grounded in the general culture than in America, with a tradition of questioning the past and the future rather than cheerleading them and a post-imperial understanding of the complexities of all possible worlds that is hard to come by in a society as desperately confident as the United States. British sf can take as a model one of its first great characters,

the despised area where the pretentious meets the profound

the Time Traveller. From an oak-panelled, gaslit study filled with books and Victorian clutter, he steps into an untidy but modern laboratory and sits astride his crystal-powered machine, essentially a magic bicycle, then takes off into the timestream. He might be expected to visit Camelot (like Mark Twain's Yankee) or Gloriana's court, but instead he thrusts himself into the far future, desperate to discover how the great story of humanity will turn out.

Significantly, in the end, by choice or through misfortune, he doesn't come back.

CHAPTER 1
FROM PROSPERO'S BOOKS TO KUBRICK'S MONOLITH

MIRANDA: O, wonder! How many goodly creatures are there here! How beauteous mankind is! O brave new world, that has such people in't!
PROSPERO: 'Tis new to thee.

William Shakespeare, *The Tempest*, Act V, Scene I

It's well known that William Shakespeare's play *The Tempest* provided the uncredited inspiration for the 1956 science fiction movie *Forbidden Planet*, yet the bawdy bard of Stratford Upon Avon deserves more than a grudging footnote in the history of the genre, especially on his home ground. There is a case for regarding Shakespeare as the founding father of UK science fiction. Robby the Robot be damned, Shakespeare's influence discernible in such landmark examples of the genre as *Doctor Who*. Conceived nearly three centuries before H G Wells shaped what is now regarded as science fiction 'proper', *The Tempest* deploys many of genre's standard elements: a perilous voyage in a state-of-the-art vessel; a mysterious, 'unnatural' setting; a secluded man of secret learning with strange powers (and a lovely young daughter); bizarre creatures both friendly and malevolent, and some not very funny comedy relief (strictly optional). The creators of *Forbidden Planet* knew good source material when they saw it, though one suspects Shakespeare would have given the scriptwriter a good kicking.

Employed for around a dozen years of his career at the Globe Theatre, Bankside, London, writer in residence Shakespeare knew how to please all classes of audience, his patrons including both the educated nobility and the illiterate, thrill-hungry masses. Those not entirely appreciative of the narrative dexterity, in-depth characterisation, political commentary, psychological insight or poetic subtleties in his plays could still enjoy the often risqué humour and plotlines featuring star-crossed lovers, conspiracies, mistaken identities, lost relatives, violence, mutilation, homicide, suicide, regicide, patricide,

multiple identical twins and underage sex. Plus a woman waking up to find herself in bed with a headless corpse (*Cymbeline*, for the record). Similarly, science fiction spans the entire cultural spectrum, from fatuous absurdity (Sean Connery's matching orange bandoliers and loincloth in John Boorman's *Zardoz* 1973) to the most profound philosophical reflections (the inevitability of stagnation, apathy and despair in a society without death, also in *Zardoz*). Sometimes the two occur simultaneously, as when the spectacular giant, flying stone head from *Zardoz* cruises to the Second Movement of Beethoven's Seventh Symphony, spews out weapons to its followers and then comes out with the line: 'The gun is good. The penis is evil'. (If all the above sounds a little off the wall, bear in mind that the film was originally going to star Burt Reynolds).

Dated at around 1611, *The Tempest* is among the last of the Shakespearean canon, which has led some to equate the central character, single parent and part-time magician Prospero, with the middle-aged playwright, both men looking to enjoy a peaceful retirement once their remaining business is set in order. Compared to his high-tech descendants, gnostic spell-weaver Prospero is remarkably modest, and largely benevolent, in his aims. Formerly the Duke of Milan, he let his interest in 'the liberal arts' dominate his life, unwisely leaving the actual governing to his untrustworthy brother, Antonio. 'Being transported and rapt in secret studies', Prospero was understandably peeved when Antonio organised a coup and set him and his infant daughter Miranda adrift in a leaky boat to die at sea. By good fortune, they were deposited on an uncharted island, inhabited by an aggressive, rapacious man-beast named Caliban, son of a former spell-casting resident, the 'damn'd witch Sycorax'. While Prospero's research into secret knowledge was non-malevolent, Sycorax's interests lay only in the black arts, 'mischiefs manifold, and sorceries terrible', which proved too much for her slave Ariel, now Prospero's servant, 'a spirit too delicate to act her

The Tempest: *Prospero warns Ariel, 'Dost thou forget/From what a torment I did free thee?'*

earthy and abhorr'd commands'. Marooned for a dozen years or so, Prospero has developed powers Victor Frankenstein would envy: 'graves at my command have wakened their sleepers, oped, and let 'em forth by my so potent art'. (At the risk of veering into anorak nit-picking, where on this remote, uninhabited island would Prospero find graves?) Aided by Ariel, on temporary lease after being rescued from agonising imprisonment within a tree, Prospero realises that commanding the forces of nature gives him a chance to regain his Dukedom, an understandable, if disappointingly earthbound ambition. Interestingly, Prospero's relationship with Ariel

Shakespeare certainly knew how to play the crowd

anticipates later science fiction in its dealings with the master/servant, human/non-human theme that tends to figure whenever artificial lifeforms are on the scene (Frankenstein's monster, Lieutenant Commander Data, and so many others). A product of neither man nor nature, Ariel exhibits a sense of humanity as keen as Prospero's after spying the latter's shipwrecked captives trembling in a cave.

ARIEL: ...if you now beheld them, your affections would become tender.
PROSPERO: Dost thou think so, spirit?
ARIEL: Mine would, sir, were I human.

'I prithee, be my god.' Trinculo and Stephano teach Caliban the pleasures of intoxicating liquor. The Tempest, Act 2, Scene 2, from Bell's illustrated Complete Works of Shakespeare, 1774.

Unlike the majority of subsequent alchemists, magicians and scientists, Prospero does not lust after wealth, power or conquest beyond the dreams of ordinary man. Rather than transform the outside world in his own visionary image, he yearns only to rejoin the society of men denied him for so many years, once the small business of his brother's treachery has been resolved. While later master scientists regard the existing status quo with barely veiled contempt, Prospero embraces it. Then again, he is a Duke. All the powers of enchantment are just a means to this end, to be discarded without hesitation once he sets sail for Milan: 'But this rough magic I here abjure ... I'll break my staff ... I'll drown my book'. Man, it seems, has no need of supernatural or superhuman powers in the everyday world, especially when his daughter is engaged to the King of Naples's son. Still, there is at least a small note of regret in Prospero's closing speech: 'Now my charms are all o'erthrown, and what strength I have's mine own, which is most faint.' The Tempest concludes with Prospero directly addressing the audience, pleading for his freedom: 'As you from crimes would pardon'd be, let your indulgence set me free.' The once all-powerful becomes powerless, dependent on the benevolence of the paying public for his liberty. Shakespeare certainly knew how to play to the crowd.

Anyway, onto Forbidden Planet. It's as American as a slightly suspect apple pie, it stars Leslie Nielsen before he was intentionally funny, it's a key film in the science fiction genre and, to some, it's grossly overrated. Released by a major studio, Metro-Goldwyn-Mayer, the film was the first science fiction epic in both Technicolor and Cinemascope, boasting striking futuristic sets and special effects that pushed the budget to over $1 million. The 'original' story was devised by writer Allen Adler and special effects man Irving Block, who were aiming for a higher level of sophistication than the genre usually exhibited. The Tempest, an undeniably classy act, happened to be Block's favourite play and its 'castaways on an enchanted island' storyline seemed ideal for science fiction adaptation, combining the fairytale quality of the original with some challenging, provocative ideas about future technology and the power of the human mind. According to some accounts, MGM didn't draw attention to their story source at the time, worried that middle-American audiences would be turned off by highbrow material. Nor did they have quite enough confidence in their first science fiction project to go the full 'A' budget route – one reason why the striking visuals are complemented by a decidedly 'B' grade script and cast.

The story parallels are certainly blatant. Set in the year 2200, the film charts a military space expedition to a mysterious, uncharted region, the planet Altair-4, where an elderly scientist, Dr Morbius (Walter Pidgeon), has been stranded for close on 20 years with his young, naive daughter, Alta (*Rocky Horror* favourite Anne Francis), the only survivors of an entire earth colony. Like Prospero, Morbius has a large measure of power over his adopted home, thanks largely to the technology left behind by the planet's former inhabitants, the Krells, who mysteriously disappeared. In place of spirit servant Ariel, Morbius enjoys the services of the more earthbound Robby the Robot (an impressive, if less than agile piece of robotic design that has become one of the great icons of the science fiction genre). The film departs from the original play in several major respects, turning some story points around completely. While Prospero deliberately shipwrecks his former allies to settle old scores, Morbius is deeply resentful of the United Planets Cruiser setting down on his planet, its crew asking awkward questions. Prospero is, on the whole, a balanced individual, but Morbius seems on the edge of sanity.

Commander Adams (Nielsen) already has more than a few suspicions about Morbius when the killings start.

Of course, the idea of exploring strange new worlds is present in *The Tempest*, given that Shakespeare was writing at a time when adventurers – to put it politely – were invading and colonizing the 'New World' of America with indecent haste and scant regard for the native population. By all accounts a keen investor in real estate, Shakespeare had shares in a company founded to reap the rewards of this rich virgin territory, displaying a shrewd business sense if questionable morals. The brutish Caliban, referred to in the play's dramatis personae as 'a savage and deformed Slave', has been interpreted by some as a symbolising an Elizabethan view of Native Americans: lustful, subhuman beasts to be enslaved or killed. Despite being introduced as a potentially threatening character, Caliban is rapidly transferred to the comedy relief department, his initial menace diffused with drunken antics. While the monstrous presence in *Forbidden Planet* is a full-blown homicidal maniac, Caliban is rendered meek and harmless by Prospero's power: 'I'll rack thee with old cramps, fill all thy bones with aches.'

On the planet Altair IV, Morbius (Walter Pidgeon) and Robby the Robot confront the visitors from Earth, led by Commander Adams (Leslie Nielsen). A scene from Forbidden Planet (1956), MGM's futuristic interpretation of The Tempest.

In July 1956 Robby visited New Malden as part of a trip to promote Forbidden Planet.

Much Hollywood-produced 1950s science fiction reflected the all-pervasive fear of the looming Communist menace. Alien invaders, Martian or otherwise, equated with another kind of 'Red Peril' as they slashed and burned through contemporary America. Set nearly three hundred years into the future, when the United Nations has expanded into the United Planets (did Gene Roddenberry ever see this movie?), Forbidden Planet is, by implication at least, rather more optimistic about mankind's ability ultimately to resolve his ideological and political differences. The film seems less sure about man's control of himself, especially in the case of someone as uptight, repressed and resentful as Morbius. Forbidden Planet's Freudian twist reveals the murderous, invisible attacker as an 'Id' monster unwittingly conjured by Morbius from the dark recesses of his own mind, massively IQ-boosted by exposure to technology left behind by the Krells. This monster of the subconscious is stirred into life by negative feelings, especially jealousy, towards others.

Thus when Alta falls for Commander Adams, Morbius's possessive, near-incestuous feelings towards his daughter awake the beast within with messy results (unfortunately, Cyril Hume's trite script, coupled with some post-production cuts, largely obscures this crucial plot point).

For all its faults, Forbidden Planet offers a prime example of a science fiction warning on the twisting, forked path of human progress (with a little alien help). Technology may make the world a fabulous place or cause disaster. At the movie's climax, Adams confronts Morbius with the awful truth: 'That thing out there. It's you!' Having taken his brain to places where the human mind just shouldn't go, Morbius has no way back. The force is within him, ferocious and uncontrollable. By contrast, Prospero's power, embodied in Ariel, is only temporary ('then to the elements be free, and fare thou well!'). More to the point, while monster Caliban grudgingly serves as Prospero's slave, he is in no way a projection of the magician's personality, acting out the latter's suppressed desires. When Caliban boasts of his attempted offstage rape of Miranda ('O ho, O ho! would't had been done! I had peopled else this isle with Calibans'), Prospero reacts with the disgust of a loving, protective father ('Abhorred slave, which any print of goodness wilt not take'), not the dark rage of a guilt-ridden man unwilling to confront his own incestuous urges. Something of a Machiavellian schemer, Prospero is blessed with knowledge, self-awareness and control, his mind unblighted by inner demons. Morbius, despite his vast IQ, is ultimately lacking in all these attributes. Unlike Caliban, the Id monster, briefly rendered visible under laser fire, cannot be controlled by Morbius's threats. Cornered with Alta, Adams and a disappointingly inactive Robby, Morbius attempts to vanquish his personal demon: 'I deny you! I give you up!', but it's too little, too late. Scientist and psychic offspring die together. Dr Morbius exhibits elements of both Victor Frankenstein, tampering with dubious science to create new life, and Henry Jekyll, messing with his mind to unleash the beast within. Compared to both these ill-fated medics, however, he seems appallingly ignorant.

Twenty-five years before *Forbidden Planet* hit the screens, *The Tempest* inspired another key work of science fiction, Aldous Huxley's 1932 novel *Brave New World*. Picking up on Prospero's ironic response to Miranda's ingenuous utterance, Huxley depicted a drug-controlled future society where the population is genetically selected and graded from Alpha to Epsilon. Fifty years later, *The Tempest* was reclaimed for eighties Britain as the cult hit musical *Return to the Forbidden Planet*, which replays the film's basic plot as the framework for over two dozen hit songs, an eclectic line-up ranging from The Surfaris' 'Wipeout', through The Zombies' 'She's Not There' to Patti Smith's 'Gloria'. Shakespeare, who slotted a musical interlude or two into *The Tempest*, would surely have approved.

MONSTROUS KNOWLEDGE

Two hundred years after Prospero put away his books, his rough magic thoroughly abjured, concerns about man's relentless, unquestioning pursuit of scientific knowledge came together in definitive form: Mary Wollstonecraft Shelley's 1818 novel *Frankenstein; or, The Modern Prometheus*. By the shores of Lake Geneva, in the Villa Diodati, the nineteen year old Mary Godwin spent a wild night or two during the summer of 1816 in the company of her poet boyfriend, Percy Bysshe Shelley, and their host Lord Byron, George Gordon to his friends.

According to Mary Shelley's own account, written for the 1831 edition of the book a good fifteen years after the event, following a few thunderstorms, some frank discussion of deep personal fears (and perhaps a little laudanum), the talk turned to composing ghost stories. Both Percy Shelley and Byron soon gave up, impatient with the restrictions of mere lumpen prose (or just plain idle). Dr John Polidori, Byron's personal physician, devised *Ernestus Berchtold, a Modern Oedipus* (not *The Vampyre*, which came later), a story now as obscure as its creator.

Aside from drawing on Greek myth for a classical parallel, Mary Godwin's own effort proved to be on a different plane entirely, reworking such legendary figures as the Golem, the homunculus and Faust to create a cautionary tale that would take root as an authentic modern myth. (For whatever reason, the late 1980s produced three cinematic restagings of this particular house party: Ken Russell's amusingly ludicrous *Gothic* 1986; the intriguing low key Spanish production *Rowing With the Wind* 1989, featuring both Hugh Grant and Liz Hurley, and *Haunted Summer* 1988, an adaptation of Anne Edwards's 1972 novel that sank without trace.) Though not the most accessible piece of literature for the contemporary sf

man's usurpation of God; the failure of science to assume responsibility for its creations

thrill seeker, *Frankenstein*'s underlying themes remain provocative and compelling: 'forbidden' knowledge; unnatural 'birth'; man's usurpation of God; the failure of science to assume responsibility for its creations. Filtered through scores of adaptations into the popular imagination, the basic story is straight-forward. Victor Frankenstein, a young student driven by the desire to push back the boundaries of knowledge, creates a man who is intelligent but hideously ugly (not to mention eight foot tall). Rejected by Frankenstein and the rest of humanity, the essentially good-natured 'monster' becomes seriously embittered and swears vengeance upon its creator, a reluctant and decidedly absentee father.

As science fiction, *Frankenstein* is extremely skimpy on technical specifics, offering little more than 'I collected the instruments of life around me'. It's likely that Mary Shelley drew her inspiration from the then fashionable 'science' of galvanism, apparently one of the topics of discussion at the Villa Diodati, where both Percy Shelley and Byron expressed a fascination with discovering 'the principle of life'.

Paul Krempe
(Robert Urquhart)
and his brilliant
protégé Victor
Frankenstein (Peter
Cushing) attempt
to revive a dead
puppy in Hammer's
The Curse of
Frankenstein
(1957).

Named after an Italian scientist, Luigi Galvani, this school of thought argued that electricity was some form of fluid chemical element, capable of flowing through wires like liquid. Thus an electric current run through a severed frog's leg would momentarily restore the spark of life (rather than merely produce a reflex muscle spasm). Percy Shelley himself had been intrigued by the life-giving properties of electricity, especially lightning bolts, though his undergraduate experiments at Oxford produced little more than a few mild shocks. As related to Arctic explorer Robert Walton, who discovers the half-crazed Frankenstein wandering the frozen wasteland, the story of the creation is coloured by revulsion and self-disgust. Frankenstein refuses to give away more than the merest hints: 'After days and nights of incredible labour and fatigue I succeeded in discovering the

cause of generation and life; nay, more, I became myself capable of bestowing animation upon lifeless matter.' Sadly, he just doesn't like what he sees: 'the beauty of the dream vanished, and breathless horror and disgust filled my heart.'

For all his initial success in the laboratory, Victor Frankenstein is hardly striking an impressive blow for scientific objectivity when he reacts to his twitching creation by screaming in terror and disappearing into the night at speed.

Frankenstein's subtitle, 'The Modern Prometheus', is a nod to Greek mythology that subsequent adaptations of the book largely disregarded. One of the Titans, an ancient race of giants, Prometheus took a handful of earth, a few drops of water, and moulded the resultant clay into man, created in the image of the gods (with or without divine approval, depending on the version being read). Realising that man needed a little help if he was to rise above the beasts and attain civilisation, Prometheus climbed up to Mount Olympus and stole fire from the hearth of the gods, returning to earth to grant man the precious gift. Chief Olympian Zeus, no friend of the Titans at the best of times, didn't take kindly to this unauthorised redistribution of divine power and decreed a severe punishment. Prometheus was chained to a rock on Mount Caucasus, where his liver was daily torn out and devoured by an eagle (or possibly a vulture), only to grow back during the night in time for the next day's feeding. Despite his unceasing agony, Prometheus remained defiant towards Zeus, until Hercules happened along and broke his chains. The Prometheus legend was a favourite with both Byron and Shelley, whose 1819 poem *Prometheus Unbound* is widely regarded as his masterwork, and probably seemed an ideal starting point for Mary Godwin's tale of over-reaching man. While the gift of fire sets mankind off down the path of technology, the subsequent wrath of the gods brings about grief and destruction.

Victor Frankenstein, like a few others in the medical profession, is afflicted with a god complex of his own: 'it was the secrets of heaven and earth that I desired to learn.' Naive and idealistic rather than coldly ambitious, Victor is very much the humanitarian: 'I had begun life with benevolent intentions, and thirsted for the moment when I should put them into practise, and make myself useful to my fellow beings.' Frankenstein stands at the head of a long line of scientific trailblazers whose undeniably good, or least non-malevolent, intentions soon run into deep trouble. Stamping out disease, curing illness and prolonging life are admirable ambitions, but creating new life is a calling that should be reserved either for God (creator of all things seen and unseen) or woman (biologically equipped for childbirth). As outlined in Shelley's novel and its countless variations, the reasons for this taboo are brutally simple:

1) *Medical pioneers working in the early nineteenth century can't create new life without robbing graves or collecting spare body parts, sometimes from living donors.*

Both Universal's *Frankenstein* (1931) and Hammer's *The Curse of Frankenstein* (1957) feature scenes where the corpses of executed criminals are furtively cut down from the gallows for a little recycling. As film historian Rudy Behlmer points out, in Universal's film, Frankenstein literally throws dirt in the face of

Death during the opening grave-robbing scene, excavated soil striking a nearby figure of the Grim Reaper. In the Hammer version, Frankenstein subsequently murders an elderly professor in order to appropriate the man's brain for his creation. In Paul Morrissey's *Flesh for Frankenstein* (1973), the Baron and his standard issue idiot assistant hang around the local brothel looking for some top breeding stock, casually decapitating one customer they take to be a sex fiend with a pair of giant shears (unfortunately for them, they picked a trainee monk). Even in the book, Frankenstein begins his work with a sense of detachment from the more unsavoury aspects of his research: 'a churchyard was to me merely the receptacle of bodies deprived of life, which, from being the seat of beauty and strength, had become food for the worm'. Put simply, if one's chosen occupation involves body snatching and murder, it's probably wise to seek retraining. The living shouldn't mess with the dead.

2) *The creature will almost certainly look hideous and, shunned by mankind, turn against its creator, unless a mate is provided.*

Leaving aside the hideous element, the creation of a female monster raises issues that most film versions preferred to avoid (yes to monster horror; no thank you very much to monster sex). Shelley's creature offers Frankenstein a bargain which seems, on the face of it, reasonable: if the monster is given a mate, he will leave mankind alone and spend the rest of his days in a remote part of the world far from civilisation. Frankenstein reluctantly agrees, only to lose his nerve once the full implications of this

yes to monster horror; no thank you to monster sex

monstrous union become clear: 'one of the first results of those sympathies for which the demon thirsted would be children, and a race of devils who would be propagated upon the earth who might make the very existence of the species of man a condition precarious and full of terror.'

A race of monster children sounds an alarming prospect, to be sure, yet it should have occurred to the medically trained Frankenstein that he could create a female being without the capacity to reproduce (the original monster's own fertility is never discussed). One suspects that Frankenstein – and Mary Shelley – just couldn't stomach the idea of the creature having a carnal good time. Whatever the case, Frankenstein wastes no time breaking his side of the deal: 'I thought with a sensation of madness on my promise of creating another like to him, and trembling with passion, tore to pieces the thing on which I was engaged.' Thus to save future human generations, Frankenstein commits an act as brutal as any of the creature's misdeeds. In Kenneth Branagh's *Mary Shelley's Frankenstein* (1994), one of the closest film adaptations of the book, Frankenstein (Branagh) goes through with the operation, creating the 'bride' from the body of a lynched servant girl and the head of his murdered wife, Elizabeth (Helena Bonham Carter). As it happens, the servant, Justine, was 'executed' for a crime committed by the monster, who more recently ripped out Elizabeth's heart, so the chances of the union blossoming are remote. The resulting female creature, with a necklace of stitches and a weird fleshy eyepatch, sets herself on fire with

The monster undergoes virtual crucifixion by the mob

indecent haste. Universal's *Bride of Frankenstein* (1935), prudently assembled from anonymous donors, is a hissing seven foot amazon with Queen Nefertiti-style hair, a tent-like white dress (partly to disguise the fact that actress Elsa Lanchester was on stilts) and a distinct lack of interest in her intended mate. The original script supposedly added Elizabeth Frankenstein (Valerie Hobson) to the bridal ingredients, but Universal never seriously considered this perversely logical idea. When Hammer got around to *Frankenstein Created Woman* (1967), male and female were ingeniously fused within the same body, a drowned girl invested with the vengeful soul of her wrongly executed boyfriend.

Kenneth Branagh directed and co-starred in Mary Shelley's Frankenstein (1994), a faithful retelling of the original story.

3) *Ordinary townsfolk, unfamiliar with the tenets of Enlightenment rationalism, will very likely get the wrong idea when the Creature takes a dubious interest in their close relatives.*

The book doesn't make too much of this, aside from the creature's encounter with the De Lacey clan. Having been extensively educated by kindly (and blind) old Mr De Lacey, the creature gets short shrift from his sighted son, who beats him out of their cottage. The more familiar image of the angry, torch-bearing mob marching through the darkness on the old windmill or Castle Frankenstein (or wherever) is a creation of the 1931 film, reused several times during the Universal series.

Audience sympathies tend to be with the monster by this stage in the proceedings, the villagers resembling nothing more than a lynch mob, thirsty for blood. Director James Whale described the chase sequence in the first Universal film as 'the pagan sport of a mountain manhunt'. In *Bride of Frankenstein*, the monster undergoes virtual crucifixion by the mob, a blatant Christ parallel thoroughly in keeping with the film's high-camp tone.

The theme of dangerous childbirth, natural or otherwise, held a particular resonance during the early nineteenth century (and beyond), when the infant mortality rate was extremely high, even among the privileged classes who could afford medical treatment. Mary Shelley's mother, the pioneering feminist Mary Wollstonecraft, died shortly after her daughter was born. Mary Shelley herself gave premature birth to a daughter, who soon died, lost her young son William to illness, and later suffered a miscarriage. Only one child survived: Percy, born in 1819 – a year after the publication of *Frankenstein*. Where nature so often failed, science could hardly hope to prosper.

While the failure of Victor Frankenstein's experiment comes as no great surprise, it's notable that Mary Shelley never really explains the reasons for the disastrous outcome. It's often argued that Victor is prejudged for 'playing god' and therefore doomed right from the start, though Mary Shelley probably shared her husband-to-be's then scandalous atheist convictions. Shelley certainly spends an inordinate number of pages stressing how both the monster and Frankenstein himself feel that the latter is to blame for his failure to take responsibility for what he created.

While this apparent uncertainty could be counted as one of the book's flaws, it leaves open the possibility that, had Victor attempted to care for and educate his creation, its benevolent nature would have been allowed to develop and even permitted it to exist with some measure of happiness. Lacking any sense of parental instinct or duty, Frankenstein abandons both his 'child' and any hope of proving his theories correct. There is a real sense of both opportunity and

For all the boldness of its themes, Frankenstein *is in the end a strikingly reactionary work*

innocence lost here. Joss Whedon describes *Frankenstein* as a story of responsibility: 'It's really about the consequences of having given life'. The novel certainly makes for a scathing indictment of absentee parents. Unfortunately, Mary Shelley fails to pursue this line of thought, opting instead for a safer route: man goes up against nature and gets his fingers burned to a crisp. Whether Frankenstein should be blamed for his blasphemy or his irresponsibility, his work is still fated to go wrong. The very nature and circumstances of the monster's birth mean that it is fated to live a life of misery and hostility. Any inherent goodness it may possess is outweighed by the conditions under which it was produced. For all the boldness of its themes, *Frankenstein* is in the end a strikingly reactionary work, its dying scientist berating himself for having tampered with that old science fiction standby, Knowledge Best Left Alone: 'Learn from me, if not by my precepts, at least by my example, how dangerous is the acquirement of knowledge, and how much happier that man is who believes his native town to be the world, than he who aspires to become greater than his nature will allow.'

So much for progress. Universal's *Frankenstein* plays just as safe, spelling out its moral stance in a censor-friendly prologue. Worried about offending powerful religious groups, the studio

A poster promoting a re-issue of Universal's Frankenstein (1931). British actor Boris Karloff played the Monster when Bela Lugosi and John Carradine both turned the role down.

added this sequence months after the finish of principal shooting. Delivered by actor Edward Van Sloan, who plays the conservative Dr Waldman in the film proper, this address to the audience informs us that the film-makers 'are about to unfold the story of Frankenstein, a man of science [already dubious], who sought to create a man after his own image [monstrous]… without reckoning upon God [blasphemous]'. There is no sense of confusion or ambiguity here, though the script later complicates the issue by having 'Henry' Frankenstein (Colin Clive) unwittingly transplant an abnormal, criminal brain into his creation, which despite this does not seem automatically inclined towards violence or evil (Given Waldman's earlier demonstration of the clear distinctions between a normal and abnormal brain, it's surprising that former student Frankenstein doesn't spot the difference). The scientist is attempting a task not meant for mortal men. Frankenstein's line at the climax (so to speak) of the creation sequence, the much-censored 'Now I know what it feels like to be God', underlines his blasphemy, which cannot go unpunished. Like the original Frankenstein, Henry soon repents his scientific obsessions and turns on his creation: 'I made him with these hands and with these hands I shall destroy him.' The Baron Frankenstein of the later Hammer sequence would surely despise this attitude. As Peter Cushing points out in *Frankenstein Must Be Destroyed* (1969): 'If man were not given to invention and experiment' we would all still be living in caves. However harshly we judge the amoral, occasionally murderous antics of Hammer's Frankenstein, Shelley's conclusion is as conservative and orthodox as could be wished.

It's long been the received wisdom that *Frankenstein* the novel does not lend itself to ready adaptation, whether for stage, film or television. There are plenty of elements in the story with the potential to generate narrative excitement: the creation of the monster from corpses (a major setpiece in most retellings of the story); Victor Frankenstein's flight from his creature; his gradual descent into madness; the creature's systematic elimination of Victor's friends and family, culminating in the murder of his bride; Victor's pursuit of his creation, leading to their deaths in a remote frozen wasteland. This is potentially gripping stuff, yet doesn't really read that way in the book. Shelley seems to have been more interested in ideas than character or story, treating the plot as a vehicle for her moral lessons, which wouldn't matter so much if she had a surer grasp of narrative.

The otherwise fascinating monster is a particularly problematic figure in this respect. While as imposing, ugly and, on occasion, murderous as any of its cinematic counterparts, the creature is less a plausible character than a sounding board for the author. Writing at the tail end of the eighteenth-century Gothic tradition, which valued gruesome atmosphere above storytelling, Mary Shelley wanted to draw less than subtle parallels with John Milton's *Paradise Lost* and God's responsibility towards his creation, the fallen angel Lucifer. Described by British Gothic specialist David Pirie as a variation on Rousseau's 'noble savage', the monster is given to lengthy speeches on the misery of his existence (don't we know it) and philosophical justification for his acts of violence. As the human race will not love him, he'll settle for stark terror.

Mary Shelley's subsequent fiction never came close to repeating the success of *Frankenstein*. Few have even heard of her later science fiction novel *The Last Man* (1826), which envisages the human race destroyed by pestilence (given the amount of tragedy in her own life, Mary Shelley's preoccupation with mortality, especially of the premature variety, is not hard to understand). Bearing this in mind, it's hardly surprising that early adaptations of the book radically altered the characters. By 1823, there were five stage versions doing the rounds, including Richard Brinsley Peake's influential *Presumption, or: The Fate of Frankenstein*, which reduced the creature to an inarticulate brute and introduced a new character called Fritz, Frankenstein's assistant (elements taken up in many subsequent versions). Attempts to produce faithful screen versions of the original novel never quite seem to click. Universal's largely forgotten small screen retelling *Frankenstein: The True Story* (1973), made for NBC, was touted as a definitive adaptation of the Mary Shelley novel, which explains the odd, not to say misleading subtitle (it might be scary but it didn't really happen). Based on a screenplay co-authored by respected writer Christopher Isherwood, this 200 minute epic certainly uses elements of the book previously discarded by adaptors, notably the Arctic finale, yet the end result strays a long way from the original, with very uneven results. Isherwood and co-writer Don Bachardy fell out with Universal early on in preproduction, especially over the appointment of director Jack Smight, and the script was extensively rewritten without their input or consent. Leonard Whiting's tortured young doctor is closer to the original than either Colin Clive or Peter Cushing but lacks their fierce passion (it doesn't help that, thanks to production delays and reshoots, Whiting's Frankenstein gains and loses a beard in the space of one scene). The introduction of James Mason as fellow monster-maker 'Dr Polidori', complete with acid burned hands and Chinese servants, suggests that Universal simply lost confidence in their material. There is, however, a chance to see Jane Seymour get her head torn off. Four years later, the Swedish-Irish co-production *Victor Frankenstein* (1977), starring Stanley Kubrick regular Leon Vitali, offered the first genuinely faithful retelling of Shelley's novel, toning down the expected horror elements in favour of brooding, melancholy atmosphere. Misleadingly retitled *The Terror of Frankenstein* for American release, the film had no real place in the shock-hungry 1970s horror market and received scant distribution. In truth, any serious attempt to recreate accurately the book for a mass audience is likely to end up as *Mary Shelley's Frankenstein*, overloaded with dialogue for the hard-of-understanding, caricature performances and frenetic direction.

HIGHER INTELLIGENCE

It's tempting to link Shelley's fable of an overreaching scientist, daring to play god, with the ideas of nineteenth century German philosopher Friedrich Wilhelm Nietzsche, who declared god dead and promoted man to the supreme being slot. Best known for this concept of the 'ubermensch' – literally the 'overman', or 'superman' – Nietzsche's public image tends towards the unsavoury. Mentally unstable for much of his life and a popular figure with the Nazi Party, his vision of the 'superman' has been so mistranslated, misinterpreted and generally

Nietzsche would have had little time for the doctor's moral pangs and ultimate repentance

twisted that its exact meaning has never been clearly established. It's generally agreed that Nietzsche saw the ultimate aim of man as the enhancement of the human species. This sounds fair enough, but only a select group of elite individuals could attain such enhancement, those 'of a high, independent intellect, a will to stand alone … a great understanding'. Victor Frankenstein certainly qualifies on these three counts, and his creation of an artificial lifeform has major implications for the possibility of a new, improved race, yet Nietzsche would have had little time for the doctor's moral pangs and ultimate repentance.

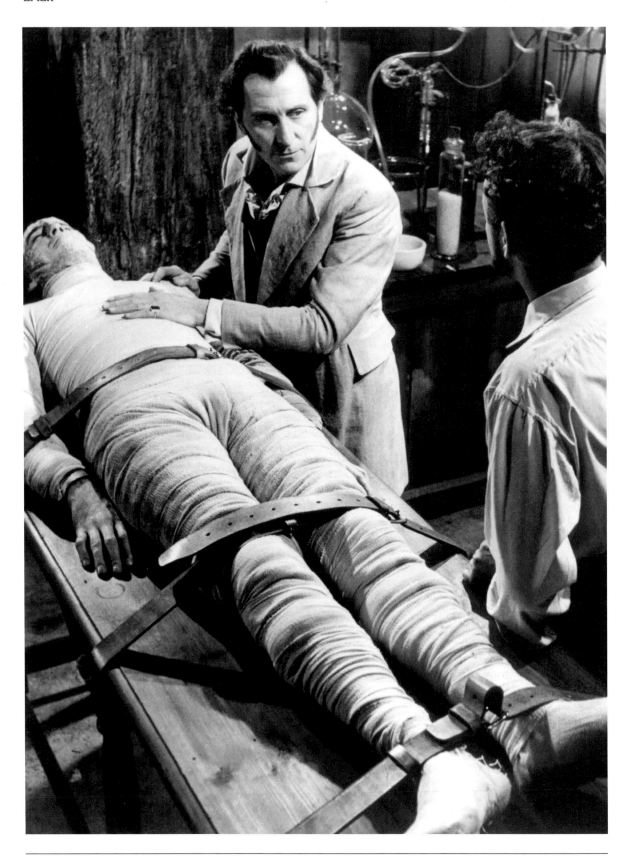

Rejecting Christian and liberal ethics, along with all despised democratic ideals, Nietzsche argued that the superman must not be limited by conventional morals, which are the provenance of the weak and feeble-minded. An authentic superman must be capable of almost anything, especially with technology, the modern Ariel, to aid him. Lacking Nietzsche's apparent brutalist streak, Shelley invests neither creator nor creature with the characteristics of the 'true' superman. Despite his initial disregard for graveyard decorum, young Frankenstein sees his work as benefitting all mankind, not just a select few. He neither regards himself as belonging to any intellectually superior group nor harbours the desire to create a race of supermen. For the creature's part, far from despising the 'inferior' human race, he craves the acceptance and society of the ordinary man.

Nietzsche's concept of the 'elect self' or 'higher' being provides a more profitable comparison with the figure of Frankenstein as envisaged by Hammer Studios. Kicking off with the surprise hit *The Curse of Frankenstein* in 1957, Hammer turned out a total of seven *Frankenstein* films, six of which starred the inimitable Peter Cushing as the ethically dubious Baron. (1970's *The Horror of Frankenstein*, featuring Ralph Bates in the title role, is a clumsy black comedy remake of *Curse* of interest only to completists.) Having shifted the emphasis from creature to creator, Hammer developed the character with impressive consistency, especially given that only the first two films, both scripted by Jimmy Sangster, have linked narratives. Horror maestro Terence Fisher, who directed all but one of the Cushing *Frankensteins*, always looked for the best in the character. He explained in a 1964 interview: 'Baron Frankenstein wants to create something ... He was after perfection – the tragic pursuit of perfection. He's ruthless only because of his ideals... Maybe I didn't plug his idealism enough.' On the plus side, this more mature Frankenstein is cultured, charismatic, fiercely intelligent and an obviously dedicated man of science. He's also cold, arrogant, manipulative, obsessive, utterly amoral and ruthless to the point of murder. Short on natural modesty, Frankenstein flaunts his genius: 'I always had a brilliant intellect'. He derides his fellow man – and woman – as ignorant, contemptible creatures to be used and discarded. As Nietzsche puts it in *Beyond Good and Evil*: 'the greater, more complex, more comprehensive life lives beyond the old morality; the individual is forced to make his own laws.'

Baron Frankenstein sees himself as a man whose intellect and idealism lifts him above the normal run of humanity. He relentlessly pursues his desire to create a perfect human being, an amalgam of the best parts of various bodies, as outlined in *Curse*: 'a man with perfect physique, with the hands of an artist and the matured brain of a genius'. The social conventions and morality of his time carry no weight in his thinking as far as this work is concerned. Cushing himself liked to compare the Baron with pioneering heart transplant surgeon Christian Barnard – a two-edged compliment if ever there was one – yet the 'superman' parallel seems more apt. Cushing's Frankenstein has no time for either God or his representatives on Earth. Visited in his condemned cell by a pompous priest at the start of *Curse of Frankenstein*, the Baron is dismissive: 'Keep your spiritual comfort for those who think they need it.' This same priest has his head chopped off by a guillotine on Frankenstein's instruction in *The Revenge of Frankenstein* (1958; given the censorious climate of the late fifties, it's surprising Hammer got away with this).

Unlike Shelley's Frankenstein, the Baron is more than happy to take responsibility for his work, indeed, things invariably start to go wrong for him once his creations escape from his control (one

Cushing's Frankenstein has no time for either God or his representatives on Earth

dissolved in acid, one savagely beaten, two consumed by fire, one drowned and one shot and disembowelled). After Christopher Lee's memorably pathetic, childlike creature – described by Fisher as 'some wandering, forlorn minstrel of monstrosity' – is shot in the eye in *Curse*, Frankenstein lovingly restores it to life. Anyone worried that the Baron might be getting sentimental is reassured a few scenes later when his maid, a spurned lover pregnant with their child, threatens blackmail. Frankenstein locks her in with the creature and calmly waits for the screaming to start (thus the prized man-made 'offspring' terminates the unwanted natural child). While *The Revenge of Frankenstein* tones down the Baron's vicious streak, he has no problem treating his charity hospital, run under the pseudonym 'Dr Stein', as a private organ depository, amputating a healthy limb now and then for his new creation. As an insurance policy, the presumed dead doctor constructs a lookalike body to house his brain, a wise precaution given the general lack of good will once Dr Stein's cover is blown. Beaten to a pulp by his charity

Frankenstein (Peter Cushing) and Krempe (Robert Urquhart) with their bandaged Creature (Christopher Lee) in The Curse of Frankenstein (1957).

Working undercover in a poor hospital, Baron Frankenstein (Peter Cushing) evaluates a potential limb donor (Michael Mulcaster) in The Revenge of Frankenstein (1958).

patients (including one still resentful about the loss of his legs), the Baron is resurrected in his new shell as Harley Street's dashingly moustachio'd Dr Frank, who opens for business as the closing credits roll. Thus Frankenstein becomes his own creation, the one shining, if ironic success in an otherwise frustrating career.

Having turned a neat full circle, the Hammer Frankenstein saga would seem to have come to a suitable finish, but the studio had other ideas. An immediate follow-up, *(And Then) Frankenstein Created Woman*, was announced in the Hollywood trade journal *Variety* in July 1958, to star Cushing and imported French sex goddess Brigitte Bardot. An obvious spin on Bardot's 1956 hit *Et Dieu Crea la Femme/And God Created Woman*, this tantalising blend of Gothic horror and continental sexploitation never reached audiences in its intended form. For whatever reason, either Bardot's unavailability or *Revenge*'s disappointing American box office, the project stalled for eight years. When *Frankenstein Created*

Woman did finally reach the screens, it depicted the Baron as a more or less heroic figure, a persecuted man of science whose sometimes questionable methods pale next to the unfeeling cruelties of the 'normal' outside world that condemns him as a black magician: a crippled, deformed girl taunted by wealthy bullies; the drunken murder of her protective father; the wrongful execution of her boyfriend, also Frankenstein's assistant; the girl's subsequent suicide. Having united the deceased lovers via his revolutionary soul transplant (it sounds risible but plays well onscreen), the Baron is reduced to a helpless onlooker as his seductive polysexual creation goes on the bloody vengeance trail.

Sadly, this softer, caring-sharing side of Frankenstein was conspicuous by its absence in the sequel, *Frankenstein Must Be Destroyed*, which opens with the latter casually decapitating a fellow medic with a sickle. A thief, blackmailer, murderer and rapist, the Baron appears incapable of seeing his actions as in any way wrong. When his shocked assistant points out that obtaining a healthy body to house the prized brain of an insane former colleague will involve murder, Frankenstein merely replies 'Of course, Karl. How else?' The last film of the Hammer series, *Frankenstein and the Monster from Hell* (1974), ends with the Neanderthal giant of a creature, fitted with the regulation brain of a mathematical genius and hands of an artist, being torn to pieces by a crowd of lunatics. 'Best thing that could have happened to him' the Baron comments, concluding that his work went wrong this time owing to 'too much surgery and not enough biochemistry'. Enough.

THE MOVIE MONSTERS

When Nietzsche first postulated the idea of a higher being, he probably wasn't thinking in terms of artificial intelligence, a concept that Mary Shelley raised in *Frankenstein* without really exploring its more sinister implications. Victor Frankenstein builds a creature with a level of intelligence, self-awareness and physical strength far greater than that of the average man. All these qualities count for little, however, when the creature, denied any place in human society, succumbs to self-pity and self-destruction (there are a few murders along the way, to be sure, but it's minor

league stuff). More assertive and aggressive man-made beings, whether robotic, cybernetic or ersatz organic, would fuel the dreams, and nightmares, of science fiction writers and artists for years to come. When Isaac Asimov laid down the ground rule that no robot lifeform could harm a human being, much

'too much surgery and not enough biochemistry'

like Robby in *Forbidden Planet*, he was whistling in the dark. HAL 9000, the *Bladerunner* replicants, even the Terminator, can all be seen as updated versions of Frankenstein's monster, what could happen when men attempt to play god with artificial lifeforms or even try to make gods out of machines.

Designed to oversee man's deep space travel, where the crew spend long periods in suspended animation, 2001's HAL computer possesses a good deal more character than the bland, emotionless astronauts he serves. Unfortunately, this 'personality' also exhibits neurosis, breakdown and homicidal mania, leading to a kill-or-be-killed showdown between HAL and sole surviving astronaut David Bowman (Keir Dullea). It's notable that HAL falls apart when he acts like a man, not a machine. The replicants, android fugitives pursued by Harrison Ford's reluctant blade runner in the year 2019, are as murderous as HAL when cornered, yet remain oddly sympathetic, even when snapping Mr Ford's fingers. Designed to serve as off-world slave labour, they are given offbeat human names, notably Roy Batty and Pris, implanted memories of non-existent pasts, and a lifespan of only a few years. Pleading with his creator, Dr Tyrell (Joe Turkel), for just a little more time, Batty (Rutger Hauer) is denied by the smug cyber mogul and responds by crushing Tyrell's head (offscreen). The rooftop showdown between dying android and bloodied blade runner is touching, Batty allowing his pursuer to live, suggesting at least the possibility of man and intelligent machine achieving peaceful co-existence (unless, of course, the blade runner is another replicant, in which case only the androids are going to make it). Arnold Schwarzenegger's original Terminator, however, is an unmitigated sonofabitch, a relentless, emotionless killing mechanism with dubious dress sense. Starting off in the year 2024, when computers have usurped man's place as rulers of the earth, this time

Baron Frankenstein (Peter Cushing) and Dr Hertz (Thorley Walters) prepare to revive and remake the drowned Christina (Susan Denberg) in Frankenstein Created Woman (1967).

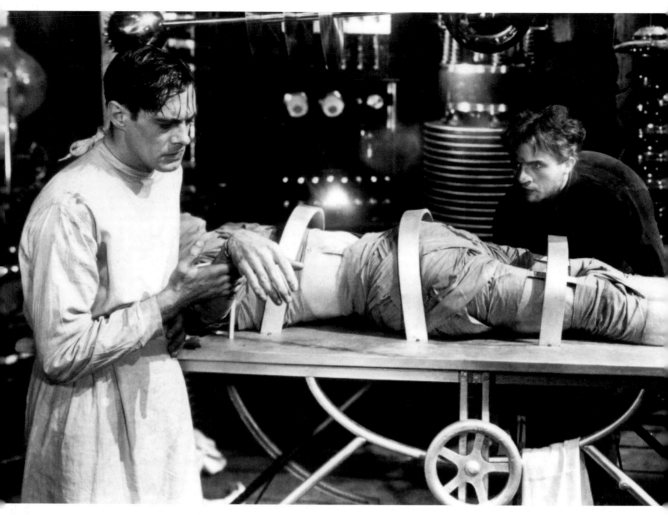

Henry Frankenstein (Colin Clive) assesses the results of his research in Frankenstein (1931).

travel-paradox saga makes the interesting point that human reliance on technology will inevitably lead to machine revolution if this technology ever achieves self-awareness. A point forcibly demonstrated when the Terminator punches its fist into an arrogant street punk's chest and pulls out his still beating heart (a scene recreated to somewhat risible effect in *Mary Shelley's Frankenstein*). Even future worlds, where mankind is a more or less sorted species, tend to contain artificial lifeforms just waiting for a chance to get nasty. The wholesome, non-megalomaniac crew of the Battlestar Galactica had regular problems with the robotic Cylons, despite the latter's lumbering, arthritic movement and Metal Mickey voices.

The ongoing *Frankenstein* saga is a classic example of the strange but true. Mary Godwin, known for most of her brief life as Percy Bysshe Shelley's mistress, then second wife, then widow, came up with a story, a modern myth, that became far better known to the wider public than anything Shelley himself ever

wrote. Having served as Mary's consultant and editor on the manuscript, Shelley was credited by some as the novel's true author, following its initial, anonymous publication. Shelley's name remains inextricably entwined with the *Frankenstein* legend: Universal's 1931 film credits the source novel to 'Mrs Percy B Shelley'. In *The Bride of Frankenstein*, they both appear as characters in an amusingly fey prologue. In *Gothic*, Shelley (Julian Sands) stands naked on the roof of the Villa Diodati as an electrical thunderstorm rages around him, the laudanum-stoned poet transfixed by the supposedly life-giving force.

Whatever the faults of Mary Shelley's debut novel as literature, it provides an archetypal demonstration of science fiction's two faces: the pulp and the profound. Filmgoers entirely ignorant of her novel have sat through such varied offerings as *Frankenstein Meets the Wolfman*; *Abbott and Costello Meet Frankenstein*; *I Was a Teenage Frankenstein*; *Frankenstein's Daughter*; *Jesse James Meets Frankenstein's Daughter*; *Frankenstein Meets the*

Space Monster; Frankenstein Conquers the World; Dracula versus Frankenstein (there are three different films with this title); Santo versus the Daughter of Frankenstein; Lady Frankenstein; Frankenhooker and Blackenstein (honest to God). In fact, the Abbott and Costello version is pretty good. Tim Burton, director of the melancholy Frankenstein variant Edward Scissorhands (1990), started his career with Frankenweenie, the touching 27 minute tale of a small boy restoring his beloved pet dog to life.

The Frankenstein saga took on a sinister real-life note following World War II, when it was revealed that Nazi scientists, given a ready supply of human research material, had attempted to emulate the title character with their own 'Frankenstein'-style experiments. Of course, the Nazi Party had officially embraced the ideas of Nietzsche, albeit in vastly simplified and twisted form, promoting their own 'superman' in the guise of the Aryan ideal (blonde hair, blue eyes, athletic physique and so forth). Short of earthbound evidence for this version of the superior being, especially after black athlete Jesse Owens's victories at the 1936 Berlin Olympic Games, the Nazis advanced one theory that their celestial ancestors had been brought to earth in drifting 'cosmic ice', an entirely different species from the rest of humankind. In Ira Levin's Hitler-cloning fantasy The Boys from Brazil, filmed in 1978, Dr Joseph Mengele idles away his South American exile turning the native children's brown eyes to the prerequisite blue, an image perhaps more disturbing than the brood of budding young Hitlers.

Intentionally or not, the Italian-French-American co-production Flesh for Frankenstein, often known as Andy Warhol's Frankenstein, deftly blends Shelley, Hammer, Nietzsche and neo-Nazism into a compelling, if deliberately stomach-turning whole. Directed by Warhol regular Paul Morrissey, with a little assistance from Italian exploitation veteran Antonio Margheriti, the film is sumptuous, ludicrous, gross, witty and even tender. (Warhol happily confessed that his only contribution to the production was turning up for the press parties). Portrayed by mad-eyed, slick-haired German actor Udo Kier, the incestuous, necrophiliac and extremely mad Baron wants to create the perfect male and female as the Adam and Eve for his projected Serbian master-race (extremely chilling in the light of 'ethnic cleansing'). Lest anyone should take the proceedings seriously, Morrissey throws in some deliberately 'bad' performances, notably Joe Dallesandro's displaced New York shepherd-stud, and such pithy dialogue as 'to know death you have to fuck life in the gall

bladder', delivered by Kier in heavily-accented English. By the end of the film, his right hand severed and his entrails dangling off the end of a pole, the Baron still has no regrets, talking wistfully of 'a laboratory and a dream'. His male creature begs to differ, ripping open his freshly stitched torso to let his innards run out.

For many, the definitive version of Frankenstein is still the 1931 Universal film, though no-one has yet worked out exactly where and when it's supposed to be set (one of the cinema's most intriguing spacial-temporal limbos). Produced in Hollywood, the movie drew heavily on imported British talent, notably actors Colin Clive and Boris Karloff – cast as creator and creature – and director James Whale.

Born in Dudley, near Birmingham, respected theatre director Whale had served in the British Army during World War I, experiencing first hand the horrors of the first truly technological war. The product of a working class background, Whale more or less changed his identity after the war, reinventing himself as a cultured English gentleman (and appalling snob, by some accounts). Openly, if discreetly gay, Whale certainly cut an unusual figure in 1930s Hollywood. Having scored a major success with his debut film, the World War I drama Journey's End (1930), Whale was Universal's new golden boy, offered the pick of the studio's best properties by production chief Carl Laemmle Junior. Whale decided on Frankenstein, attracted to the 'strong meat' subject matter, the story's visual potential and the two strong, decidedly offbeat leading characters. Unlike Mary Shelley, Whale considered the lengthy, detailed creation sequence absolutely crucial to the story's success, arguing that audiences had to really believe in the man-made monster. Filmed over 35 days, Frankenstein cost Universal a grand total of $291,000, a pretty good investment.

The laudanum-stoned poet transfixed by the supposedly life-giving force

For all its intrinsic merit, the 1931 Frankenstein's biggest contribution to popular culture in general and science fiction in particular is the image of the monster: the deathly pallor, the squared-off head, the low, almost neanderthal brow, the heavy eyelids, the sunken eyes, the narrow, black-lipped mouth, the electrodes – often mistaken for bolts – in the neck. Whale, a former cartoonist, claimed much of the credit, having 'discovered' little known bit part actor

Karloff in the Universal canteen: 'I made drawings of his head, added sharp bony ridges where I imagined the skull might have joined.' Whatever Whale's disputed contribution to the design, the monster's appearance was put into effect by top make-up artist Jack Pierce, who could therefore claim to have

'I made drawings of his head, added sharp bony ridges where I imagined the skull might have joined'

influenced the twentieth century's view of science fiction – and horror – with his iconic rendering of the Frankenstein monster, which built on and exaggerated Boris Karloff's gaunt, lugubrious features to startling effect. Pierce didn't have much to work from in Mary Shelley's novel, though there is some description of the creature in the book: 'His yellow skin scarcely covered the work of muscles and

James Whale, the British director of Universal's Frankenstein (1931) and the Bride of Frankenstein (1935).

arteries beneath; his hair was of a lustrous black, and flowing; his teeth of pearly whiteness; but these luxuriances only formed a more horrid contrast with his watery eyes, that seemed almost of the same colour as the dun-white sockets in which they were set, his shrivelled complexion and straight black lips.'

Shelley preferred, by and large, to leave the monster to her readers' imagination (a tradition followed by much low budget British film and television science fiction, if only for reasons of expedience). Aside from the lips and the eyes, Pierce pretty much began again from scratch, reasoning that a non-surgeon such as Frankenstein would lack the skill to reassemble human body parts with any degree of finesse (though why this lack of expertise would result in a flat head is anyone's guess; Peter Cushing always managed a rounded cranium). Revised slightly for Karloff's subsequent turns in *Bride of Frankenstein* and *Son of Frankenstein*, Pierce's copyrighted make-up was later modelled by Lon Chaney Junior, Bela Lugosi (who claimed to have rejected the monster role in the original film) and stuntman Glenn Strange. None of these pretenders to the Universal monster throne came close to equalling Karloff, who invested the creature with an innocence and curiosity that made his frustrated acts of brutality tragic rather than appalling.

The monster's famous scene with the small girl Maria (Marilyn Harris) best expresses his own fundamentally child-like quality. Playing by the side of a lake, the completely unafraid Maria greets the creature as an equal, inviting him to help her make flower 'boats' to float on the water. Running out of flowers, the monster drops Maria into the water, assuming she will also float, reacting with uncomprehending alarm and panic when she drowns. For years, most available prints of *Frankenstein* ended the scene with the smiling monster reaching towards Maria, implying that her subsequent killing is a wilful act of murder. Not only does this completely misrepresent the creature's character, it adds undue force to Frankenstein's utter rejection of his 'child'. As Karloff explained: 'I always saw my monster as something inarticulate, helpless and tragic. To him, Frankenstein was God.' A god, it might be added, who disowns his creation, unable to cope with the responsibility.

Just as Frankenstein couldn't bear to be associated with his creation, so James Whale came to loathe being labelled a 'horror' director, abandoning the genre after *Bride* for more 'weighty' dramatic films that reflected genuine human experience.

Unfortunately, his tenure at Universal became very shaky once Carl Laemmle Junior lost control of the studio, despite hits such as *Show Boat* (1936). Following the commercial failure of *The Road Back* (1937), a much hacked-about sequel to the World War I classic *All Quiet on the Western Front*, Whale's career went into irreversible decline, grinding to a permanent halt in the early 1940s after such forgettable programmer fare as *Green Hell* (1940). Universal reused the temple set from the latter film for *The Mummy's Hand* (1940), a shambling creature feature a long way from Whale's original monster hit a decade earlier.

The relationship between James Whale and his screen monster is explored in Bill Condon's 1998 film *Gods and Monsters*, based on Christopher Bram's 'factional' 1995 novel *Father of Frankenstein*. Karloff's sympathetic creature is persecuted and shunned for his 'abnormal' nature, though he can't help himself, something which is clearly paralleled with Whale's own homosexuality. In one sequence, Whale, now a largely forgotten figure in the movie business, is mischievously invited to a garden party held for visiting British royalty by esteemed director George Cukor. Cukor, a model example of a closeted gay filmmaker, is unamused by Whale's pointed references to queens. Accompanied by his resolutely straight gardener, whom the director knows will be taken for his lover, Whale agrees to pose for a picture with actors Karloff and Elsa Lanchester, accepting that he is as much a screen ghost from the past as their characters in *Bride of Frankenstein*. Black and white dream sequences depict Whale's memories as a confused mix of reality and fantasy, the body-strewn trenches of World War I blending with the monster rampaging across a barren landscape. At one point, Whale becomes the monster, assuming the identity that his life and career could never escape. While the gay subtext to Whale's *Frankenstein* has probably been overstated, the wartime echoes are undeniably pervasive. Aside from the multitude of blasted, stunted landscapes on view, the monster is dressed in shabby, cast-off clothes, resembling a destitute war veteran, forgotten and unwanted.

Science fiction has a long history of taking a hold on those who feel marginalized and alienated by family, peers or society as a whole. The classic image of the bullied playground nerd or misfit finding both solace and escape in dreams of stars, space exploration and superhuman beings has accompanied the genre for years, which goes some way to explaining its less-than-cool reputation. Some of science fiction's most commercially successful practitioners, notably Steven Spielberg and George Lucas, have specifically mentioned this as a key element of their childhood experiences. Those opposed to the genre might argue that it nurtures isolation and fantasising to a prolonged and potentially harmful degree.

DIVIDED SELVES

Throughout the nineteenth and twentieth centuries, the deep ambivalence to scientific and technical progress expressed by Mary Shelley was strongly in evidence, particularly in stories like Robert Louis Stevenson's *The Strange Case of Dr Jekyll and Mr Hyde* (1886). Here, the dedicated doctor develops a chemical formula that temporarily releases the primitive, animalistic side of man's nature, with predictably messy consequences. If not quite on a par with creating a new life from scratch, unleashing the beast within is still an act of extreme social irresponsibility. Both Shelley and Stevenson convey the true horror of their protagonist's reckless dabbling in the great unknown by having the resultant monsters attack children. The creature strangles Frankenstein's younger brother William as part of his vengeance on the creator. Mr Hyde tramples a small girl in the street, inflicting serious injuries, and is nearly lynched as a consequence. Stevenson tended to dismiss the pseudo-scientific aspects of his story, especially the mysterious chemical potion, as 'so much hugger mugger', a mere narrative device in a salacious, money-spinning morality tale that the higher-minded could interpret as a metaphysical exploration of the nature of evil.

Jekyll's split personality certainly cries out for some form of analysis, psycho or otherwise. The shabby doorway into which the loathsome Hyde disappears after his often violent nocturnal wanderings is at the back of the respected Jekyll's supposedly elegant house, two sides of the same dwelling. Conceived before the advent of Freudian theory, the Jekyll story is perhaps a prime example of what happens when Superego allows Id full sway, the same theme that powers *Forbidden Planet*. Having put his faith in the 'hugger mugger' potion, Jekyll initially believes that Hyde is under control, giving way to his better half once his – and Jekyll's – more sordid appetites have been sated. However, it is not in the nature of the beast to be willingly caged. Stephen King argues, with some conviction, that Edward Hyde is a werewolf pure and simple, a step down the evolutionary ladder who prompts instinctive disgust in all who lay eyes on him. As one character, Richard Enfield, memorably puts it: 'There is something wrong with his appearance, something displeasing, something downright detestable. I never saw a man I so disliked, and yet I scarcely know why.'

While Victor Frankenstein is a misguided idealist, Henry Jekyll ultimately seems little more than a classic Victorian hypocrite. Far from using science to purge man of his baser instincts, of which the Victorians exhibited plenty, Jekyll deploys his Hyde persona as a supposedly foolproof means of indulging all vices without risk of detection. Maintaining a facade of utmost social respectability, the 'good' doctor presents himself as a man of pure virtue, a near saint offering an example few can hope to follow. Unless, of course, they get their hands on his potion. From this perspective, Jekyll's sorry fate seems more or less deserved.

As with the *Frankenstein* movies, the numerous film versions of *Dr Jekyll and Mr Hyde* tend to be treated as horror rather than science fiction – not that these genres have ever been mutually exclusive by any means. The dual title role quickly became established as a worthwhile challenge for the most serious

There is something wrong with his appearance, something displeasing, something downright detestable

dramatic actor – in a way the part of Frankenstein never did – and the numerous screen Jekylls include such big names of their day as John Barrymore (1920), Fredric March (1932) and a reluctant Spencer Tracy (1941). Barrymore's Hyde, supposedly conceived with minimal make-up, is a long-haired, pointy-headed creep, with elongated fingers and a scuttling, arachnid-style movement (the similarity is emphasised in a dream sequence, where a giant spider crawls onto the sleeping Jekyll's bed). March, who won an Academy Award for his performance, plays Hyde as regressive ape-man, Wally Westmore's heavy make-up design only just staying the right side of absurdity. Eagerly pawing his wretched prostitute lover, Ivy (Miriam Hopkins), this Hyde is all rampant animal lust, both for sex and violence. Filmed before the Hays Office and Catholic Legion of Decency gained their iron grip on the American film industry for three decades, this version of the story is remarkably upfront about Hyde's sheer nastiness, the scenes where he torments, beats and finally murders Ivy still disturbing today. Produced in more restrictive times, the Spencer Tracy version opts for intricately staged Freudian dreams and low key debauchery (set visitor W Somerset Maugham

claimed he couldn't tell Jekyll and Hyde apart).

Hammer's *Two Faces of Dr Jekyll* (1960), scripted by novelist and playwright Wolf Mankowitz, puts an interesting spin on the story. Far from being a respected and admired public figure, Jekyll (Paul Massie) is a meek, middle aged loser, despised by his wife and cuckolded by his supposed best friend. Hyde, by contrast, is young, suave, handsome and aggressive, nearly beating a club bouncer (a young Oliver Reed) to death when the man shows lack of respect. A notable box-office failure for the studio, the film seemed to run into a curious problem with its transformation sequence: Jekyll is bearded, Hyde cleanshaven. While the public could buy smooth-faced Fredric March suddenly turning apeman, they just couldn't accept Paul Massie's abrupt loss of facial hair. Hammer's later *Dr Jekyll & Sister Hyde* (1971), initially conceived by former *Avengers* producer Brian Clemens as a throwaway joke, hiked up the science fiction element, Jekyll (Ralph Bates) discovering his less-than-warm feminine side via hormone experiments.

According to director Roy Ward Baker, by the early 1970s the creative forces at Hammer had become fairly desperate in their search for new ideas, feeling that the traditional Gothic monsters had been vigorously flogged to death. Baker rated Clemens's initial pitch: 'He drinks the magic potion and turns into a woman' as 'a very astute idea', ingeniously playing on gender themes. Experiencing both sexual confusion and a new ruthless streak, Jekyll turns to slaughtering East End prostitutes for their hormonal glands, creating mass panic and the Jack the Ripper legend. This is a long way from Stevenson and not necessarily in the right direction, though Martine Beswick makes a striking Sister Hyde, the effect accentuated by her more than passing resemblance to Ralph Bates. Jekyll perishes in mid-transformation, having robbed himself of both identity and gender. A year earlier, Hammer's chief horror rival Amicus had opted for a more low key Freudian approach in *I, Monster* (1970), starring Christopher Lee as Dr Marlowe and Mr Blake (this name change is curious, given that Stevenson's novel was long out of copy-right). Having enabled his repressed patients to shed their emotional inhibitions, Marlowe discovers that his own hidden self should have stayed that way.

SCIENCE WITHOUT A CONSCIENCE

Both *Frankenstein* and *Dr Jekyll and Mr Hyde* suggest that unorthodox scientific research conducted in lonely isolation is likely to have dangerous

consequences. Another archetypal British science fiction tale, H G Wells's 1897 novel *The Invisible Man* – also filmed by James Whale for Universal Studios – further endorses the two themes of alienation and the abuse of science and technology. The book also demonstrates that the profession of mad scientist is not necessarily a dignified one. Prancing around stark naked, albeit unseen, in his pursuit of world domination, scientist Griffin is as absurd as he is frightening. Whale's 1933 film version, which made a star of Claude Rains after Boris Karloff declined the lead, captures both elements with impressive ease. At one point reduced to a pair of floating trousers skipping down a country lane, Griffin sings 'Here we go gathering nuts in May' as he gleefully pushes startled villagers off their bicycles. Later on he plots

cold blooded mass killings to demonstrate his power: 'We'll start with a few murders. Big men, little men – just to show we make no distinction.'

Wells's earlier anti-vivisection fantasy *The Island of Dr Moreau* (1896) is even more extreme, with its gruesome animal-into-man surgery in the dreaded House of Pain. Working from his remote island base, Moreau, described by castaway narrator Prendick as possessing 'an expression of pugnacious resolution', has dedicated his life to 'the study of the plasticity of living forms'. Worshipped with extreme fear and trembling by his 'manimal' subjects, Moreau is the ultimate example of the mad scientist as self-appointed god, in this case a malignant, callous god given to acts of Old Testament-style wrath and retribution. He even has his own list of commandments, as recited by

Paul Massie starred in The Two Faces of Dr Jekyll (1960). Hammer's inventive re-interpretation of Robert Louis Stevenson's story was directed by Terence Fisher and scripted by Wolf Mankowitz.

Although H G Wells was dismissive of his early science fiction novels, the ideas he originated served as the foundation for the genre throughout the 20th century.

his creations, notably: 'Not to go on all-Fours; that is the Law. Are we not Men?... Not to eat Flesh nor Fish; that is the Law. Are we not Men?' Having mutilated and adapted the animals' physical forms into hideous travesties of men, Moreau seeks to break their remaining instincts, an approach that would surely appal even the most passionate vegetarian. The ominous chant of the man-beasts says it all:

> His is the House of Pain.
> His is the Hand that makes.
> His is the Hand that wounds.
> His is the Hand that heals.

Far from being a card-carrying, whip-wielding sadist, however, Moreau seems utterly indifferent to the sufferings of his creatures, dismissing the very notion of pain: 'Oh! but it is such a little thing. A mind truly opened to what science has to teach must see that it is a little thing.' Over a century after he first appeared, Moreau remains one of science fiction's most disturbing figures, not to mention an extremely bad advert for pioneering medical research.

Moreau seems utterly indifferent to the sufferings of his creatures

The Island of Dr Moreau was the first of Wells's novels to be officially adapted for the screen. Paramount's 1932 film version, Island of Lost Souls, starred Charles Laughton as Moreau and Bela Lugosi as the Sayer of the Law, spokesman for the man-beasts. Capturing the gruesome, not to say offensive, spirit of the book, the film gains particularly from

Laughton's performance, more overtly sadistic than Wells's Moreau, which he supposedly based on his dentist. Unfortunately, the film was banned by the horror-loathing British film censor on the grounds that its content was too gruesome and its theme 'against nature'. Wells considered the film a vulgar travesty of his book, disliking Laughton's portrayal of Moreau in particular, and applauded the decision. British cinemagoers were denied a chance to appraise the film for themselves until 1958. Later screen adaptations seem a little timid by comparison, the much derided 1996 version starring Marlon Brando better known for its troubled production history than any intrinsic interest. AIP's 1977 film with Burt Lancaster drops the disturbing surgery angle altogether in favour of implausible chromosome experiments (in 1911). Not only does this seem a spineless cop-out – squarely aimed at a family-friendly 'PG' rating – it makes nonsense of Moreau's deeply chilling line in the book: 'The stubborn beast flesh grows day by day back again'. For all his scientific and surgical genius, Moreau is ultimately nothing more a coldly vicious small boy pulling the wings off flies. Prendick's verdict on the doctor's reckless, amoral and ultimately pointless research seems just: 'Had Moreau had any intelligible object I could have sympathized at least a little with him ... But he was so irresponsible, so utterly careless. His curiosity, his mad, aimless investigation, drove him on, and the things were thrown out to live a year or so, to struggle, and blunder, and suffer; at last to die painfully.'

Regarded by many as the 'father of modern science fiction', Wells's vision, above all others, reflects a specifically British schizophrenia about the future and scientific progress, his work covering just about every theme common in the genre today. His socialist utopian politics inspired him to the ultimately optimistic imaginings of the anti-fascist The Shape of Things to Come (1933), where by 2030 technology and humanity are walking hand in hand in a world where war has – finally – been abolished and everyone can achieve their potential. Under the benevolent rule of scientists, of course, technocracy being far more desirable than democracy – and more desirable than the Luddite artistic types terrified of progress (Wells had a few axes to grind). Coming late in Wells's career, this is a vision of the future that his readers could comfortably embrace, especially those, like the Americans, who were relatively unscarred by the devastating effects of technological warfare. A few years later, British-based Hungarian-born film mogul Alexander Korda recruited Wells for a lavish screen version, Things to Come (1936), almost certainly the most expensive science fiction production of the 1930s. Notoriously dubious of the film medium, especially such 'rubbish' as Fritz Lang's *Metropolis* (1926) and the *Dr Moreau*-inspired *Island of Lost Souls*, the 70-year-old Wells not only gave the project his blessing, but agreed to provide the screenplay, though he disowned the finished film, following extensive rewrites by an uncredited Lajos Biro (in fairness to Wells, much of the dialogue is risible).

In *Things to Come*, decades of war and pestilence lead to a regressive, near feudal society that is finally brought to order by Wings Over The World, an international organisation of pilots dispensing technological salvation (an interesting, if unlikely, choice for the saviours of mankind). Peaceful civilisation rises again and man enjoys health, wealth, happiness and extensive leisure time, his interests eventually turning to space exploration. At the climax, a young couple are shot into the heavens in a rocket fired from a gigantic electronic space gun. Visionary scientist Oswald Cabal (Raymond Massey)

gets the last word (and how): 'Man has no rest and no ending ... when he has conquered all the deeps [sic] of space and all the mysteries of time, still he will be beginning.' Directed by American set designer William Cameron Menzies, who had a fine eye for futuristic detail but little idea how to handle actors, *Things to Come* is both naive and horrendously dated, yet retains more than a passing fascination. It's certainly preferable to the ultra low budget 1979 Canadian film *The Shape of Things to Come*, which reverts to Wells's original title but is otherwise completely unrelated, uninspired and almost unwatchable (the special effects highlight is Jack Palance's disembodied head slowly rotating).

MARTIANS, MORLOCKS, AND THE FIRST MEN IN THE MOON

However much Wells believed in mankind's potential for a utopian future, he was more persuasive dealing with the idea of technology put to malevolent use by beings notably short on humanity. Even the opening

Alexander Korda's Things To Come (1936) was realised on an unprecedented scale by director William Cameron Menzies.

Colossal three-legged machines gave way to flying saucers in George Pal's War of the Worlds (1953).

section of *Things to Come* depicts the outbreak of another World War in 1940 (talk about prescient), British viewers of the film version getting the chance to see their country bombed flat on screen just a few years before it happened for real. In *The War of the Worlds* (1898), probably Wells's most famous work, Earth suffers a near apocalyptic fate at the hands (or claws) of invading Martians and their dreaded Red Weed. Interpreted by some as a prefiguring of World War I, this novel was to have a profound effect on the British science fiction tradition: the first of many dark, dystopian and frequently tortured visions of armageddon. Key literary works such as M P Shiel's *The Purple Cloud* (1903), John Wyndham's debut novel

The Day of the Triffids (1951) and John Christopher's *The Tripods Trilogy* (1967-68) all owe a major debt to Wells. Wyndham, a Wells fan from early childhood, shared the latter's interest in human behaviour when faced with the breakdown of social and moral order in the aftermath of extraordinary, unimaginable events.

In *The War of the Worlds*, Wells offered a graphic depiction of the destruction of a society too absorbed in its petty conventions and hierarchy to appreciate its extreme fragility in the face of an alien onslaught: 'so vain is man, and so blinded by his vanity'. The opening paragraph of the book exhibits a sneaking, almost Nietzschean admiration for the fiercely intelligent Martian invaders, with 'minds that are to our minds as ours are to those of the beasts'. Once the invasion has begun, however, any respect for the aliens is swept away by sheer revulsion: 'Those who have never seen a living Martian can scarcely imagine the strange horror of their appearance. The peculiar V-shaped mouth ... the Gorgon groups of tentacles ... the extraordinary intensity of the immense eyes – culminated in an effect akin to nausea...'

Chapter titles such as 'The Heat-Ray in the Chobham Road' and 'What I saw of the Destruction of Weybridge and Shepperton' chart the Martian's murderous progress through England, anyone standing in their way instantly vaporised in a flash of 'luminous green smoke'. A more subtle, if deeply unappealing, theme is the notion that the Martians represent mankind's future self, foul blobs of fierce intellect and insatiable appetite.

Along with Mary Shelley and Robert Louis Stevenson, H G Wells was among the first British science fiction writers to have his work regularly adapted by the Americans. Having done well out of *Island of Lost Souls*, Paramount Studios bought the film rights to *War of the Worlds* for top director Cecil B DeMille, only for the project to stall in preproduction. On 30 October 1938, Orson Welles and John Houseman's 'Mercury Theater on the Air' company broadcast a memorable radio dramatization of *War of the Worlds*, scripted by Howard Koch. Intended as a sly Halloween treat, with Welles himself in the lead, the documentary-style drama proved plausible enough to cause a minor panic, not to mention wildly exaggerated tales of hysterical masses fleeing to the hills to escape the Martian menace, recreated in the 1975 tv movie *The Night That Panicked America*. (Nicholas Meyer, scriptwriter on the latter, later transposed both H G Wells and Jack the Ripper to 1970s America in *Time After Time* 1979.)

Post World War Two, producer George Pal's 1953 film version of *War of the Worlds* updated the story to the present day and changed the setting from London to Los Angeles, ostensibly to increase American audiences' identification with the protagonists. Shorn of its original backdrop, the movie slotted comfortably into Hollywood's ongoing alien invasion cycle, distinguished largely by its vibrant colour and elaborate special effects, which won an Academy Award. The impressive scenes of Martian carnage, including one – not in the book – where a bible-

'Those who had never seen a living Martian can scarcely imagine the strange horror of their appearance'

toting, psalm-quoting minister is zapped by an alien death ray, were considered sufficiently horrific to merit an adults only 'X' certificate from the British censor (never mind that the Martian battlecraft are visibly supported by wires in some shots). For all the BBFC's concern, Pal and Paramount Studios toned down the pessimism and brutality of the book, where the hero is forced to strike his companion, a deranged, raving curate, with a meat-cleaver to avoid detection by the Martians. Oddly, the movie is marginally more downbeat than the novel in its overall depiction of humanity under fire, the selfish, brutal mob mentality on display leaving the viewer to wonder if the conquest of this Earth is really something to be lamented. In Wells's novel, the hero searches war-torn England for his wife, recalling events, places and people from his past that he has only come to truly appreciate now that everything seems lost. The fall of human civilisation is a tragedy, for all its faults. In fairness to Pal, Paramount demanded major changes to the story, losing the

Harry Brandon, Ann Robinson and Les Tremayne in War of the Worlds (1953). Production company Paramount shifted the action to southern California.

theme of the forcibly separated couple and transforming the hero into a square-jawed scientist attached to the US Military. Though not as wooden as some have claimed, bargain basement leads Gene Barry and Ann Robinson are fighting a losing battle to draw audience attention away from the Martians (George Pal got his big break with the 1940s *Puppetoon* series and, as with Gerry Anderson a generation later, many felt his switch to live action did not result in noticeably more animated performances). Heavy with religious imagery, mawkish heavenly choirs and Cedric Hardwicke's stentorian narration, the film's *deux ex machina* conclusion, where a disease-ridden Martian crash-lands its war machine next to a church full of praying humans, is regarded by many as an unforgivable betrayal of Wells's vision. In truth, the basic idea is present in the novel, the Martians 'slain, after all man's devices had failed, by the humblest things that God, in His wisdom, has put upon this earth'. Bacteria, in fact. Atheist movie-hater Wells would probably still have turned in his grave. But fifties Hollywood was not the place for 'feelbad' science fiction, Allied Artists subsequently ordering director Don Siegel to tack a happy, or at least reassuring ending onto his nightmare fantasy *Invasion of the Body Snatchers* (1956).

One of the most enduring, if unusual adaptations of *The War of the Worlds* is American Jeff Wayne's 1978 concept double album, recorded in England for CBS, which uses the full gamut of musical effects and dramatised scenes to recreate the stark horror of Wells's original. Offering an eclectic star line-up – Richard Burton, Julie Covington, David Essex, Justin Hayward and Thin Lizzy frontman Phil Lynott – this epic production proved a major hit, even generating a hit single with the Hayward song 'Forever Autumn'. The impressive artwork for the album is dominated

Veteran actor William Hartnell starred as a slightly ill-tempered unnamed time traveller

by the image of a three-legged Martian war machine blasting a fleeing ship with its heat ray. Only a complete killjoy would point out that this tripodal structure wouldn't actually be able to move without toppling over, let alone conquer the earth.

At the start of the 1960s, *War of the Worlds* producer George Pal released a second H G Wells adaptation, *The Time Machine*, starring Australian actor Rod Taylor as a slightly unlikely Victorian time traveller named George. Three years later, the British

Broadcasting Corporation launched a modestly-produced science fiction drama series, *Doctor Who*, as part of their Saturday teatime schedule. Veteran actor William Hartnell starred as a slightly ill-tempered, unnamed time traveller who dressed like a Victorian but claimed to be a visitor from another planet, far beyond the known galaxy. While it's unlikely that the Pal film provided a direct inspiration for *Doctor Who*, the series certainly owed a passing debt to Wells's original book, the author later appearing as a character in the 1985 story *Timelash*. Incidentally, Pal had the same idea 25 years earlier, the name 'H G Wells' clearly visible on the control board of the time machine in one shot.

A distinct improvement on *The War of the Worlds*, Pal's 1960 *Time Machine*, which he also directed, stands on its own merits. Unlike *The War of the Worlds*, the film retains the 1895 novel's period setting, moving forward a mere five years to set the events against the start of the exciting new century, full of technological promise. Pal regarded the film as a personal favourite, claiming that 'it had a lot to say about a man who was born in the wrong century and wasn't happy about it'. Travelling forward just over a decade, George soon has his faith in future mankind dented, catching England in the middle of the First World War. A trip to 1966 finds the world being torn apart by nuclear war, which can't have reassured audiences at the time. The most disturbing section of Rod Taylor's trip through the ages is the far future, 802,701 AD, where he comes across the Eloi, a race of docile, unthinking and self-absorbed prototype flower-children (with regulation Aryan blonde hair) who are in thrall to the Morlocks, a neanderthal race of whip-wielding, cannibal troglodytes. While the Eloi might be regarded as a prescient forerunner of the hippie counterculture then seven years distant, their utter lack of feeling for either their environment or each other would have gone down badly during the Summer of Love. Wells envisaged the Eloi-Morlock relationship as a logical, if unsavoury consequence of the class system, the exploited, downtrodden Morlock workers turning the tables on the idle decadents who feed off them in the most literal way possible: 'These Eloi were mere fatted cattle, which the ant-like Morlocks preserved and preyed upon.' Contrary to popular belief, the film doesn't drop this idea entirely, though Hollywood good taste blunted some of its impact. Regularly lured underground to serve as both hard labour and a tasty snack, the apathetic Eloi are eventually shown how to fight back by time traveller George, who demonstrates the value of self-determination and a strong right hook. As

The lurid British quad poster of MGM's The Time Machine (1960).

with *War of the Worlds*, George Pal shied away from the novel's bleaker elements, including the death – and possible ingestion – of the time traveller's Eloi girlfriend at the hands of the Morlocks.

Having ended his *Time Machine* with the hero returning to the future (as in the book), George Pal intended to make a sequel but could never raise the backing. Nearly two decades later, director Nicholas Meyer sent H G Wells time travelling once again in the ingenious, if uneven *Time After Time*. Pursuing a supposed friend who's turned out to be Jack the Ripper, Wells (Malcolm McDowell) ends up in modern day San Francisco, his machine part of an exhibition honouring the long dead author ('A Man Before His Time'). Still optimistic about mankind's future, Wells initially believes he's found Utopia in 1979, McDonalds and all, a view largely reversed after a miserable night spent sleeping on a hard park bench. Meanwhile, the object of Wells's space-time pursuit, Mr Ripper (David Warner), flips through a dozen television channels in his cheap hotel room, taking in a world obsessed by its capacity for

violence, and concludes he's found his natural habitat. Wells, on the other hand, seems as lost and disoriented as any 'genuine' alien visitor, before befriending a broadminded female bank clerk (Mary Steenburgen), who makes the author's once controversial views on 'free love' seem positively quaint. Inventive, charming, and surprisingly gory in parts, *Time After Time* has a great premise but stumbles over its contrast of past with present. While life in the big city circa 1979 would certainly have had its perils, to argue that this present is infinitely more dangerous, callous and downright cruel than Victorian London is absurd. The film's upbeat ending, where Wells's girlfriend returns with him to the past and becomes the second Mrs Wells in 1895, certainly irritated those familiar with the genuine H G Wells' personal life, which included numerous affairs (for the record, Herbert was slightly broader and a good foot shorter than screen incarnation McDowell).

The success of *The Time Machine* movie was due in large part to its special effects, an element that would play an increasingly important role in the

development of British science fiction. Working with relatively lavish Hollywood resources, Pal's team came up with some memorable images: day and night speed by in a matter of seconds, rock entombs then crumbles away from the time machine, a dead Morlock decays into a pile of black dust, an ancient

attempting to boost the world's food supplies with genetically modified oversized animals

Arnold Bedford (Edward Judd) and Joseph Cavor (Lionel Jeffries) explore a new world in the 1964 adaptation of First Men In The Moon. Nigel Kneale co-wrote the screen-play, based on H G Wells' 1901 story.

book falls apart in the traveller's hands. Another Wells classic, *First Men in the Moon* (1901), was filmed in Britain a few years later by the American partnership of producer Charles H. Schneer and special effects man Ray Harryhausen, with a script co-authored by acclaimed television writer Nigel Kneale (there is an earlier film version dating from 1919, long out of circulation). A longtime UK resident, model animation genius Harryhausen is to many one of the most important figures in the history

of movies, let alone science fiction. Having begun his solo career with such low budget, American-shot sf offerings as *The Beast From 20,000 Fathoms* (1953), *Earth Versus the Flying Saucers* (1956) and *Twenty Million Miles to Earth* (1957), Harryhausen scored a major hit with the Technicolored mythological fantasy *The Seventh Voyage of Sinbad* (1958), which offered cyclops, a snake woman, a dragon and a living skeleton in place of the now standard dinosaurs and UFOs.

Though best known for his excursions into man's imagined ancient past, notably *Jason and the Argonauts* (1963), Harryhausen made a few returns to science fiction, albeit with period settings. The Jules Verne-derived *Mysterious Island* (1961) features Captain Nemo attempting to boost the world's food supply with genetically modified oversized animals (it'll never happen). *First Men in the Moon* (1964), similarly reworked as a showcase for Harryhausen's animation set-pieces, is an odd hybrid. Hoping to cash in on the mounting public interest in the Apollo moon programme, the film-makers added a modern-day framing story to Wells's Victorian tale, American astronauts beating their Russian rivals to the lunar surface only to find a tattered Union flag already in place (there's wishful thinking). Rating H G Wells as 'one of the greatest geniuses we've ever produced in this country', Kneale found adapting his work for the screen something of a mixed experience, the initial sense of 'fun' soon evaporating. 'It got rather a typical Hollywood treatment ... it rather put me off films for a bit'.

Better reviewed than many Schneer-Harryhausen efforts, largely for an engaging performance by Lionel Jeffries as the bumbling Professor Cavor, *First Men in the Moon* has its share of spectacular lunar creations: the spindly, insectoid Selenite leaders, a giant caterpillar-like mooncalf and the vast, subter-ranean Selenite city (mostly miniature work). They are, however, a little thin on the ground for a Harryhausen film, which might explain the film's disappointing box office. There are bigger problems with the storyline, Kneale and Jan Read's screenplay extensively rewritten by producer Charles Schneer 'to no visible improvement'. (Fours years earlier, Schneer had produced a factually dubious biopic of German rocket pioneer Wernher von Braun, *I Aim at the Stars*, starring future Bond villain Curt Jurgens, which probably didn't endear him to Kneale – see below.)

A little heavy on comic relief, *First Men in the Moon* also falls down on elementary science, with earth-type gravity on the moon and sound waves travelling through a vacuum (in fairness, the latter also occurs in 2001, *Star Wars* and scores of others). More

seriously, there is the deeply unappealing image of burly moon explorer Edward Judd killing scores of diminutive Selenite drones (played by children in suits) for no great reason other than extreme xenophobia. Reasoning that the real-life moon programme was extremely unlikely to discover any sentient lunar lifeforms, Kneale elected to wipe out the entire Selenite race, *War of the Worlds*-style, with humble common cold germs unwittingly spread by Cavor. The lunar civilisation is long gone by the time the American astronauts touch down. Whatever this achieves for the film's sense of scientific verisimilitude, it casts a slightly sour note over the proceedings. Far from being hostile towards their uninvited visitors, the Selenites seem merely curious, reducing leading lady Martha Hyer to one of Harryhausen's

trademark living skeletons in their X-Ray machine. At least the Martians had it coming.

OH BRAVE NEW WORLD!

However much he was softened, sanitised or downright distorted by film-makers, H G Wells's original work offered highly persuasive glimpses of hellish dystopias, whether brought about by global war, alien invasion or basic human stupidity, and British science fiction has a strong track record in creating visions of grim totalitarian futures where individuals are held in slavery by the state. Aldous Huxley's *Brave New World* offers a future of genetic engineering and selection, the earth's population replenished in the Fertilising Rooms and graded at conception from Alpha to Epsilon. Divorced from any sense of morality by his

Bedford and Cavor become the First Men In The Moon, a film that promised to present 'H G Wells' astounding adventure in Dynamation!'

relentless pursuit of 'pure' science, mankind has reduced himself to little more than an organic automaton. Tranquillised with the drug soma, a forerunner of Prozac, the human race is intellectually and emotionally controlled by the World State, with its motto: 'COMMUNITY. IDENTITY, STABILITY'. No one can be ill or isolated or unhappy because any affliction of body and mind will lead to instability, threatening the carefully nurtured status quo. Promiscuity is actively encouraged by the state to divorce sexual activity from any sense of emotional attachment, reproduction no longer being the provenance of the outmoded family unit. Interestingly, the World State has not attempted to eradicate man's aggressive impulses via genetic tampering, merely to unleash them in a controlled environment via the

Promiscuity is actively encouraged by the state to divorce sexual activity from any sense of emotional attachment

compulsory monthly VPS treatment, the Violent Passion Surrogate: 'All the tonic effects of murdering Desdemona and being murdered by Othello, without any of the inconveniences.' Note the further Shakespearean analogy: Huxley was a man who liked to keep his cultural references highbrow. The idea of rendering 'happiness', in its State-approved version, as synonymous with the submission of individual will is deeply unsettling. Most editions of the book quote moral philosopher Bertrand Russell on the cover: 'It is all too likely to come true'. Let's hope not.

Now often overlooked by genre devotees, *Brave New World* has inspired few direct adaptations, aside from a mediocre American television film first screened in 1980. Presumably looking for a little quality by association, the producers included 2001 actor Keir Dullea in the cast, inviting comparisons that their bland, uncertainly toned small screen offering just couldn't bear. Elsewhere, Huxley's influence can be seen in the less portentous future-world of Woody Allen's 1973 sci fi comedy *Sleeper*, set in 2173, which mixes satire and slapstick with such pseudo-*Brave New World* notions as the pleasure orb, the orgasmatron, and the attempted cloning of Earth's largely assassinated dictator from his sole surviving body part (the nose). George Lucas's *THX 1138* (1970), a prize-winning student film reworked into a flop theatrical release, offers a future so bleak and arid as to be almost risible. Like Huxley, Lucas presents a totalitarian society, where people

have numbers instead of names and reproduction is controlled by the state. Shaven-headed human drones, doped to the eyeballs, work for the general good under the close supervision of robot policemen ('We only want to help you'). Televised sex and violence keep the sedated masses content and desensitised. Futuristic hardware (circa 1969) combines with white on white imagery, the human figures often disappearing against their cold, clinical backdrops. With all impulses and emotions, including sexual appetite, completely suppressed by the daily drug cocktail, human intimacy has become the prime form of rebellion (that and stomping up and down on an android lawman's head). The film's most effective touch is having the robot police pursuit of the title character called off when the budget allocated for his capture runs out. Lucas's rather better known *Star Wars* series, described by some as '*Lord of the Rings* in Space', avoids sexual matters until Episode V, *The Empire Strikes Back* – where Han Solo and Princess Leia get it together, only for the former to be carbon frozen before they can act on their lustful impulses. Is the Dark Empire attempting to suppress sexual activity among the Rebel Alliance?

DOWN WITH BIG BROTHER

Sex as rebellion is one of the central conceits of George Orwell's *Nineteen Eighty-Four*, largely written in 1948 (note the cunning switch of digits), which gave the world 'Newspeak', the thought police and the catchy slogan 'Big Brother Is Watching You'. Unlike *THX 1138*, *Nineteen Eighty-Four* depicts rebellion as a futile act, a brave but feeble gesture against an all powerful state that can manipulate both the bodies and minds of its people without recourse to drugs. History is rewritten daily to complement the Party line, former national heroes turned into public enemies or expunged from the records altogether. Language is being reduced, reshaped and revised to make it impossible to even question the doctrine of the state, succinctly expressed in a mere nine words: 'War is Peace. Freedom is Slavery. Ignorance is Strength'. Doomed rebel Winston Smith, who dares to write 'Down with Big Brother', dreams of attaining heroic martyrdom once captured, only to be quickly disillusioned by party official O'Brien: 'You are imagining that there is something called human nature which will be outraged by what we do and will turn against us. But we create human nature. Men are infinitely malleable.' Even Smith will be rapidly broken, manipulated through a carefully planned programme of torture into relinquishing any semblance of free will. The last lines of the book say it all: 'He had won the victory over himself. He loved Big Brother.'

The endless propaganda broadcast by *Nineteen Eighty-Four*'s Ministry of Truth, whether on film, television, radio or in print, has been interpreted as Orwell's heartfelt dig at his former employer, the British Broadcasting Corporation. Comparing the BBC to a lunatic asylum combined with a girls'

school, Orwell served his time with the organization in Broadcasting House, a building adorned with such symbols of the future as *The Tempest*'s Prospero and Ariel. Orwell paid further dubious homage to the BBC, naming *Nineteen Eighty-Four*'s ultimate torture chamber after his old office, Room 101. There is, arguably, more than a hint of embittered self-indulgence to Orwell's unrelentingly horrible parable

The doomed Julia (Jan Sterling) beneath the watchful eye of Big Brother in 1984, the 1956 film adaptation of George Orwell's novel.

of a fascist world, humanity literally crushed under the jackboot: 'If you want a picture of the future, imagine a boot stamping on a human face – for ever.'

Writing shortly after the end of World War II, his own health in terminal decline, Orwell was hopefully offering a veiled commentary on the contemporary world situation rather than a heartfelt vision of the future. When the year 1984 actually came around, received with an air of mildly apprehensive anticipation, the reality of this significant date proved something of a disappointment. Closed circuit television bought a vague feeling of surveillance

'Imagine a boot stamping on a human face – forever'

without Orwell's sense of menace, resentment of CCTV's intrusion into people's personal lives tempered by an appreciation of its security value. There is a strong case for characterising the Prime Minister of the time, Margaret Thatcher, as an aspiring 'Big Mother' – although she couldn't make everyone love her. The year also brought a new film version of *Nineteen Eighty-Four*, well acted and true to the book's depressing (lack of) spirit yet ultimately a little redundant. The score included inappropriate tracks by the then-fashionable New Romantic band the Eurythmics, added against the producer's wishes. In 1984, the Modern Romantics held sway.

PLANKTON OF THE ETHER

In 1954, four years after George Orwell's death, BBC producer/director Rudolph Cartier staged a live television version of *Nineteen Eighty-Four*, starring Peter Cushing as the ill-fated Winston Smith. The project had been knocking around for several years, generally regarded as too difficult for small screen adaptation. Scripted by BBC staff writer Nigel Kneale, who had recently scored a major hit with *The Quatermass Experiment* (also produced by Cartier) the play made few concessions to delicate audience sensibilities. Though unable to replicate the graphic sex and violence of the original book, Kneale still captures the nihilistic force of Orwell's vision, right down to the Room 101 sequence where Smith finally breaks when confronted with his worst nightmare – rats. The scurrying creatures are shown eagerly awaiting the chance to eat into Smith's face. Having obtained genuine sewer rats for the scene, Cartier discovered that the rodents simply panicked under studio lights, then fell asleep. Specially-bred laboratory rats were successfully substituted, their cage smeared with apple juice to ensure lively curiosity and a hint of sinister appetite. Though regarded by Kneale as 'purely a technical challenge', the production proved hugely controversial, the BBC even receiving death threats. Thankfully, the corporation stuck to its guns, restaging the play for a live 'repeat', which was recorded for posterity (though Cushing felt the first performance was superior). Ably supported by actors such as Yvonne Mitchell, André Morell and Donald Pleasence, Cushing's anguished performance is still effective, transcending the production's crude technical aspects. Kneale, not an easy man to please, gave the end result his seal of approval: 'It was very, very good indeed'. The success, and notoriety, of the BBC play prompted a film version the following year, which substituted second rank American stars Edmond O'Brien and Jan Sterling for Cushing and Yvonne Mitchell and added a defiantly upbeat ending, Smith still yelling 'Down with Big Brother' as the firing squad takes aim.

Five decades on from *Nineteen Eighty-Four*, Nigel Kneale remains one of the key names in the history of British science fiction, a man who can be said to have influenced virtually everything that came after him. Focusing on human curiosity, scientific investigation, bizarre, seemingly supernatural phenomena and hostile 'alien' intelligence, his work is not invariably downbeat but tends to suggest that man's unrelenting attempts to

Julia (Yvonne Mitchell) and Winston (Peter Cushing) unwisely place their trust in O'Brien (André Morell). The BBC's original adaptation of Nineteen Eighty-Four, performed live in December 1954, caused a national sensation.

explore, rationalise and control the unknown leave him vulnerable to forces he can barely comprehend, let alone withstand. Kneale is rated by many as the most significant creator of science fiction to have worked primarily in television, praise indeed given such competition as Gene Roddenberry (*Star Trek*), Rod Serling (*The Twilight Zone*) and Gerry Anderson (*Thunderbirds*).

Kneale's major achievement is the trio of *Quatermass* serials produced by the BBC during the 1950s: *The Quatermass Experiment* (1953), *Quatermass II* (1955) and *Quatermass and the Pit* (1958), better known to contemporary audiences in the pared-down, simplified Hammer film versions. A charismatic man of science, Professor Bernard Quatermass of the British Rocket Group is another hard-headed idealist, forced to question his scientific zeal after a pioneering space flight goes badly wrong. While Kneale picked his hero's unusual surname from the London telephone directory, the Professor's first name was a tribute to the esteemed British radio astronomer Bernard Lovell, later head of Jodrell Bank. Kneale envisaged Quatermass as the polar opposite of controversial German rocket scientist Wernher von Braun, creator of the V2 rocket. Employed by the Nazi regime during World War II, von Braun subsequently switched his allegiances to the United States, re-establishing his credentials as a 'respectable' figure by working on the American space programme, before falling from favour. As ruthless as he was wealthy, von Braun represented to Kneale all that is worst about scientific progress, a man with 'no perceptible morality of any kind ... I'd hate to have met him.'

Kneale's own interest in the burgeoning space race was echoed by the general public and the events forming the backdrop to the first *Quatermass* serial barely seemed like science fiction at the time. In fact, Britain's real rocket research programme lagged far behind those of the superpowers and there was no actual British Rocket Group. Throughout the *Quatermass* saga, the professor constantly found himself in conflict with both his government superiors and the military establishment, whose respect for Quatermass's intelligence and integrity was equalled only by their distrust of the scientist (at the start of *Quatermass II*, funding for the rocket group is abruptly cut). Kneale brilliantly captured the atmosphere of British paranoia, departmental rivalries and government cover-ups brought about by the proliferation of shadowy experimental state research facilities in remote, forbidding settings. If Quatermass couldn't find out what his employers were up to, the general public stood little chance.

Writer Nigel Kneale scripted the BBC's 1954 production of Nineteen Eighty-Four and created the character of space pioneer Professor Quatermass.

Even before the alien trouble, Quatermass felt his work was being corrupted, Kneale dwelling on the time-honoured science-military conflict: 'His rocket group was going to be taken over for warlike purposes, which he did not like.'

According to Kneale, who received around £250 for his script, Professor Quatermass's debut appearance stirred little initial excitement within the BBC, which still viewed radio as its prime medium.

Kneale brilliantly captured the atmosphere of British paranoia, departmental rivalries and government cover-ups

(The BBC subsequently ventured into science fiction on the wireless with *Journey Into Space* (1954), starring future all-purpose media pundit David Jacobs.) As Kneale explains: 'The BBC itself didn't believe in television ... television had no class at all.' With very few sets in existence and only a limited amount of transmission time per day, this struggling medium had yet to capture the public imagination. In *The Quatermass Experiment*, starring Reginald Tate, the first manned rocket flight brings back a hostile alien, described as 'a sort of plankton of the ether', that has absorbed two of the crew and infected the third. Capable of ingesting all terrestrial life-forms, the creature gradually grows to maturity, reaching the point where it can release its spores and wipe out humanity. Probably the first television drama that genuinely gripped the entire nation, *Quatermass* was a milestone production, though the show scored more

Bureaucracy is shown to be secretive and untrustworthy, the upper class establishment easily infiltrated

strongly with the public than the critics. With only the one television channel available, *Quatermass* had an impact in the fifties that the medium can't have now, contemporary audiences able to choose from scores of terrestrial, satellite and cable networks or watch pre-recorded material on video or DVD.

Whether for reasons of public service responsibility or simple good PR, the BBC chose to broadcast a warning before the transmission of each episode, shown after eight o'clock in the evening when younger viewers were supposedly not watching. (It's probably for the best that the BBC vetoed Kneale's original title: *Bring Something Back*, an audience non-starter if ever there was one.) The marked pessimism of the show was very much a reaction to the feelgood climate at large during the year, which Kneale presumably felt to be downright un-British. As the writer later explained in his introduction to a 1979 publication of the script: '1953 was an over-confident year. Rationing was coming to an end. Everest had just been climbed, the Queen crowned, and our first Comet jets were being deceptively successful. A sour note seemed indicated.'

And duly provided. Not that Professor Quatermass himself was intended as an addition to the ever-growing pantheon of mad men of science, indifferent, if not downright hostile to his fellow human beings. On the contrary, Kneale saw Quatermass as 'a rather worried and bothered man who'd brought something horrible to the world without intending to' (one reason the writer disliked Brian Donlevy's bluff, authoritarian portrayal in the first two Hammer films). Kneale set the story's climax, where Quatermass convinces the still partly human hybrid-creature to destroy itself, in Westminster Abbey, scene of the recent coronation. Lurking in Poets' Corner, the seemingly unkillable monster presented an insurmountable challenge to the appointed BBC designer, who simply refused the task. Kneale stepped into the breach, ingeniously crafting and operating a more than respectable creature made out of two gardening gloves and assorted rubber strips in front of a blown-up photograph of the Abbey interior. Still working on the scripts as the first episodes went out live from Alexandra Palace, Kneale felt the BBC remained unsure about the series until the viewing figures came in. Kneale himself got a buzz out of knowing that all operating television sets were tuned into his show: 'There was a very strong feeling of talking to an audience, addressing an audience, through television. That was new.' *The Quatermass Experiment* struck a collective nerve, viewers drawing perverse delight from the possibility of humanity's imminent extinction. Even the freshly rejuvenated British monarchy, offering the start of a new Elizabethan age, stood helpless in the path of the alien spores.

Highly credible as Kneale's troubled scientist, Reginald Tate agreed to repeat the role in *Quatermass II*, only to die two weeks before the start of production, necessitating the last minute substitution of John Robinson (who had to work off cue cards for the first episode). Happy with the bigger studio, improved technical facilities and the newly established BBC Visual Effects Department, Kneale remained unsure about the numerical title, 'which wasn't very clever really'. The plot deals with a marginally more subtle invasion, a localised shower of meteorites containing a parasitical alien hive-mind species that infects and controls humans as a first step towards complete planetary takeover. Kneale's inspiration derived partly from rumours of covert

Judith Carroon (Isabel Dean) joins Peter Marsh (Moray Watson, left) and Professor Quatermass (Reginald Tate) as they await news of her astronaut husband in the first episode of The Quatermass Experiment, broadcast in July 1953.

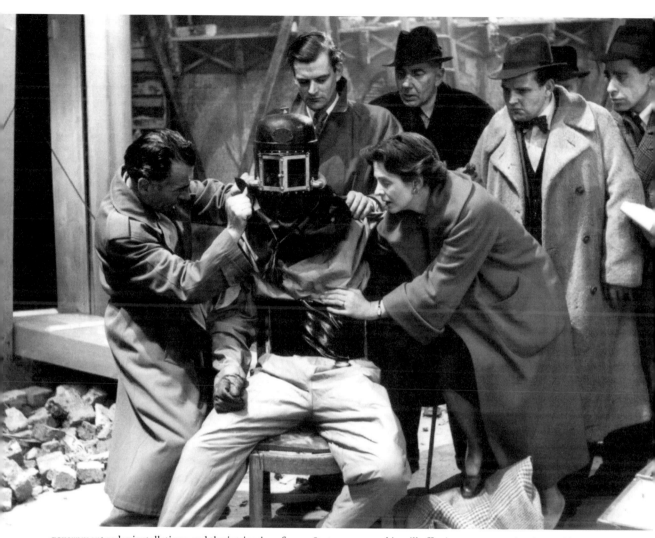

government radar installations and the intricacies of the Official Secrets Act, which he'd been obliged to sign as a BBC employee. 'It had a considerable, I suppose, sociological political element', he recalls. Bureaucracy is shown to be secretive and untrustworthy, the upper class establishment easily infiltrated, a possible reference to the latter's sympathetic attitude towards fascism two decades earlier. The story centres on Winnerden Flats, one of the new towns that has sprung up as part of the post World War II rebuilding programme, perfect cover for an alien invasion. Winnerden Flats is home to both human and extraterrestrial life, the latter residing in a secret government processing plant, supposedly producing synthetic food, that the aliens' human slaves have built to enable atmospheric acclimatization.

Opening each episode with smoking titles, accompanied by the 'Mars' suite from Gustav Holst's *The Planets* (Mars being the Bringer of War), the first

Quatermass sequel is still effective 45 years on, low key and atmospheric. The bleak location work for the Winnerden Flats sequences was filmed, like the subsequent Hammer version, at the Shellhaven oil refinery on the Essex coast. Largely devoid of human staff, the semi-automated chemical plant provided exactly the right kind of eerie atmosphere. While Kneale has so far vetoed any complete television repeat or video release of *Quatermass II*, his script is well constructed and full of perceptive touches. A probing working class member of Parliament – Labour by implication – helps Quatermass investigate the apparent government cover-up, only to be infected himself. Kneale saw nothing particularly improbable about establishment figures being taken over by aliens: 'some of them are halfway there anyway'. Quatermass, who has stumbled onto the alien plot a full year after the initial invasion, holds a secret conference with his few remaining allies in a deserted

Victor Carroon (Duncan Lamont, seated) is the sole survivor of the British Rocket Group's disastrous mission into space in The Quatermass Experiment *(1953).*

Espresso bar, coffee having lost its chic status to tea. In one scene, a picnicking family is ordered away from a beach near the plant by thuggish 'zombie' guards. The father's principled refusal to abandon their usual eating place on the brute command of dubious authority proves fatal. Offscreen machine gun fire is followed by shots of the picnic strewn over

Not only are the alien invaders already here, they've been around since the dawn of man

the beach, a grim testament to their brutal murder. The aliens' total disregard for human life is further illustrated in extremely gruesome fashion when pulped corpses are used to block a pipeline in the plant, blood dripping from the metal tube onto the floor below.

Quatermass and the Pit, with André Morell, boldly explores the theme of cosmic atheism, Kneale chillingly suggesting that man's evolution was

Following the sudden death of Reginald Tate, John Robinson starred as Professor Quatermass in Quatermass II, broadcast in 1955.

manipulated five million years ago by visiting Martians. Rated by Kneale as the best of the 1950s Quatermass serials, the last of the original trio had a top-line cast to match the more lavish production values and ingenious storyline. The assured visuals were complemented by some atmospheric, if strange sound effects courtesy of the BBC Radiophonic Workshop, which later provided *Doctor Who* with a succession of eerie, odd and downright risible noises. It's worth pointing out that Morell had been offered the lead in the original series, politely turning it down as just not his kind of thing. Kneale suspected the real reason lay with the lowly status of both the medium and the genre: 'television wasn't taken seriously by anyone … science fiction had become a very spat upon term.' Six years on, things had changed: 'we gained the respect of really good actors.'

According to *Quatermass and the Pit*, with the Red Planet heading for extinction, the Martians sought to preserve their species by implanting their race memory into the minds of the primitive ape-men then inhabiting the earth. Marginally more benevolent than the invaders of *War of the Worlds*, Kneale's alien scientists nevertheless invested humanity with a race memory of mass culling in the name of genetic purity (this racism theme caused a little friction within BBC management). Even Quatermass is affected by this resurgence of the long dormant Martian gene that returns to haunt the present in the shape of a huge horned creature, popularly known as The Devil, collectively projected by berserk, rioting Londoners. Not only are the alien invaders already here, they've been around since the dawn of man. *Quatermass and the Pit* shows us that the Martians were ourselves all along, a prospect arguably far more alarming than H G Wells's Red Planet war machines. Impressionable viewer Anthony Daniels, later to achieve sf icon status himself as the prissy android C-3PO in the *Star Wars* saga, was both terrified and transfixed by the ominous, threatening monochrome images: 'I actually hid behind the sitting room sofa.' Even the BBC Martian creatures, which could be dismissed as 'really hokey preying mantises', took on a highly sinister quality as the 'possession' theme unravelled.

A huge success with television audiences, Professor Quatermass rapidly found his way to the big screen in the 1955 sleeper hit *The Quatermass Xperiment*, a respectable mini-budget adaptation that put Hammer Film Productions on the map at a time when few British filmmakers regarded science fiction as a commercial prospect, despite the genre's popularity in America. Always happy to capitalise on

established hits, Hammer had previously drawn on radio favourites such as *Dick Barton* and *PC49* for film material, making television a logical progression. The less than subtle title change, rated 'about as cheap as you can get' by Kneale, reflected the film's expected 'X' certificate, duly conferred by the British Board of Film Censors (often cited as the first for a British-made film, though the 1952 'baby farming' melodrama *Women of Twilight* received an 'X' three years earlier). While most British film companies regarded an 'X' as a box-office kiss of death, Hammer hoped to make it a major selling point, the financially stricken company in desperate need of a hit (without *The Quatermass Xperiment*, Hammer probably wouldn't have survived to embark on its Gothic horror renaissance). The studio had already dabbled in bargain basement science fiction, such as the Cold War espionage drama *Spaceways* (1953) and *Four Sided Triangle* (1953), a modestly successful story of human cloning, released just a couple of months before the BBC broadcast the first episode of *The Quatermass Experiment*.

Quatermass director and co-writer Val Guest, who claimed not to have seen the television serial, aimed

to give the black and white film the low key style of a newsreel documentary, taut and fast-paced. Hammer and American partner Robert Lippert were counting on a US distribution deal for the film, which necessitated the use of an inexpensive American lead. No stranger to this expedient form of casting, Hammer selected experienced screen heavy Brian Donlevy, whose fading Hollywood career and serious

Professor Quatermass (André Morell) discusses the discovery of ancient alien life-forms with Dr Roney (Cec Linder) in Quatermass and the Pit (1959), the final story in the original BBC trilogy.

Marsh (Maurice Kauffman) and Professor Quatermass (Brian Donlevy, right) discover the startling consequences of The Quatermass Xperiment (1955), Hammer's remake of the BBC serial.

drink problem left him open to overseas offers. After a false start with Columbia, which didn't want competition for its homegrown sci fi hit *It Came From Beneath the Sea* (1955), Lippert eventually made a deal with United Artists, who released the *Quatermass* film in March 1956 as *The Creeping Unknown*. Nigel Kneale hated the choice of Donlevy, dismissing his version of Professor Quatermass as an unscrupulous, bullying egomaniac who gets his way by shouting.

'There's no room for personal feelings in science ... some of us have a mission'

Displaying an emotional range that ran from annoyance to fury, Donlevy's 'cold mechanic' was closer in spirit to Wernher von Braun than the original television Quatermass. Val Guest rejected

Kneale's criticism of his star, feeling that Donlevy's abrasive, no-nonsense acting blended in well with the overall film, despite the actor's inability to remember his lines. Reduced by alcoholism to reading off cue cards, Donlevy's bullish Quatermass is a fairly one-note creation, yet his performance contrasts effectively with those of the more genteel British supporting cast. Dismissing his assistant's concern for astronaut Victor Carroon's catatonic condition, Quatermass refuses to waste time on mere details: 'There's no room for personal feelings in science ... Some of us have a mission.'

As played by gaunt, sad-eyed actor Richard Wordsworth, the alien-infected Carroon, unwilling martyr to Quatermass's scientific crusade, exhibits far more humanity than the Professor. Having witnessed the creature's death by electrocution in Westminster Abbey, a simplistic, if spectacular rewrite of Kneale's original ending (Kneale wasn't pleased), Quatermass walks away with total indifference, his mind already on the next rocket launch: 'I'm going to start again.'

As a BBC staff writer whose contract didn't permit outside freelance work, Nigel Kneale had been excluded from the first Quatermass film deal, receiving no money and very little credit. In response to this, both Quatermass II and Quatermass and the Pit were devised with possible film versions in mind. Having quit the BBC by the time Hammer got round to the subtly retitled Quatermass 2 (1957), Kneale was able to have some say in the production, adapting the original television scripts himself. Kneale also prevented Hammer from turning his character into a mini franchise. The studio intended the Quatermass-influenced X the Unknown (1958), scripted by Jimmy Sangster, as an official sequel until Kneale refused them use of the character name. A solid commercial success, Quatermass 2 was not as big a hit as The Quatermass Xperiment, its thunder largely stolen by another Hammer production released earlier in the year. Boasting glorious Eastmancolor, Gothic settings, bright red gore and an all-British cast, The Curse of Frankenstein proved a worldwide box-office smash, taking Hammer in a new direction. In the largely austere, not to say drab, climate of 1950s Britain, the Curse formula provided a real jolt for audiences, particularly the full-colour blood.

Hammer optioned Quatermass and the Pit in 1961, but it was another six years before director Roy Ward Baker commenced filming with Scottish actor Andrew Keir in the title role. Baker's previous hits had included The One That Got Away (1957), the story of German POW escapee Franz Von Werra, and A Night to Remember (1958), the best reconstruction of the Titanic disaster. One of the British film industry's most respected veterans, Baker had trained at Gainsborough Studios,

"QUATERMASS II" starring BRIAN DONLEVY "X"
with JOHN LONGDEN · SIDNEY JAMES · BRYAN FORBES · WILLIAM FRANKLYN · VERA DAY
Produced by ANTHONY HINDS   Directed by VAL GUEST   A HAMMER FILMS PRODUCTION

specialists in lush period melodramas such as The Wicked Lady (1945), edited by fellow Hammer director-to-be Terence Fisher. While the Gainsborough style has been cited as an influence on Hammer's own rich period Gothic look, its immediate value to Baker was the experience of 38 films in six years, which he followed with Army service, making instructional films and propaganda. Having spent most of the 1960s directing television episodes, notably The Saint and The Avengers (see Chapter 2), Baker felt more than happy to take on Quatermass and the Pit, despite some puzzlement over Hammer's blatant recycling of old material: 'I've never quite understood how they got away with it' (it probably helped that the original television serial was now nearly a decade old).

Baker certainly enjoyed his Hammer experience: 'How to make films for nothing ... quite a jolly time.' Baker hadn't seen either of Hammer's previous Quatermass films, but rated Nigel Kneale's screenplay for Pit as 'a fireproof script, an absolute humdinger ... you'd need to be a very bad director to muck it up'. The dialogue seemed sharp, with both clarity and edge, the central Man-as-Martian premise 'very intriguing ... awfully bogus but in fact it's plausible'. His only worry was creating a believably scary 'devil' for the film's climactic sequence: 'I was terrified it was going to look comical.' The glowing, nebulous end result proved difficult to achieve but did the job, more a ghost from mankind's past than a living creature. Baker also liked Hammer's choice of Quatermass:

Broadhead (Tom Chatto) pays a terrible price for investigating the mysterious domes at Winnerden Flats in Quatermass 2 (1957).

A shocked chemist (Toke Townley) discovers the horrifyingly afflicted Victor Carroon (Richard Wordsworth) in The Quatermass Xperiment (1955).

Professor Quatermass (Andrew Kier) faces his demons in the fiery climax of Hammer's *Quatermass and the Pit* (1967).

'Andrew was absolutely dead right for it ... the ideal man to play the part... He got to be a real professor.' Keir's Scottish accent seemed tailor made for the role, Baker believing that it rendered the character authoritative, without being arrogant. 'He came from an ordinary background. He was not posh.'

Feeling that he'd got on well with Keir during the film's production, Baker was surprised when, years later, the actor claimed that their working relationship had gone badly. Never a believer in 'overdirection', Baker now suggests that Keir probably wanted more guidance than he felt was necessary. Despite this apparent unhappiness with his director, Andrew Keir met with Nigel Kneale's unqualified approval: 'He was very, very good. It was the character as I'd always seen him.' Light years away from the Brian Donlevy version, Keir's Professor Quatermass had, in Baker's words, 'a

deeply felt conscience about society', all too aware of the potential disaster facing mankind when the Martian gene was reactivated. An intelligent, well-handled distillation of the three hour original, Hammer's *Quatermass and the Pit* would be the Professor's last appearance for over a decade. Writer and editor Stephen Jones, author of *The Essential Monster Movie Guide*, sneaked into the film at the tender age of 14, leaving with a lasting regard for the power of Kneale's vision: 'Nigel Kneale tapped into these basic fears we have in this country of technology, of looking forward.' Roy Ward Baker concurs: 'Nigel's views were very sound and very principled. He knew what he was writing about and he knew what the undercurrent was.'

When Kneale finally revived his character for the Euston Films/ ITV television serial *Quatermass* (1979, aka *The Quatermass Conclusion*), the result was a curious, extremely downbeat sequel lacking some of the urgency and edge of the original 1950s trio. First mooted in 1969 as a Hammer-BBC television co-production entitled *Quatermass IV*, the project went through various stages of semi-development. Kneale claims to have had both a finished script and a producer by 1972, only for the BBC to drop the whole production on grounds of cost. Seven years on, the pseudo-hippie 'Planet People' element central to the story seemed dated, and star John Mills made no secret of his uneasiness in the title role. Produced on a relatively high budget, with location work ranging from Wembley Stadium to Stonehenge, and hundreds of extras, *Quatermass* is still quite powerful viewing. Having planted proprietorial markers on the earth centuries before in the form of stone monoliths, an alien race returns with the intention of harvesting the human race, which it regards as little more than a plaything. While the impressionable youth are transfixed by the extraterrestrial visitors, setting up a cult of alien worship, the older generation is less impressed. Professor Quatermass nobly sacrifices himself to save humanity with a strategic nuclear explosion. In 1996, Andrew Keir reclaimed the title role for the BBC Radio 4 serial *The Quatermass Memoirs*, an impressive resurrection.

Whatever Kneale's reservations about the Hammer *Quatermass* films, their overseas release –

particularly in America – brought his work to a wider audience than BBC television could have offered at the time. Kneale's far-reaching influence remains visible to this day, not least in more or less every other episode of Chris Carter's megahit *The X-Files*, with its unending series of alien manifestations, 'supernatural' events, hideous mutations, genetic tamperings, hidden agendas and government

'Nigel Kneale tapped into these basic fears we have in this country of technology, of looking forward'

cover-ups (Kneale and the Roswell Incident have a lot to answer for). This is one instance where imitation has not been taken as flattery: 'I hate *The X-Files* ... very dull'. When asked recently if he'd ever been approached to write for the show, Kneale confirmed that he'd received a phone call or two and made his refusal very clear. Mulder and Scully are not the new Quatermass: 'They turn me off straight away.'

A decade earlier, American director John Carpenter, a major fan of Kneale's work, commissioned the writer to provide the screenplay for *Halloween III: Season of the Witch* (1983), which he promptly rejected as both too costly and insufficiently

Kickalong (Ralph Arliss) addresses the Planet People at the Ringstone Round stone circle, while Professor Quatermass (Sir John Mills) looks on in Quatermass (1979).

horrific. Following extensive rewrites by Carpenter and director Tommy Lee Wallace, Kneale took his name off the credits, leaving Wallace listed as the sole author. Kneale is diplomatic about the whole business, arguing that 'John was too busy on another project' (The Thing 1981, which Kneale likes). The end result still bears traces of Kneale's influence, if not his input. Insane but practical mask manufacturer Dan O'Herlihy attempts to recapture the true, bloodily pagan spirit of the overly commercialised Halloween festival by issuing a series of fright masks fitted with special micro-chips incorporating slivers of a genuine Stonehenge monolith. This unlikely use of the sacrificial stone enables O'Herlihy to deploy a nifty piece of high-tech witchcraft: activated by a special television signal, the masks bloodily implode on their wearers. Kneale claims that the story elements commonly attributed to him, notably the extra-special computer chips, were in fact added to the script by Carpenter and Wallace.

Carpenter's later Prince of Darkness (1987) borrows from both Quatermass and the Pit and Kneale's similarly outstanding television play The Stone Tape (1972), a blend of ghost story and rash scientific investigation. Messy in both conception and execution, the film depicts Satan as a not quite dormant extraterrestrial entity trapped in a Los Angeles church basement by The Brotherhood of Death, a Catholic sect that doesn't advertise. Carpenter penned the screenplay under the pseudonym 'Martin Quatermass', a homage that slightly backfired. Unimpressed with the end result, Kneale feared that he would be mistakenly (dis)credited as the film's true author. Professor Quatermass himself seemed on the verge of a movie

Human evolution is apparently directed by extraterrestrial forces

comeback several times during the last decade, both in Britain and the United States. In the early 1990s, Alien co-author Dan O'Bannon wrote a script for an American remake of The Quatermass Experiment, which Kneale rated highly but regarded as far too intellectual for the Hollywood market. A proposed Hammer remake of Quatermass and the Pit failed to materialise, largely because of complications over the rights.

KUBRICK'S COSMOS

The Martians who rewrite man's genetic code in Quatermass and the Pit do so for a largely selfish reason: the preservation, by proxy at least, of their own species. In Stanley Kubrick's 2001: A Space Odyssey (1968), human evolution is apparently directed by extraterrestrial forces out of general inter-galactic benevolence. The apemen seen in the film's opening section are not whisked off to the Red Planet for a little radical surgery, merely confronted with a featureless black monolith that seems to impart knowledge, or at least an improved instinct for self-preservation. Progress equates with acts of violence, however, whether for food or territory, and man's path is set. A bleached animal bone becomes a lethal tool of hunting and warfare, then transmutes – via a justly famous jumpcut – into a sleek spacecraft travelling towards the populated moon in the twenty first century. Underneath the calm, detached hi-tech surface, little has changed, civilised man displaying all the hostility, ignorance, suspicion and aggression of his apeman ancestors. Still a primitive, childlike race, mankind is in need of further help.

Co-written by Kubrick and science fiction novelist Arthur C Clarke, 2001 is one of the most celebrated, derided and analysed films of all time. Financed by struggling Hollywood giant MGM, this self-styled space epic is authentic trans-Atlantic science fiction in both credentials and outlook, filmed in England with largely homegrown talent under the direction of an ex-patriot American auteur. The groundbreaking futuristic sets and effects, which cost the then-extraordinary sum of $6.5 million, established a new benchmark for the genre, seldom equalled to this day.

Whether the viewer finds 2001 profound and uplifting, or shallow, pretentious and trite, its potency to provoke has barely diminished after three decades. Employing minimal, often deliberately banal dialogue, Kubrick expresses the film's themes in largely visual terms, augmented by an impressive, if mostly ornamental medley of classical music, ranging from Johann Strauss's 'The Blue Danube' to Richard Strauss's 'Thus Spake Zarathustra'. Anyone tempted to read neo-Nietzschean themes into the film should bear in mind that this pop classics soundtrack was a last minute choice, supplanting the original Alex North score. Kubrick's refusal to spell out his ideas in definitive, easy-to-follow form led those in search of hard answers to turn to co-writer Clarke, whose short story The Sentinel was credited as the film's source. Clarke worked on the novel 2001 in tandem with the movie script, in the process carefully clarifying many elements that the film left open to interpretation. Other elements of the novel simply diverge from the film, and no attempt has been made to bring the two versions of the story into alignment. (For example, in the film the spaceship Discovery is heading for the planet Jupiter. In the novel, Jupiter is

visited, but only en route to the *Discovery's* final destination, Saturn). There is certainly no shortage of conflicting interpretations of the story (Kubrick and Clarke themselves didn't completely agree as to what it all meant). But it seems reasonable to argue that 2001 the film deals, in part at least, with the guidance and possible salvation of the listless, petty, technologically dependent human race through alien intervention, an idea that probably provided much needed comfort in the unsettled global climate of the late 1960s.

Never a great believer in humankind, Kubrick probably felt he had taken the theme of man's capacity, not to mention yearning, for self-destruction as far as it could go in his Cold War black farce *Dr Strangelove: Or, How I Learned to Stop Worrying and Love the Bomb* (1964). Here, US General Jack Ripper (Sterling Hayden), a paranoid psychotic obsessed with bodily fluids, blames the Russians for his sexual impotence and launches a nuclear strike against the Soviet Union, which in turn triggers the Russian's top secret Doomsday Machine, with apocalyptic results. This impending Armageddon is greeted with ill-disguised glee by Dr Strangelove (Peter Sellers), a former Nazi scientist co-opted by

the Americans for their own weapons research. Convinced that the political and scientific elite assembled in the President's War Room will be quite safe in their bomb shelter, Strangelove seems more concerned with the opportunities for selective breeding than the impending destruction of the earth. (Ronald Reagan, whose own Presidential vision of the world appeared to be a seamless melding of reality and fantasy, was sufficiently impressed with Ken Adam's designs for *Strangelove* to request something on the same lines for his own War Room.)

By contrast, 2001 seems almost optimistic, if not in mankind then at least in humanity's potential to transcend its in-built flaws under pseudo-divine patronage. The discovery of a second monolith on the moon triggers a signal, alerting man's unseen alien benefactors that the time has come for Phase II. Having taken on and defeated homicidal computer HAL, astronaut David Bowman makes a psychedelic trip through the stargate to meet his destiny. The Academy Award winning special effects, still impressive today, were devised by an Anglo-American team that included Wally Veevers, Tom Howard, Con Pederson and Douglas Trumball. Kubrick originally approached *Thunderbirds* creator-producer Gerry

General Turgidson (George C Scott) urges the American president to annihilate the opposition in Stanley Kubrick's apocalyptic black comedy Dr Strangelove or: How I Learned to Stop Worrying and Love the Bomb (1964).

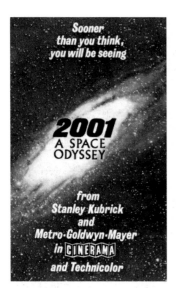

Production of Stanley Kubrick's 2001: A Space Odyssey was announced in February 1965. It would be over three years until the film reached cinemas.

The counter-culture influence of the Summer of Love is apparent in this psychedelic poster promoting 2001: A Space Odyssey (1968).

Anderson to supervise the numerous effects sequences, only to find that Anderson would not loan out his talent on other people's projects. David Lane, one of Anderson's regular editors and directors, later saw the finished film and rated it 'The finest day's rushes I've ever seen', an opinion Anderson felt little urge to contest. Interestingly, Kubrick's odyssey failed to find favour with another of Britain's premiere science fiction names. Nigel Kneale, who rated Dr Strangelove as 'a masterpiece... very clever, totally true', felt that 2001 fell into the common sf trap of getting ideas above its station: 'It can claim too much profundity, which it can't deliver.' Kneale has also voiced suspicions over the buried lunar monolith's passing resemblance to the Martian spaceship discovered in Quatermass' pit.

The most obviously dystopian element in 2001, the deranged computer HAL 9000, represents artificial intelligence as a rebel angel – a man-made artefact that turns on man. Or does HAL represent the next logical stage in human evolution, the ongoing process of mechanization that began with the apeman's bone club? As voiced by Canadian actor Douglas Rain, HAL is helpful, informative and courteous, even showing a polite interest in Bowman's burgeoning artistic talent, generously praising his sketches of fellow crewmen (whom it subsequently kills). The astronauts, on the other hand, are anonymous, subservient drones as mechanised and programmed as their spaceship. Disconnected by Bowman, HAL 'expires' to the plaintive tones of 'Daisy, Daisy, Give Me Your Answer Do', inspiring a sense of loss entirely absent from the earlier human deaths (for the record, Daisy said no). Critic and cult film chronicler Danny Peary suggests that the aliens may have deliberately triggered HAL's 'breakdown' to test the crew. By vanquishing the previously omnipotent computer, Bowman both

rediscovers his human potential and proves himself worthy to move on to the next evolutionary stage.

Many regard 2001 as a pessimistic vision. Critic Peter Nicholls describes the film as 'a lament for the sterility of human achievement', yet it surely contains more hope than such recent dystopian visions as The Matrix (1998), where mankind's perception of the world is nothing more than a virtual reality environment generated by the all-powerful computers that now rule the earth. Having encountered a third monolith, Bowman dies in human form and is reborn as the star child, a celestial infant (angel?) floating back towards the earth, possibly to help the rest of humanity evolve to the next phase of existence (alternatively, the Bowman star child is taking a last look at a world and species it has now outgrown). While Nigel Kneale revealed the Devil as a Martian with an intelligible, if selfish, plan for survival after corporeal extinction, Stanley Kubrick preferred to redefine God as an enigmatic, unfathomable, almost playful alien presence.

Shortly before 2001: A Space Odyssey received its American premiere in 1968, MGM held a press launch for the film, with Arthur C Clarke as guest of honour. (The air travel wary Stanley Kubrick would not fly out of Britain to attend.) Modestly downplaying his own contribution to the film – 'I acted as a first-stage booster and provided occasional guidance' – Clarke outlined Kubrick's as-yet unseen space epic as a major new departure in the much-maligned and misused science fiction genre. Dismissing most previous sf films as 'junk' that had prejudiced audiences against the form, Clarke described 2001 as 'a mature treatment of the theme of space exploration, this great new frontier that's opening up in our age.' The Apollo space programme management team had re-scheduled an important meeting to attend 2001's premiere, surely the ultimate reflection of the film's significance. Going beyond the known universe, 2001 also entered the realm of metaphysical speculation, 'an attempt to convey the possible, indeed the probable place of man in the hierarchy of the universe ... we are probably pretty low on the cosmic totem pole.'

While Arthur C Clarke's desire to depict 2001 as the start of a new and exciting approach to cinematic sf is understandable, in many ways the film marks the end of an era, a definitive summation of the major themes developed in British science fiction since the time of Shakespeare, that leaves little to be added. We have The Tempest's non-human lifeforms, secret knowledge and pseudo-divine power deriving from techno-alchemy. The film also stirs memories of

Frank Poole (Gary Lockwood) waits while his colleague David Bowman runs a fool's errand in 2001: A Space Odyssey (1968).

Frankenstein's Faustian pursuit of forbidden learning and the creation of artificial life that proves uncontrollable. H G Wells's themes of interplanetary travel, and the humbling superiority of alien beings, and Nigel Kneale's extraterrestrial commandeering of human evolution are also clearly present in the mix.

Subsequent major sf films would largely look to other genres for their inspiration rather than the 2001 template, whether it be the western (Star Wars), the horror movie (Alien), the noir thriller (Blade Runner) or the war film (Aliens). Even Close Encounters of the Third Kind (1977), which re-packages the alien-contact theme with a sense of reassuring, middle-America-friendly warmth, is ultimately more concerned with the idea of a regular guy attaining his dream against the odds – even if it does mean upsetting his family at

the dinner table and flying off in a spaceship: sf meets the world of Frank Capra. Whatever its faults, 2001: A Space Odyssey will remain the ultimate in intellectual, near abstract science fiction speculation on the big screen, from the man-ape rumbles of pre-history to the tastefully furnished white limbo

God as an enigmatic, unfathomable, almost playful alien presence

where David Bowman observes his physical degeneration and death. For those still wondering, the star child's eyes do move at the end, taking in both the earth and the audience.

CHAPTER 2
SUPERMARIONATION, SUPERSPIES AND CAR SICKNESS

By the time Stanley Kubrick began production on 2001 in late 1965, the low budget British science fiction film cycle initiated by *The Quatermass Xperiment* had largely palled. Producers had switched their attentions to the gothic horror revival, spurred by the success of Hammer's *Curse of Frankenstein*.

This is not to say that the public appetite for 'pure' science fiction had disappeared altogether. *Quatermass* writer-director Val Guest enjoyed another hit with *The Day the Earth Caught Fire* (1961), where American and Soviet nuclear testing knocks the earth out of its orbit into the path of the sun. As *Daily Express* investigative journalist Edward Judd discovers, man's only chance of survival is to detonate further nuclear bombs in the hope of reversing the original effect (the science may be bad but the storytelling is quite gripping). Even Hammer briefly returned to sf with *The Damned* (1963), where a government scientist keeps a group of deliberately irradiated children in an isolated, hermetically sealed environment, conditioning them to serve as the Earth's chosen survivors in the event of nuclear war. Directed by reluctant Hollywood exile Joseph Losey, a shunned 'Red' previously removed from *X the Unknown* on the insistence of its American star, Dean Jagger, this provocative, incredibly cynical melodrama didn't please studio executives looking for another *Quatermass*. Delayed, hacked about and pointlessly retitled *These Are the Damned* for the American market, Losey's film died a quiet box-office death, but is now regarded by many as one of Hammer's finest achievements. On the downside, the 1962 film version of John Wyndham's *The Day of the Triffids*, overseen by American producer-writer Philip Yordan, proved so underwhelming in its first cut that new scenes were added using a different cast and director. When it came to television, however, science fiction fantasy would enjoy an unprecedented boom during the 1960s. While the trendsetting Professor

Quatermass had departed from the small screen, he didn't lack for successors.

On the face of it, the ingredients for *Doctor Who* didn't look especially promising: an ill-tempered humanoid, banished from his home world, arrives on present day Earth with his slightly strange granddaughter in a malfunctioning space-time machine, the TARDIS (Time And Relative Dimension In Space), disguised as a police call box. Though far more intelligent than the average human, granddaughter Susan enrols at the local secondary school for a taste of a solid British education. Two teachers, commendably concerned for their mysterious new pupil's welfare, are virtually kidnapped by the dubious Doctor (he won't give his real name) and transported back to the less than hospitable Stone Age. From these offbeat beginnings, *Doctor Who* progressed from surprise hit to national institution, finally coming to a halt after an impressive 26 years, gone from the studio floor but by no means forgotten.

On 23 November 1963, the BBC transmitted the first episode of their new series, which arrived on the screens after a slightly bumpy ride. Conceived by a team headed by BBC Head of Drama Sydney Newman as a canny blend of entertainment and education, slotted in between the Saturday afternoon sports coverage and *Juke Box Jury*, the show was originally intended to employ science fiction trappings without an 'excessive' amount of fantasy content. The Doctor would regularly transport his human companions to various points in Earth's past, where they would encounter famous historical figures in an adventure story format.

Opposite: William Hartnell as the original Doctor Who in the 1964 serial Inside the Spaceship.

A British trade advertisement for the 1963 film adaptation of John Wyndham's The Day of the Triffids.

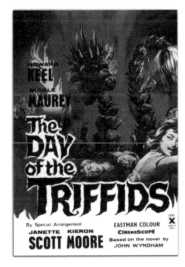

Though not entirely adverse to the occasional sf story, Newman had little time for what he regarded as the clichés of the genre, especially 'bug-eyed monsters'. The series might not aspire to the intellectual heights of Nigel Kneale's *Quatermass* trilogy, but there would be no 'B' movie-style ray gun antics. It's notable that the early *Doctor Who* asked its family audience to buy into some fairly tricky concepts, such as the TARDIS being dimensionally transcendental, or, put another way, bigger on the inside than the outside. The first season, devised as seven linked but self-contained stories, was entrusted to novice producer Verity Lambert, Newman's former production secretary at ABC Television and one of the first women elevated to the post at the BBC. Interviewed by the *Radio Times* for the programme's

twentieth anniversary, Lambert recalled Newman's determination to get his vision for the show on screen: 'Sydney told me it was to be a show that stretched television, using all the newest technology and that it should be educative as well as entertaining. When we travelled back in time, every detail had to be accurate ... When we went into the future, it had to be based on what was known then about space and other planets.'

Having persuaded an initially doubtful William Hartnell to take the lead, Lambert ran into problems with the original pilot episode, which was rejected by the management and reshot from scratch. On transmission night, audiences were still reeling from the assassination of President Kennedy the day before and were in a probably less-than-receptive mood.

Schoolteachers Barbara Wright (Jacqueline Hill) and Ian Chesterton (William Russell) grow curious about their unusual pupil Susan Foreman (Carole Ann Ford) in An Unearthly Child *(1963), the first episode of* Doctor Who.

Writer Terry Nation with two of his most notorious creations in a picture taken to publicise the 1964 serial The Dalek Invasion of Earth.

Viewed nearly four decades after it was first shown, the early *Doctor Who* is undeniably creaky at times, but the flickering black and white images of the surviving episodes retain a strong fascination. (Existing copies are crude 16mm film transfers made for overseas sales; the original master tapes were erased). Secretive, mischievous, unpredictable and arrogant, Hartnell's aged Doctor is hardly a comforting paternal figure, leaving even his granddaughter dismayed by his often selfish attitude. In the second serial, *The Daleks*, the Doctor resorts to sabotaging the TARDIS when his companions vote to leave the radioactive planet of Skaro rather than continue their hazardous exploration. Impatient with those less intelligent than himself, the Doctor makes little effort to hide his contempt for human ignorance. On the other hand, he is a lonely figure, a self-proclaimed 'wanderer in the fourth dimension', with no particular reason to be benevolent towards the human race (ironic, given his later exile on the planet). Like Shakespeare's Prospero, he possesses secret, mysterious knowledge – not to mention power – that he wields for largely benevolent ends, fearlessly pitting his wits against hostile forces.

Hartnell's Doctor softened a little during his tenure in the role, treating his succession of human companions with grudging affection, though his philosophy of self-preservation remained pragmatic: 'I never take life unless my own is threatened'. When his granddaughter Susan falls in love with a man from Earth's future, the Doctor spares her the agony of conflicting loyalties, locking her outside the TARDIS and departing.

Like Shakespeare's Prospero, he possesses secret, mysterious knowledge

Hartnell's portrayal of the Doctor offered a unique, if uneasy, blend of character and actor. Fatigued by the fast pace of weekly television work, he stumbled over his lines at times, the absentmind-edness, hesitation and occasional irritability of his screen character probably quite genuine (time was money, and retakes were frowned upon).

The first *Doctor Who* story, *100,000 BC*, faithfully followed Sydney Newman's original brief, involving

The 1966 film *Daleks' Invasion Earth 2150 A.D.* gave the Daleks a more impressive effects budget than that afforded to their television counterparts.

the time travellers in a Stone Age tribal struggle and the inevitable quest for fire. Whatever the educational value of this story, when reluctant passenger Ian Chesterton (William Russell) shows caveman Za how to make fire by rubbing two sticks together, he's surely disrupting the natural course of history, a point the story chooses to ignore. *Doctor Who* really hit its stride with the follow-up tale, *The Daleks*, written by Terry Nation, which drew an average eight million viewers over its seven episodes and left the BBC management wondering how an educational family show had somehow managed to transform itself into an anti-nuclear, anti-fascist allegory in the space of two stories. The planet Skaro, reduced to a petrified wasteland after centuries of neutronic warfare, is home to two races, both transformed by generations of mutation. While the Thals, blonde-haired pacifist humanoids, struck it relatively lucky, the Daleks are hideous, warped lumps of seething

intellect reduced to travelling within the confines of their city in personal armoured transports. The Daleks, violently xenophobic to the nth degree, are obsessed with perpetuating the race warfare (their much parodied cry of 'Exterminate! Exterminate!' has definite Nazi connotations).

Subsequently toned down for the more juvenile film remake *Dr Who and the Daleks* (1965), this is fairly heavy duty material for a family show and didn't meet with universal approval. A deeply annoyed Newman initially hated the Daleks, 'absolutely not what I had wanted', and summoned Verity Lambert for a fierce dressing down. As Newman later admitted, he was very much in the minority. Constructed by designer Raymond Cusick from Terry Nation's original outline, the Daleks are a superb piece of cost-conscious alien hardware. Abandoning the familiar man-in-a-rubber-suit look of most screen monsters, they glide along like miniature upright tanks, eye stalk looking straight ahead, laser gun at the ready. The effect is greatly enhanced by the Daleks' harsh, electronically distorted voices, devised by Brian Hodgson of the Radiophonic Workshop. Far from being flat and devoid of emotion in the standard robot tradition, the voices are filled with malice and aggression. The only downside to the Thal-Dalek dichotomy is the implication that humanoid lifeforms will invariably act humanely, whereas a creature as utterly alien as the Dalek can only be malevolent. Throughout its long run, *Doctor Who* would continue to touch on potentially controversial subjects, dressed up in allegorical form. Terry Nation's first Dalek sequel, *The Dalek Invasion of Earth* (1964) depicted a desolate, semi-ruined future London ruled by the vicious aliens and their 'Robomen' thugs, human beings reduced to near zombies by severe brain tampering. Nigel Kneale, no stranger to scaring audiences with visions of England under extraterrestrial siege, felt this story was unacceptably horrific for juvenile viewers. Scriptwriter William Emms, who came up with the third season opener *Galaxy Four* (1965), once explained that no one in BBC management could be bothered to scrutinise the scripts for a 'mere' science fiction show, enabling the writers to tackle themes forbidden to more respectable mainstream drama. Incidentally, in Emms's story, the humanoid, physically attractive Drahvins are vicious aggressors, whereas the 'ugly' ammonia-breathing Rills want only peace. The former are an Amazonian, female dominated race, which throws up issues of its own.

In the event, the first season of *Doctor Who* was an even mixture of science fiction and history, offering encounters with Marco Polo, the Aztec civilisation and the French Revolution. The post-Dalek 'monster' species were conventionally human-shaped but still quite effective. *The Keys of Marinus* offered the Voords, anonymous thugs with a penchant for black rubber. *The Sensorites* were bald-headed telepaths with amusing feet, wary of mankind but essentially harmless. William Hartnell always preferred the historical stories, claiming he got a kick out of the Doctor meeting famous figures from history. Audiences begged to differ, the series's ratings taking a nosedive whenever it returned to earthbound costume drama. One point these stories invariably made was that however much the TARDIS crew interacted with figures from Earth's past, they could not alter the course of history. In *The Aztecs* (1964), companion Barbara Wright (Jacqueline Hill) is hailed as the reincarnation of High Priest Yetaxa, only to find that her understandable opposition to human

sacrifice stirs strong resentment among the locals. In the third season story *The Massacre of St Bartholomew's Eve* (1966), set in 1572, the Doctor and his companion Steven (Peter Purves) can do nothing to prevent the St Bartholomew's Day Massacre of French Protestants.

Feeling that the series needed more guts, not to mention healthy ratings, producer Innes Lloyd decided to phase out the historical stories after the 1966/67 Patrick Troughton instalment *The Highlanders*, set in the aftermath of Culloden. The 1975 Tom Baker story *Pyramids of Mars* took a more flexible approach to possible futures, the Doctor showing companion Sarah Jane Smith an alternative present day earth

Doctor Who declared war on malevolent lifeforms without offering victory as a foregone conclusion

reduced to a wasteland by Sutekh the Destroyer. In *Earthshock* (1982), Doctor number five Peter Davison saw his fellow traveller Adric blown up in a spaceship, but refused all entreaties to take the TARDIS back in time for a rescue operation. While it's an oversimplification to argue that *Doctor Who* and *Star Trek* are key examples of British pessimism versus American optimism, the latter's sf coated lessons in humanistic ethical behaviour tended to end on a reassuring note, everything being largely for the best in the best of all possible universes. Doctor Who declared war on malevolent lifeforms without offering victory as a foregone conclusion.

SUPERMARIONATION STATION

While *Doctor Who* did the rounds of historical personages and bizarre alien lifeforms for the BBC, independent television came up with some notable science fiction shows of its own, both with and without live performers. Producer Gerry Anderson, once described as the man who perfected the miniature explosion, carved himself a distinctive, if unexpected niche in small screen fantasy with a series of puppet shows employing high-tech marionettes against intricate scaled-down backdrops. Even those unmoved by the drama of Century 21 Productions' *Stingray* would have to admit that the models were pretty fine. Avoiding the relatively low-tech look of *Doctor Who*, recorded on low resolution 405 line black and white videotape, Anderson opted to work on film and in colour at a time when colour television (in the UK) was still several years away. An extremely astute move when it

Gerry Anderson, the producer of some of Britain's best-loved science fiction shows.

skyscraper. The pilot episode of *Thunderbirds*, 'Trapped in the Sky', involved a 2000 person atomic-powered airliner, a logical extension of contemporary jet aircraft. Aware of the research into jump-jet fighter planes, Anderson gave *Thunderbirds'* International Rescue vehicles the power of vertical take-off. Aside from Stanley Kubrick's short-lived overtures (see Chapter 1), Century 21's impressive array of magnificent flying machines attracted at least one unexpected job offer, Anderson agreeing to provide a model shot of the as yet unfinished Concorde supersonic airliner for a promotional film. Initially wary of mentioning his day job, Anderson soon discovered that the Concorde project staff were big *Thunderbirds* fans.

Gerry Anderson first broke out the marionettes for the 1956-7 children's series *Twizzle*, the adventures of a boy doll with extendable limbs. *Torchy the Battery Boy* (1959) featured a clockwork toy who travels by rocket to Topsy Turvy Land, where all toys are alive. Both series dealt with toys either neglected or mistreated by their child owners, a somewhat ironic theme given Anderson's later emphasis on all-out miniature destruction. Anderson introduced more human-looking puppets in the western series *Four Feather Falls* (1960), which starred the unlikely duo of Nicholas Parsons as Sheriff Tex Tucker and *Carry On* regular Kenneth Connor as Fernando, a shifty Mexican bandit. The proud possessor of four magic feathers given him by a grateful Indian Chief, Sheriff Tucker's armoury included a strange fusion of sorcery and technology: self-operating pistols that could aim and fire while still attached to his gunbelt. International Rescue would probably not have approved. The American setting would prove significant, Anderson largely forsaking English 'locations' over the next decade.

Gerry Anderson's prototype sf puppet show was *Supercar* (1961-62), featuring a futuristic all terrain vehicle equally at home on land, in the air and underwater. Granada Television, which had funded Anderson's previous shows, turned this new idea down, Lew Grade's Incorporated Television Company (ITC) stepping in to save the series and benefit from the puppet boom to come. Operating from a secret base in the middle of the Nevada Desert, inventors Professor Popkiss and Doctor Beaker monitor dashing pilot Mike Mercury, the first of Anderson's many square-jawed hi-tech 'American' heroes, as he puts Supercar to the test. The jump from folksy western to slick science fiction left Anderson unfazed: 'Why I don't know, but I seem to have a capability of making a story out of anything.' The

came to international sales and reruns, Anderson's chosen medium also matched his material. While *Doctor Who* ventured into dark, quite sinister territory on a regular basis, Anderson made his name with resolutely upbeat juvenile science fiction fantasy aimed squarely at the American market, typified by the positive family values of the smash hit series *Thunderbirds* (1965-66).

Aware of the 'natural' resentment and resistance to progress embodied in much British science fiction, Anderson never shared it, despite an appreciation of the risks: 'I support all technological progress... I don't see how it's possible to have progress without that sort of danger.' His own

'the idea of making a science fiction action adventure series starring puppets is crazy in the extreme'

speculations on man's progress were confined to the fairly near future: 'I can only really think a hundred years ahead.' Most Anderson series are set roughly a century on from their date of production, hence the Century 21 tag for his company. Having dined in a revolving restaurant, Anderson took the idea one step further in *Fireball XL5*, featuring a revolving

first of Anderson's 'Supermarionation' series, *Supercar* had more sophisticated puppets than *Four Feather Falls*, with moving eyes and mouths, yet there were problems. Still relatively crude, the eighteen inch human marionettes were difficult to operate in a believable fashion, at least by Anderson's exacting standards. One thing the *Supercar* cast couldn't do with much success was walk, a problem readily solved by keeping them on board their futuristic vehicle. Forty years on, Anderson still feels that 'the idea of making a science fiction action adventure series starring puppets is crazy in the extreme', yet

the combination seemed to work and Anderson found himself more or less typecast. *Supercar* sold worldwide, including to the all-important American market.

By the early 1960s, manned space travel seemed an imminent development rather than a distant possibility. Aiming to catch the mood of the times, Anderson followed *Supercar* with *Fireball XL5* (1963), an endearingly clunky space opera 'starring' ace pilot Steve Zodiac and a less than dazzling DIY robot, called Robert (a very English homage to *Forbidden Planet*'s Robby?). Cruising the Solar System in the

Mike Mercury is prepared for a scene in an episode of Gerry Anderson's 1959 series Supercar.

Steve Zodiac says goodbye to his crew-mate Venus and their pet lazoon Zoonie in an episode of Gerry Anderson's Fireball XL5 (1961).

year 2067, Zodiac's craft was part of the World Space fleet, operating from Space City back on Earth. The show's villains included the unsubtly named Mr and Mrs Spacespy, which made covert operations a little tricky. If the inspiration for the catchy title was disappointingly earthbound: Mobil XL motor oil, the lyrics to the theme song expressed a proper sense of cosmic yearning: 'I wish I was a spaceman, The fastest guy alive, I'd fly you round the universe, In Fireball XL5.' Fireball XL5 was the first Anderson show to be acquired by one of the major American networks, NBC, and pointed the way to the future of puppet television. If nothing else, the series taught Anderson two valuable lessons: don't work in poky black and white, and, in the case of lead Mr Zodiac, make the puppets good looking rather than alarmingly ugly.

Shooting the follow-up Stingray (1964-65) in colour at a cost of around £1 million, Anderson

switched from outer space to the ocean depths, feeling he needed a change of scene to avoid accusations of imaginative poverty. 'Sting' theme aside, Anderson's decision to give his marine-based heroes the misleading acronym of WASP (World Aquanaut Security Patrol) is a little strange, but the show got just about everything else right, including the technical challenges. Originally planning to film the numerous underwater sequences in a large tank, Anderson was offered an alternative method by his producer, Reg Hill. Instead of actually submerging the delicate puppets and models, a serious challenge to chief puppeteer Christine Glanville, they could be filmed 'dry' from behind a large but extremely thin water tank (around ten feet high by six inches deep), with a cyclorama backdrop completing the illusion. The tank would be filled with live fish of varying sizes, enhancing the sense of perspective. Running for a commendably economical 25 minutes per episode, *Stingray* is perhaps the archetypal Gerry Anderson series, the booming opening narration advising viewers to 'Stand By For Action!' Centring on the self-explanatory Marineville, twenty-first century home of ocean security, the storylines were mostly a prototype *Thunderbirds* mix of impending catastrophes, whether natural or man-made, and dastardly plots. One episode, 'Tom Thumb Tempest', offered an extended dream sequence that bordered on the surreal, Stingray materialising in a fish tank and the crew wandering around a giant (ie human) sized dining room (an early example of post-modern irony?). The undeniably photogenic lead puppets Troy Tempest, a dashing submarine commander, and George 'Phones' Sheridan, his lovable co-pilot, bore more than a passing resemblance to Hollywood stars James Garner and James Stewart. Though dedicated to averting major accidents and evil schemes, Tempest was a ladies' man off duty, attracting both Atlanta, daughter of his superior officer Commander Shore, and beautiful, mute sea person Marina (a dubious male fantasy if ever there was one). There is more than a touch of the Cold War ethos to *Stingray*, Marineville regularly threatened by the Aquaphibians, a green-skinned marine race with no apparent interest in peaceful co-habitation. Their leader, the stylishly bearded Titan, could have easily belonged to an underwater branch of the Soviet Bloc, hungering for the destruction of the white-bread Tempest. Years later, Tempest and Titan appeared together on a postage stamp, suggesting some form of post-Cold War reconciliation. While Phones's cigarette smoking didn't offer the best example to the kids,

the paraplegic Commander Shore's position as the head of WASP suggested that, in the future, disabled people would have equal career opportunities, in ocean security at least.

It's notable that the benevolent characters in Stingray all speak with middle American accents, some more convincing than others, a concession to US audiences that Anderson deployed for his next series, *Thunderbirds*. Producing a television series shot on expensive colour film made international sales essential, particularly to American networks. The

The futuristic submarine Stingray (top) took its orders from WASP headquarters at Marineville (above).

the benevolent characters in Stingray all speak with middle American accents

sheer quantity of US-produced shows, many of them exported to England, tended to make the television traffic a one-way stream, as Anderson discovered: 'It was very difficult to sell British product in America.' A common reason given was that American audiences simply couldn't understand British accents. Sizing up the ever so slightly nationalistic

Troy Tempest, the heroic captain of Stingray.

tendencies of his target market, Anderson soon hit on an ingenious solution, selling *Thunderbirds* as an American series that just happened to be financed and made in Britain. Cannily employing American spelling – ie 'nite' instead of 'night', the scripts were

Lady Penelope's personal mode of transport definitely belongs to the wild exaggeration school of sf speculation

even printed on US quarto-size paper rather than UK foolscap. Impressionable young American viewer Joss Whedon was totally fooled: 'I had no idea *Thunderbirds* was British until I got much older. I don't know if they had the same voices or not' (they certainly did). British audiences, weaned on scores of American films and television shows, weren't bothered either way. America also happened to lead the technological field, making International Rescue just a little more plausible if it originated from the other side of the pond (so much for Professor Quatermass's British Rocket Group). The five Tracy boys, Scott, Virgil, Alan, Gordon and John, were named after the first American astronauts to reach space.

International Rescue pilots Virgil and Scott Tracy cast a disparaging eye over their scientific advisor Hiram K Hackenbacker (aka Brains) in a publicity still heralding the first episode of Gerry Anderson's Thunderbirds (1964).

While *Stingray* was just one craft protecting civilisation from dark, damp hostile forces, *Thunderbirds* offered viewers no less than five super-vehicles used by International Rescue. With two airborne, one underwater and two in outer space, this family-run outfit had all bases covered. Given the title's origin, it's ironic that the show has come to represent the ultimate in juvenile escapism. Gerry Anderson's brother Lionel, a Royal Air Force Officer killed during World War II, had trained at Thunderbird Field, an air base in Arizona (British airbases, under regular Luftwaffe attack, were a little too dangerous for novice pilots). Back in England, Lionel Anderson piloted a Mosquito fighter, the fastest plane in the world at the time, and once buzzed the family house. The eleven-year-old Gerry Anderson was transfixed, remaining fascinated by military hardware.

Thunderbirds epitomised Anderson's attitude to producing children's entertainment. Accepting the juvenile appetite for violent mayhem as a regrettable fact of life rather than a readily exploitable market force, he refused to glorify violence: 'I cannot believe what people do to each other.' *Thunderbirds* would provide spectacular entertainment without provoking bloodlust: 'It gave

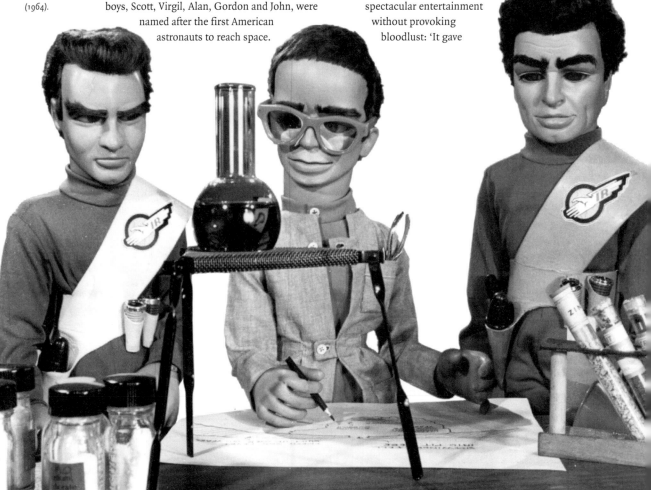

the kiddies jeopardy, death and destruction, but it was all in the aid of saving people, saving life and not destroying it.' The future depicted in *Thunderbirds* is by and large a bright one, kept safe for ordinary men by a clan of benevolent *ubermensch* (better known as the Tracys) equipped with an impressive array of advanced technology. Family patriarch Jeff Tracy, a millionaire ex-astronaut and single parent with five boys to care for, is a shining example of the White Anglo Saxon Protestant Puppet (WASPP), dedicated to the rescue work ethic. Though open to accusations of nepotism, International Rescue lives up to its name, its services available free of charge to all (admirably charitable, but no way to run a business).

Anderson liked to stress the burden of parental responsibility on Jeff Tracy's shoulders, the family head forced each week to weigh up the worth of dangerous missions that would invariably risk his sons' lives. Along with natural disasters and technological mishaps, such as a huge atomic-powered logging machine that veers off course and heads towards a dam, International Rescue also came up against deliberate sabotage, often in the person of The Hood. A bald-headed, heavy-eyebrowed villain of indeterminate Eastern origin, Mr Hood was a more blatant Cold War figure than Titan and just as unsuccessful in his wicked schemes. The storylines in *Thunderbirds* tended towards the formulaic, the plots occasionally stretched to snapping point to fill the expanded 50-minute episode length dictated by Lew Grade, but this is probably missing the point. The enduring appeal of the series is summed up by the Thunderbirds launch sequence, the countdown accompanied by a flash of lightning, rousing, if slightly discordant brass, some pretty hot drumming and the stirring announcement 'Thunderbirds Are Go!' No wonder Thunderbird 2 pilot Virgil Tracy looks so smug.

As self-appointed guardians of the earth, Jeff Tracy and his boys, including surrogate sixth son Brains, are not the most scintillating characters, though the luxury family pad on Tracy Island (there's modesty) suggests they know how to live well. More cynical observers might suggest that hiding out on a secret island base would indicate a desire to avoid the rest of the human race when not on duty. That said, the eye-catching blue uniforms with colour coded sashes would hardly provide anonymity while on the job. The only real *characters* in the show are the honourary British International Rescue members Lady Penelope and her ex-con chauffeur Parker, their contrasting posh/cockney accents done to a turn for American ears (a point superbly parodied by Peter

Paul Metcalfe, aka Captain Scarlet, the indestructible star of Gerry Anderson's Captain Scarlet and the Mysterons (1966).

Cook and Dudley Moore in a sketch for their *Not Only, But Also* television show). Then again, Jeff Tracy never thought to include a customised, fully armed pink Rolls-Royce, number plate FAB 1, in his fleet (probably not the kind of image Gerry Anderson wanted for the all-male, all-macho International Rescue). Having submitted the FAB 1 designs to the actual Rolls-Royce manufacturers, Anderson was surprised to win their approval. Fitted out with four front wheels, Lady Penelope's personal transport definitely belongs to the wild exaggeration school of sf speculation rather than the logical extension division.

TOUGH WOMEN, INDESTRUCTIBLE CAPTAIN

Subsequent Anderson puppet shows, such as *Captain Scarlet and the Mysterons* (1967-68) and the boy-agent fantasy *Joe 90* (1969), were successful without enjoying the runaway popularity of *Thunderbirds*. *Joe 90* was based on the premise of recordable brain waves, enabling its bespectacled nine-year-old hero to absorb the sum total of a person's knowledge via his special glasses, extremely handy out in the field. In the best Anderson strange acronym tradition, the brain wave transferring machine is known as BIG RAT (Brain Impulse Galvanoscope Record and Transfer).

Captain Scarlet pitted its hero against a disembodied (and therefore inexpensive) alien race, the Mysterons of the title, life as we certainly don't know it. Unlike Titan or The Hood, the Mysterons were not

Scarlet possibly miscalculated by rendering the good Captain unkillable in the first episode

Captain Blue and Captain Scarlet, members of the Spectrum organisation defending Earth from Martians in Captain Scarlet and the Mysterons (1966).

intrinsically malevolent, their aggression towards humankind prompted largely by misunderstanding, interpreting a Mars landing by Earth's Spectrum police as the start of an invasion. A member of the Cloudbase defence force, Scarlet's colour coded colleagues included Colonel White, Captain Blue and Lieutenant Green (Captain Black had been co-opted by the Mysterons, to no-one's great surprise). While

Thunderbirds offered a strong dose of social responsibility, *Captain Scarlet* is rated by some as the most violently destructive children's show ever. Specialising in reanimating dead matter, the Mysterons tended to kill hapless passers by at the start of an episode, subsequently resurrecting or 'retrometabolising' them to serve as involuntary undercover agents. Anderson did not envisage *Captain Scarlet* as a particularly dark show: 'It never occurred to me'. The series also gave juvenile audiences their first glimpse of an exploding head on children's television (a good decade before David Cronenberg's *Scanners*).

Captain Scarlet offered a more cosmopolitan flavour than previous Century 21 shows, Anderson having been asked to feature French and Italian characters for the international market. Lieutenant Green, also known as Seymour Griffiths, was Trinidadian. Serving as Colonel White's right-hand man, Green never got a promotion, despite Captain Black's forced defection reducing the number of operative Cloudbase Captains from a magnificent celestial seven to a dubious six. Anderson did give Lieutenant Green's role to a black actor, Cy Grant. Voiced by English actor Francis Matthews, Captain Scarlet himself spoke in a Cary Grant-style voice, a distinctive mid-Atlantic accent that suited American tastes (English-born, Grant's Hollywood success made him an honourary American). Scottish and Irish accents were also popular in the US, provided they remained intelligible. Captain Magenta supplied the latter, though his past interests in organised crime did little to dispel national stereotypes.

A solid hit in most departments, *Scarlet* possibly miscalculated by rendering the good Captain unkillable in the first episode, despatched and reprogrammed by the Mysterons only to recover his original human identity. As a resentful Cloudbase colleague points out: 'It's easy to be brave when you're indestructible.' Then again, the show also offers the Angels, an equally courageous quintet of glamorous female fighter pilots answering to the names of Melody, Harmony, Rhapsody, Symphony and Destiny. Viewed today, this may appear nothing more than a conventionally sexist male fantasy, yet at the time Anderson felt he was making a positive blow for equality: 'In the sixties it was very unusual for women to go out to work. It was even more unusual for them to have key jobs.' And who better to spearhead women's liberation than 'glamorous, good-looking, highly intelligent girls'.

One notable feature of *Captain Scarlet* is the puppets' more or less human proportions. While the oversized heads of previous Anderson creations possessed a good measure of charm with their caricatured features (think Parker), the main reason for this design was purely functional. In order to house the automatic mouth movement mechanisms, the heads had to be big. By the time of *Scarlet*, the mechanism had been reduced in size and could be housed in the puppet chests. While Anderson always wanted more 'realistic' puppets, the new models tended to lack the idiosyncratic character of their predecessors, resembling nothing more than de luxe Action Men (still with visible strings).

For those not enamoured of the intricate modelwork and frequent mini-explosions, *Thunderbirds'* biggest success was regular guest star Lady Penelope Creighton-Ward, one of the first notable female characters in British science fiction. Supposedly modelled on Anderson's then wife and business partner Sylvia Anderson, who also provided the character's distinctive tones, Lady Penelope seemed very much her own person (the kind of person, in fact, who would fit her Rolls-Royce with a bullet-proof space-age glass dome for all-round visibility). While *Stingray's* females tended towards the submissive, she was independent, intelligent, resourceful and courageous, not to mention well-dressed – the Penelope puppet had its own costume designer – and exquisitely spoken. Short of ready cash, Lady Penelope had been forced to open her country mansion to coach party tours, subjecting the family heirlooms to relentless public scrutiny. Whatever her opinion of the admission-paying masses, Lady Penelope's long-standing professional relationship and personal friendship with Cockney chauffeur Parker suggested that the British class divide was not insurmountable, especially when danger beckoned.

As well as Lady Penelope, *Thunderbirds* also featured two other intelligent and independent-minded female characters: Tin-Tin, Brains's glamorous assistant, and Grandma, Jeff Tracy's shrewd and on occasions brave and resourceful mother. For whatever reason, ITV was well ahead of the rival BBC in this respect, most notably with *The Avengers*. For all its undeniable merits, *Doctor Who* was not particularly strong on female characters. Granddaughter Susan, supposedly an alien being with intelligence vastly superior to man's, quickly became established as a stereotyped screaming teen, one reason actress Carole Ann Ford departed after ten stories. Her replacement, Vicki (Maureen O'Brien), inherited the childlike sense of wonder of the original character without a hint of the brains. Barbara Wright, a professional history teacher with

Patrick Macnee and Honor Blackman, the stars of The Avengers, *at a fashion show held in October 1963.*

more than her share of common sense, fared a little better, but when the Doctor needed some decisive action, he invariably turned to Ian Chesterton, her more scientifically-minded – and male – colleague. It took 14 years and the introduction of the leather-clad, knife-wielding 'savage' Leela (Louise Jameson) before the series finally got a leading lady who could kick alien butt.

Over on the other channel, a good two years before Lady Penelope first got the Rolls-Royce out of the garage, things were very different. Prior to his BBC appointment, ABC TV executive Sydney Newman had launched *The Avengers*, starring Ian Hendry and Patrick Macnee as a pair of slightly mismatched crimefighters. First broadcast in January 1961, the show chronicled the exploits of civilian doctor David Keel, who seeks to avenge the murder of his girlfriend, and a mildly shady secret service man named John Steed. Though largely devoid of the science fiction fantasy elements that would become an *Avengers* trademark, the series proved a hit. When

Georgie Price-Jones (Liz Fraser), John Steed (Patrick Macnee) and Emma Peel (Diana Rigg) in The Girl From Auntie *(1966), an episode from the fourth series of* The Avengers.

Hendry quit after the first season to pursue a film career, the producers reasoned that the show might benefit from a female replacement, adding a little glamour and sexual tension to the formula. On the other hand, they still had a number of unused scripts written for two male leads, packed with fights, espionage, intrigue and other traditionally macho activities. Though unsure whether or not a woman could bring off a 'tough' role, the producers took a chance and cast Honor Blackman, the rest being, as they say, history.

On 22 December 1962, the leather-clad, karate-chopping Mrs Catherine Gale made her *Avengers* debut in *Death Dispatch*, episode four of season two (replacing John Rollason, who had co-starred with Macnee in the first three episodes of the new series).

More by accident than design, the series marked the arrival of strong female characters in UK science fiction, Blackman later commenting: 'There had never been a woman like that on television before – in fact, there had never been a feminist creature before Cathy Gale' (though the character was partly based on *Life* magazine photographer Margaret Bourke White and anthropologist Margaret Mead). In contrast to *The Avengers*' later flights of fantasy, Cathy Gale's background was rooted in grim real-life, her late husband a victim of the Mau Mau uprising in Kenya, hence her self-sufficiency, tough outlook and expertise with firearms (Patrick Macnee took credit for the black leather outfits). An accomplished scholar with a doctorate in anthropology, Gale initially joined forces with Steed as a gifted amateur, motivated by an idealistic desire to combat evil. In many ways more likeable than her often unscrupulous, even amoral partner, Gale did not remain the amateur junior sidekick for long. The character outline circulated at the start of season three described her as a full-fledged professional undercover agent, partly in response to accusations of the show becoming too lightweight. Still far less ruthless than hardened government operative Steed, Gale's humanitarian outlook made her uncomfortable about Steed's methods on occasion – if not his increasingly rakish wardrobe.

With season four (1965-66), The Avengers gradually took on the form for which it is best remembered. While the previous three series had been recorded on black and white videotape, with occasional filmed inserts (much like Doctor Who), the producers now switched to black and white film, enabling a slicker, faster paced style with greater visual flair (not to mention the chance for retakes). New co-producer Brian Clemens, who would guide The Avengers until the end of its run, laid down a few ground rules to maintain the desired sense of fantasy: upperclass-only characters, no extras for the location scenes, no vulgar bloodshed and no dead women (somewhat ironic given David Keel's initial motivation for joining forces with Steed). This new look was complemented by a new co-star, classically trained actress Diana Rigg, formerly of the Royal Shakespeare Company, cast as the formidable Mrs Emma Peel. Keen to avoid a straightforward romantic relationship between the leads, the producers made Cathy Gale's replacement another widow, her explorer husband having perished during a particularly hazardous trip (or so she believed). Sharing Cathy Gale's passion for leather fighting suits and fast cars (a Lotus Elan), Emma Peel was similarly spirited, glamorous, intelligent, sharp-tongued, quick-witted and, when necessary, two-fisted. Like Blackman before her, Diana Rigg felt she was breaking new ground: 'Suddenly it was a woman who had the capacity for doing everything that a man can do, and that's what made the character so extraordinary.'

The Steed-Peel relationship contained a stronger element of humour than the Steed-Gale combo, the more jokey approach in keeping with the show's overall feel of light fantasy. Roy Ward Baker, who directed the first Mrs Peel episode The Town of No Return, felt the co-stars clicked straight away: 'the two of them got it together within 20 minutes ... they both understood.' Always addressed by her partner with a respectful 'Mrs Peel' rather than a familiar

'Emma', Rigg's character could occasionally dominate the proceedings without marginalizing the ever self-confident Steed, the latter happy to pull Mrs Peel along in a rickshaw at the end of one episode. Baker saw the Steed-Peel relationship as one of comfortable equals: 'Neither of them tried to demean the other ... they obviously esteemed each other.' Their spirited, intriguingly ambiguous relationship became the show's main selling point, in Baker's opinion: 'that was the story, that was really what it was about'. While Macnee assumed that Steed and Mrs Peel were occasional lovers, contraceptive pills now being readily available, others working on the show were not so sure, Roy Ward Baker feeling that 'You never quite knew what went on, if anything.' Joss Whedon, who cites Emma Peel as 'definitely a precursor' to vampire slayer Buffy Summers, deftly sums up the character's appeal: 'She was completely in charge, completely cool. She had a leather catsuit. She could take care of herself.'

Having joined up with few preliminaries, Mrs Peel's secret agent duties involved encounters with such eccentric, terribly British outfits as the Ransack Club, the Winslip Hospital for Retired and Ailing Railwaymen, Grannie Gregson's wine factory and the Arkwright Knitting Circle, invariably fronts for nefarious covert operations. A number of season four stories featured strong science fiction elements, notably The Master Minds (radio-wave induced brainwashing), Death at Bargain Prices (a nuclear bomb disguised as a department store), A Surfeit of H2O (a potentially lethal rain-making machine), The Man-Eater of Surrey Green (a carnivorous extraterrestrial plant with hypnotic powers) and The Cybernauts (killer

Emma Peel was similarly spirited, glamorous, intelligent, sharp-tongued, quick-witted and, when necessary, two-fisted

robots employed by an unscrupulous electronics mogul). First appearing on 16 October 1965, the Cybernauts beat Doctor Who's Cybermen to the screen by almost exactly a year, the latter debuting in The Tenth Planet, William Hartnell's last story, on 8 October 1966. On the other hand, the Cybernauts were mindless, remote control automata, whereas the Cybermen are intelligent, if emotionless bio-mechanical organisms (both demonstrated an impressive, and lethal, karate chop).

Aiming for a properly cinematic feel, the new-look Avengers employed a number of experienced

Are aliens killing members of the British Venusian Society? Mrs Peel (Diana Rigg) finds her investigation interrupted in From Venus With Love (1967), an episode from the fifth series of The Avengers.

film directors, including Ealing veteran Charles Crichton (The Lavender Hill Mob), Sidney Hayers (Circus of Horrors; Night of the Eagle), James Hill (A Study in Terror; Born Free) and Roy Ward Baker. An experienced hand with filmed television series, working on The Human Jungle and The Saint, Baker knew that the requirements of the medium differed considerably from the bigger canvas of the cinema screen. While inexpensive close-ups were naturally encouraged, 'one of the most effective instruments of television', more elaborate long shots tended to be frowned upon as both time consuming to set up and usually ineffective on the small screen. Technique aside, Baker had a clear sense of the show's formula: 'The idea was to create a myth, to offer a story which takes place in limbo.' No recognizable everyday characters were used, especially uniformed policeman – the more reality-bound upholders of law and order – and postmen, all letters and parcels vital to the plot delivered by unseen hands.

But Steed and Mrs Peel, while figures of fantasy, were not superbeings able to defy the laws of nature. 'Everything they did was done realistically, but always against these slightly fantasized [backdrops]... It was surrealism, I suppose, super-realism if you like.' Baker's episodes of *The Avengers* include *Too Many Christmas Trees*, where Steed has recurring Christmas-themed nightmares involving a very sinister laughing Santa Claus, and the rather more lighthearted *The Girl from Auntie*. A less than subtle take-off on *The Man from U.N.C.L.E.*, the episode featured Steed tangling with the murderous Arkwright Knitting Circle after Mrs Peel is kidnapped. Deprived of his usual partner in surreal espionage, Steed reluctantly teams up with Georgie Price-Jones (Liz Fraser), who later drives off in his Bentley. Though the quality of the *Avengers* scripts varied – Patrick Macnee once claimed that he and Diana Rigg were obliged to rewrite much of their dialogue – Baker felt the series rarely relied on obvious, well-telegraphed gags for effect: 'It was a

show in which you were permitted, indeed encouraged to be witty, and in those days that was dangerous stuff.' Refusing to pitch *The Avengers* at the lowest common denominator, executive producer Julian Wintle had no fears about going over the audience's head, allowing a throwaway reference to

'it was surrealism, I suppose, super-realism if you like'

pilot Amy Johnson during a flying scene.

One drawback to the outlandish nature of most *Avengers* episodes was the amount of detailed plot exposition involved, which could have resulted in a stagy, not to say static quality, as Baker explains: 'We were often confronted with long dialogue scenes and so the real problem was how to dress them up.' One solution involved Steed and Mrs Peel playing a game of spillikins, or pick-a-sticks, while calmly discussing the current world-threatening situation. The plot soon became secondary to the game, both for the viewer and the production team, though Baker insists 'we didn't throw the story out completely'. The switch to film also enabled the fight scenes to be

Mrs Peel (Diana Rigg) kicks off The Forget-Me-Knot *(1969), her final episode of* The Avengers.

staged with more finesse, despite a sometimes blatant use of stunt doubles in the long shots. Baker felt Diana Rigg was particularly adept at action sequences, 'very well co-ordinated', Mrs Peel's no-nonsense demolition of the numerous villains winning serious audience respect. Doubled by Cyd Child for the more demanding – and risky – stunts, Rigg's fighting woman had an edge and intensity that even Cathy Gale lacked, though directors such as Baker never went for full-on realism: 'it was not meant to be taken dead seriously, but it was fun... quite bold in its day'.

Committed elsewhere during production on the second Diana Rigg series, Baker returned for The Avengers' final season, with Macnee now partnered by Linda Thorson, cast as the much younger graduate agent Tara King. Directing the Cold War-themed episode Split!, Baker felt the series had lost its way a little: 'It got a bit silly towards the end ... too larky for words'. His overall verdict on the show remains favourable: 'It was very hard work but boy it was enjoyable.'

Season five of The Avengers (1966/67), marked the series's progression to colour film, a move made possible by its sale to American network television. One downside to the deal was the imposition of network censorship. Having studied the American Television Code, producer Brian Clemens issued a list of tongue-in-cheek guidelines, including the memorable 'We must be careful to avoid showing Emma striking or kneeing a man in his peculiarly masculine areas.' Presumably, Steed was perfectly free to kick his male opponents in the groin (though far too much of a gentleman to actually do so). There is a case for arguing that, for all the success of its 'liberated' female leads and Patrick Macnee's

this episode was initially banned in the United States, though very popular at network executive parties

insistence on his co-stars' 'hermaphrodite' quality, The Avengers remained an outrageously sexist show in many respects, Diana Rigg's famously low salary aside. Emma Peel's very name was derived from the groan-making 'M(an) Appeal', a clear indication of the producers' priorities that the cool, self-mocking style never quite eradicated. In the famous 1965 episode A Touch of Brimstone, Emma is crowned 'Queen of Sin' by the revived Hellfire Club and outfitted in long boots, basque and spiked collar, not

to mention a tastefully draped boa constrictor. (It comes as no great surprise that this episode was initially banned in the United States, though very popular at network executive parties.) In Honey for the Prince, Mrs Peel dons a bikini to perform a demure 'Dance of the Seven Veils', a gem inserted into her naval to appease US television censors. It says a lot for Diana Rigg that Emma Peel emerged from these displays with her credibility enhanced rather than diminished. Patrick Macnee has claimed that Diana Rigg eventually quit the show owing to the level of male chauvinism, declaring himself as guilty as anyone else. Roy Ward Baker's highly appreciative evaluation of Rigg's 'talent' could certainly be in terpreted as decidedly non-PC: 'an absolutely gorgeous looking woman, with a figure to match. And she could act.' Required to go undercover as a schoolteacher in The Town of No Return, Mrs Peel turned up in class (out of term-time) carrying a pair of spectacles and wearing a very mini-skirt, almost certainly a television first. Director Baker and his crew were suitably impressed: 'gosh, she looked wonderful... she was a knockout', yet their enthusiastic determination to do the ensemble justice drew executive wrath. A long shot of Rigg in her short skirt was deemed too provocative, obliging Baker to retake it in more demure medium shot. Arguably, Mrs Peel could look just as provocative sitting on a sofa, playing a tuba.

By the time The Avengers burst into colour, the show had long since perfected its depiction of the British secret agent as a cultured, witty upper class adventurer in a fantasy universe. Aside from the relative lack of gunplay (Macnee refused to have Steed carry firearms), the formula veered at times into James Bond territory, making leads Honor Blackman and Diana Rigg ideal choices for the massively popular film versions. This cunning, if obvious casting crossover did not go down too well first time round, Blackman's decision to quit the show for a co-starring role in Goldfinger (1964) causing considerable resentment, though perhaps not as much as did her duet with Patrick Macnee on the novelty single 'Kinky Boots'. Cast as Pussy Galore, ace pilot and henchperson to master criminal Auric Goldfinger (Gert Frobe), Blackman fitted comfortably into the Bond franchise, a more than worthy screen partner for Sean Connery (she deserved some kind of award for being able to say her character's name with a straight face). Resembling a cooler, amoral version of Cathy Gale, Ms Galore is initially unimpressed by Bond's standard approaches: 'You can switch off the charm.

I'm immune'. When he becomes physical, she deftly employs a little judo, throwing him into a handy pile of hay. Bond gets his way in the end, but at least Pussy's no pushover, her allegiances unclear until the big showdown at Fort Knox (Ian Fleming's book presents the character as a diehard lesbian, converted to the joys of heterosexuality by Bond: 'I never met a real man before').

Bowing to the inevitable, the *Avengers* production team incorporated a reference to both Mrs Gale and Fort Knox in one of the Emma Peel episodes. Contrary to popular belief, Pussy Galore was not the first non-submissive Bond 'girl', *Dr No*'s Honey Rider (Ursula Andress) more than capable than looking after herself. But Honor Blackman's established *Avengers* image lent her character a new element of cool. In *On Her Majesty's Secret Service* (1969), Diana Rigg plays the spirited but unhappy Countess Teresa Draco, Tracy to her friends, daughter of a cultured Italian criminal (Mafioso by implication, Corsican in the Ian Fleming novel). First seen attempting to drown herself, Tracy finds a chance of happiness with disillusioned masterspy James Bond (George Lazenby), whose pursuit of elusive master villain Blofeld seems destined for failure. Probably the only

Bond film to deal with something approaching human emotions, OHMSS is surprisingly poignant between the action set-pieces. Lazenby's inexperience as an actor is in many ways an asset, Bond appearing insecure, uncertain and vulnerable, even tendering his resignation from the British Secret Service when M appears to lose faith in him. While Tracy's suicidal despair would be anathema to Emma Peel, there are traces of the latter throughout the film, the Countess coming through when Bond needs her help. Extremely adept behind the wheel of her sports car, winning a stock car race more or less by accident, she turns to skiing like a champion and wields a pretty mean broken bottle when the occasion warrants. True love blossoms, Bond prepared to walk away from the secret agent business in the name of long-term emotional commitment.

WE HAVE AGENTS EVERYWHERE!

Despite the best efforts of Honor Blackman and Diana Rigg, the 007 series rapidly reverted to largely decorative female leads who never stood a chance of transcending such tasteful character names as 'Mary Goodnight' and 'Holly Goodhead'. The last scene of

Honey Rider (Ursula Andress) succumbs to radiation-suited assailants on Crab Key. The 1962 film adaptation of Dr. No introduced a number of science fiction elements not present in Ian Fleming's source novel.

On Her Majesty's Secret Service has the just-married happy couple forcibly separated by gunfire, Tracy taking a bullet in the head while Bond stands by, unarmed and impotent. Having surrendered his near superhuman powers for the love of a good woman, Bond is as helpless as the next man. 007 wouldn't make the same mistake again.

As embodied by Sean Connery, James Bond is a man devoid of self-doubt, frailty or troublesome emotions, shooting and screwing his way across glamorous international locations in pursuit of largely foreign cultured villains with seriously bad intentions. If nothing else, the character demonstrates the near universal appeal of the charismatic *ubermensch*, a licensed killing machine with irresistible sexual magnetism and a ready quip.

reality itself may be disintegrating but that's no excuse not to have a good time

Having pinned one of *Thunderball*'s more unpleasant badmen to a tree with his trusty speargun, Bond emphasises the lighter side of high-speed impalement: 'I think he got the point'. Not the most progressive brand of male fantasy, perhaps, but deep-rooted enough to sustain the series over four decades. A number of the Bond films flirt with science-fiction concepts, if only as a pretext for the lavish high-tech sets and hardware. Ken Adam, the premiere Bond designer, came up with the fanciful Fort Knox in *Goldfinger*, Blofeld's volcano hide-out in *You Only Live Twice* (1967), Stromberg's undersea kingdom in *The Spy Who Loved Me* (1977) and Drax's private space station in *Moonraker*. Bond's own

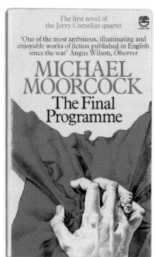

Sf becomes Literature. The Final Programme: the first part of the Jerry Cornelius tetralogy, and the only part (to date) to be filmed.

high-tech hardware backup is often relatively modest: a suitcase fitted with anti-theft gas pellets, a miniature breathing device, a magnetic watch, a combination ski-pole/gun. A notable exception is the customised Aston Martin DB5, first seen in *Goldfinger*, which comes equipped with machine guns, bullet proof windscreen, armour-plating, rotating number plates, a tyre-chewing wheel blade and the famous ejector seat. Reappearing in *Thunderball*, the Aston Martin proved disappointingly mono-functional, merely spraying a few minor henchmen with water jets.

Roger Moore's Bond got in on the act with his Lotus Esprit, which doubled as a mini-submarine, but it just didn't have the Aston's elegance. The success of *Star Wars* prompted producer Albert Broccoli to take the Bond formula deep into sf fantasy territory in *Moonraker*, complete with space shuttles, laser guns and even an outer space shoot-out. Though not the disaster of reputation, the end result suggested that Bond was better off back on terra firma.

Despite leaving a trail of demolished secret bases, dead supervillains, and sexually satisfied ladies in his wake (some of them still alive), Bond remains an establishment figure, too much of a natural born swinger in his own right to be impressed by sixties counterculture. (According to *Goldfinger*, The Beatles should only be listened to with earmuffs.) Michael Moorcock's Jerry Cornelius is the Superspy reimagined for the psychedelic age, described by his back jacket blurb as 'The English Assassin: physicist, rock star, messiah to the Age of Science.' Created by writer-editor Moorcock for his influential magazine *New Worlds*, which took off in the sixties under Moorcock's guidance after a muted start two decades earlier, Cornelius first appeared in a 1965 issue, making his book debut in *The Final Programme* (1969). Both morally and sexually ambiguous, the character typifies the high-living, thrill-seeking decadent whose battles with the forces of darkness are largely a by-product of his quest for dangerous kicks. Reality itself may be disintegrating but that's no excuse not to have a good time. A pill popping, whisky slugging hedonist, Cornelius hangs out at such hip nightspots as The Friendly Bum, before merging with shady computer programmer Miss Brunner into 'the world's first all-purpose human being', a self regenerating hermaphrodite equipped with the sum total of all human knowledge.

Prior to his wondrous transmutation, Cornelius is also something of a philosopher, given to such questionable pronouncements as 'Childhood is the happiest time of life except when you're a child'. He also lets rip with some casual existential musings: 'Jerry no longer had any idea whether the world he inhabited was 'real' or 'false'; he had long since given up worrying about it.' Transcending the standard conventions of science fiction, along with most other genres, Moorcock's needlegun-toting acid dandy scored a strong cult success. The fourth Cornelius novel, *The Condition of Muzak* (1977), won the Guardian Fiction Prize.

Eight years after his literary debut, Jerry Cornelius made the jump to the big screen in a film version of *The Final Programme* (1973, aka *The Last Days of Man on*

Earth), written and directed by the gifted, if erratic, Robert Fuest. Then riding high as the director of the Vincent Price horror hit *The Abominable Dr Phibes* (1971), a blend of art deco-style sets and gimmicky murders, Fuest had a solid background in modishly bizarre fantasy. Formerly a noted television production designer, he'd joined *The Avengers* in this capacity for the second episode of season one, his impressive work eventually securing a promotion to the director's chair for season six (1967-69). As Emma Peel made way for the younger Tara King, the series took on a more surreal, near psychedelic feel well suited to Fuest's strong, if self-conscious visual sense. His episodes as director include *Game*, *The Rotters*, *They Keep Killing Steed* and the exceptional *My Wildest Dream*, a tale of deadly psychological manipulation with a surprisingly vicious edge (the violence, including a head smashed through glass, prompted some ITV regions to schedule the episode in a late night slot). Advertised with the line 'The

future is cancelled!', *The Final Programme* starred the moody, yet uninvolving Jon Finch as Cornelius, a piece of casting that doubtless pleased the production's backers but did little for the film. (Finch had recently played the leads in Roman Polanski's *Macbeth* and Alfred Hitchcock's *Frenzy*). Having taken on the triple responsibilities of script, direction and set design, Fuest seemed to stumble, unable to invest his movie with a coherent structure or style. Set against a backdrop of impending armageddon, the outlandish costumes, camp frivolity and trendy espionage antics add up to not very much. The Cornelius-Brunner lifeform of the novel is transformed into a shuffling apeman wearing nail varnish, a weak payoff to say the least. Moorcock disliked the end result intensely.

CAR TROUBLE

While Fuest's *Final Programme* was baffling its small audience on the cinema circuit, James Graham

Jon Finch starred as the genetically superior Jerry Cornelius in the 1974 adaptation of Michael Moorcock's The Last Programme. In the United States the film was released as The Last Days Of Man On Earth.

Ballard took the idea of living for surreally dangerous kicks to a dubious extreme in his novel *Crash* (1973), an extended homage to the theme of fatal car wrecks as the ultimate sexual high. Ballard has gone on record as describing science fiction as the authentic literature of the twentieth century, 'the only fiction to respond to the transforming nature of science and technology'. His own response to technology, in this particular instance, seems to involve fractured engine blocks, shattered glass, twisted steel, spattered blood and a good helping of sperm. Car-related carnage occupies a special place in Ballard's work. His earlier novel *The Atrocity Exhibition* (1970), focuses on the Zapruder footage of the Kennedy assassination in the Dallas motorcade, turning the brief 8mm film into a metaphor for the age of medium and message.

The now-notorious *Crash* opens with the death of Vaughan, the self-styled 'nightmare angel of the highways', killed in an attempt to stage his dream car crash into Elizabeth Taylor's chauffeured limousine on the London Airport flyover. A one-time computer specialist turned media pundit, Dr Robert Vaughan – is this a homage to the *Man from U.N.C.L.E.* star ? – is also obsessed with the death of John Fitzgerald Kennedy, not to mention such youthful movie star crash victims as James Dean. His car, a ten year old Lincoln Continental, is the same make as the limousine in which Kennedy died, the Presidential brains spattering both the upholstery and the First Lady (tasteless, yes, but pretty much at the heart of *Crash*'s preoccupations). Vaughan makes highly

both Bond and Ballard seemed inclined towards the fetishistic worship of the car

detailed photographic and cine-film records of car crashes, including his own, and their victims, 'gazing at their burnt faces with a terrifying concern'. The scars incurred in auto-wrecks become the object of erotic frenzy.

On one level, this combination of gleaming technology, violent bodily rupture and sexual ecstasy is not so far from the James Bond formula. In *Live and Let Die* alone, Bond deflowers psychic virgin Solitaire, sends a rival speedboat driver crashing into a police car, and blows Harlem kingpin Mr Big to pieces ('He always did have an inflated opinion of himself'). The aforementioned Aston Martin is a four-wheeled killing machine with style to die for. Ballard simply took these elements, and concentrated them into one mind-blowing burst of auto-sado-masochism. It's

doubtful, however, that Bond would have much sympathy for what the book's narrator, James, describes as 'the perverse logic of blood-soaked instrument panels, seat-belts smeared with excrement, sun-visors lined with brain tissue' (A director of television commercials, James certainly knows how to sell his concepts). Never one for back-seat fumblings, Bond likes his car chases non-fatal, his violence directed towards an external target, and his love life straight as a die. The bisexual antics of *Crash* would merit more than a raised eyebrow; consider the gay hitmen of *Diamonds Are Forever*, prissy, hand-holding dirty fighters fit only for a climactic roasting.

Both Bond and Ballard seemed inclined towards the fetishistic worship of the car as a potent capitalist/patriotic/masculine symbol, whether Aston Martin, Mini Cooper or Vaughan's Lincoln Continental. The Empire might have crumbled, but Connery's Bond always drove luxury British: sleek, fast, elegant and no hint of engine trouble. *Crash* goes a step further, depicting its protagonists' bouts of weird car sex as an assertion of their individuality. (Once Vaughan is dead, his Lincoln quickly falls into ruin, as if kept alive only by his passion.) There is no larger object to this activity, no political or ideological stance, no protest against the sheer banality of their comfortable, futile lives. James pays final homage to his mentor in the only way possible: 'With the semen in my hands I marked the crushed controls and instrument dials, defining for the last time the contours of Vaughan's presence on the seats.'

Compared to the book, David Cronenberg's tediously controversial film version of *Crash* (1997) is fairly muted, if predictably weird, despite combining the director's recurring interest in warped sexuality with his personal passion for fast cars. Ballard's graphic couplings would qualify as hard-core pornography if faithfully restaged on film, with or without the car-crash trimmings. Here, respected name actors such as Holly Hunter, James Spader and Rosanna Arquette indulge in explicit-but-simulated emotion-free sexual shenanigans that failed to stir the notoriously sensitive British film censor James Ferman in any way. Decked out with leg callipers, fishnet tights and a selection of extremely realistic scars, disabled crash victim and auto-swinger Arquette embodies the film's main concerns, appearing sympathetic, disturbing, seductive and just a little silly. Despite some committed performances and a moody, low key, determinedly unsalacious treatment of some extremely provocative ideas, *Crash* ultimately lacks any real sense of purpose (or direction). Not that this prevented a tiresome British tabloid backlash. Condemned by then Health Minister Virginia Bottomley as pornography and banned from cinemas by Westminster Council, *Crash*'s brief status as media cause célèbre generated useful publicity but little excitement — either at the box office or on the motorways. Whatever the fears of the nation's moral guardians, the anticipated wave of auto-erotic auto-suicides never materialised.

At the time of 2001's release in 1968, the future as envisaged by H G Wells and his contemporaries seemed in many ways to have arrived. The decade of birth control, heart transplants, high-speed air travel, space exploration and excited speculation over the possibilities of extraterrestrial life suggested that much of science fiction was finally becoming science fact. Moreover, science fiction was also becoming an acceptable part of the literary scene, with 'serious' mainstream publishers such as Faber and Penguin issuing anthologies of sf short stories culled from thirty years' worth of pulp magazine fiction – with the odd highbrow author such as John Steinbeck thrown in for good measure. Introducing the landmark *Penguin Science Fiction* anthology (1960), editor Brian Aldiss captured the new outlook perfectly. 'A wonderland, that's sf, a realm of the curious, through which a twentieth-century reader wanders like a Terylene-clad Alice. Myself, I like this facet of sf greatly, preferring it to the "Popular Science" side. I'd as lief hear how crazy the world is as how fast it progresses technologically.' No longer predominantly a vehicle for prophecy, British sf concentrated instead on satire, allegory, education and, above all, pure escapist entertainment, preferably in glorious Technicolor. Much of this escapist fantasy followed the trail defined by Tolkein's *Lord of the Rings* and redefined in Michael Moorcock's quirky Hawkmoon fantasies (*The Jewel in the Skull* and so on). The world of 'Swords and Sorcery' sf had arrived, a sub-genre which many would argue has no claim to be considered as 'proper' sf at all.

Both *The Avengers* and the James Bond film series were located in a parallel, parody 1960s universe, futuristic in their hardware rather than their outlook. Gerry Anderson's puppet-based Supermarionation series, supposedly set a hundred years into the future, remained firmly rooted in their decade of origin, the supporting characters in *Thunderbirds* denied access to the technological marvels dreamed up by International Rescue's Brains. Even *Doctor Who*, theoretically free to roam the entire space-time continuum, invariably returned to the sixties era, five

of the Time Lord's human travelling companions hailing from that swinging decade. (The other six balanced each other out: three from the Earth's future, three from its past.) The notion that the future might, after all, be really just the same as the present seems to have prompted a feeling of complacency in some quarters. The sense of wonder evoked by 2001 was notably absent elsewhere, *The Avengers*, James Bond and Moorcock's psychedelic superagent Jerry Cornelius all reacting to state-of-the-art sf gadgetry with little more than mild curiosity.

Like the James Bond franchise from which it arguably draws, *Crash* operates on the borderlines of 'straight' science fiction, much as many of the stories in *New Worlds* magazine seemed only tangentially related to the genre. With the partial exception of *Doctor Who*, the emphasis in most 1960s British science fiction was on re-working established sf themes – with varying degrees of imagination – rather than any radical re-invention of the genre. While Gerry Anderson and Bond producers Albert Broccoli and Harry Saltzman didn't lack for ambition, much of it was directed towards fine-tuning their fantasy product for the international – in other words American – market. Why spend valuable time and energy on elaborate story construction when sf related plots could be drawn from the headlines? *You Only Live Twice* deploys the then-ongoing US-USSR space race as its backdrop, opening with a recreation of the exciting new out-of-the-craft space walk – which is promptly sabotaged by the machinations of SPECTRE. The image of the stranded astronaut disappearing at speed into the void of space reappeared a year later in 2001. *On Her Majesty's Secret Service* has an intriguing storyline featuring global blackmail through germ terrorism, yet the film is more often remembered for such set pieces as Blofeld's henchman falling into the path of the snowplough, prompting the Bond quip 'he had lots of guts'. *Thunderbirds*, the most successful of Gerry Anderson's shows, dispensed with the intriguing alien landscapes and lifeforms of other Century 21 series, concentrating almost entirely on the audience-pleasing high-tech vehicles of International Rescue.

Doctor Who, which drew its budget from the BBC licence fee rather than co-production finance, was largely left to carry the banner for innovative British television sf until 1967, when ITC boss Lew Grade unveiled an off-beat new fantasy series starring small-screen superstar Patrick McGoohan: *The Prisoner*. The rules of television sf were about to be re-written all over again.

CHAPTER 3
DARK SIDE OF THE MOONBASE

When *The Avengers* moved into its sixth and final season (Patrick Macnee partnered by the initially derided Linda Thorson) several episodes pulled off the unusual trick of being both surreal and hard-edged. The near-psychedelic trappings complemented storylines that dwelled on cold-blooded scheming and general human nastiness. In *Pandora*, for example, Tara King is kidnapped, drugged and imprisoned, her captors attempting to brainwash her into thinking she's living fifty years in the past. While the villains' motive is straightforward greed, the plot featuring a priceless lost family heirloom, early scenes of the disoriented, semi-comatose Tara attempting to flee are quite disturbing. Posing as concerned friends, her captors gently reassure her that she is unwell and in need of rest as they inject her with another dose of sedative. For all Tara's brains, initiative and fighting skill, she's at her captors' mercy until Steed turns up and cracks heads. We know it's going to happen but the suspense doesn't let up.

Similar, but more complex ideas are at work in *The Prisoner*, surely one of the best shows ever filmed in North Wales. Even those unimpressed by this unprecedented blend of allegory, science fiction, spy fantasy and political satire would have to admit that it gave Village life a whole new meaning. Devised by American-born actor Patrick McGoohan (star of the successful, if straightforward espionage series *Danger Man*), *The Prisoner* attempted to bridge the gap between the largely family-oriented science fiction prevalent on television and the darker, more esoteric fare aimed at adult audiences. First screened in 1967, *The Prisoner* explored the consequences to resigning from the secret service without prior consultation. Having smashed his boss's tea cup and saucer in a fit of self-righteous desk banging, the unnamed former agent heads for home and freedom, unaware that he is already doomed.

Regarded by many as the most brilliant of all 1960s cult series, the show was both startlingly original and wilfully obscure, gripping and perplexing in more or less equal measure. Audiences tuning in for standard thriller material were unprepared for the large doses of paranoid surrealism, and *The Prisoner* was initially dismissed as a self-indulgent ratings flop, particularly by production company ITC and its American partners. Initially shown in a peak-time Sunday evening slot (7.25 p.m.), the series suffered serious viewer withdrawal and was unceremoniously cancelled after 17 episodes, finishing its run in the 11.15 p.m. graveyard slot. Three decades on, *The Prisoner* stands up as that rarest of television beasts, a genuine classic, its defiantly inscrutable nature only adding to the appeal. As fan Joss Whedon explains: 'The Prisoner was a huge one for me, where nothing is solved.'

McGoohan's creative partners on the show were writer-producer David Tomblin and script editor George Markstein, who'd also worked on *Danger Man*. At one time employed by British Intelligence, Markstein had heard of special places where former spies could be safely 'retired', carefully monitored to prevent any unauthorised information leaks. Markstein saw *The Prisoner* as a logical follow-up to *Danger Man*, McGoohan still playing Agent John Drake in all but name. This didn't tally with McGoohan's own intentions for the show and viewers expecting a straightforward sequel to *Danger Man* were in for a big surprise.

Any series that employs such pithy catchphrases as 'I am not a number. I am a free man!' (THX 1138 take note), is open to accusations of high-level pretension, yet *The Prisoner* rarely put a foot wrong. At the start of every episode but one, the newly unemployed ex-secret agent is tailed home by a hearse, an unusual form of covert surveillance. Packing a suitcase, he is overwhelmed by knockout gas in his own flat, waking up to find himself forcibly relocated with a new (non)identity, Number Six. (Note to maverick former agents: once the surprise resignation has been proffered, it's probably wise not to go straight home; they're bound to know where you live).

Patrick McGoohan as The Prisoner (1967), the enigmatic individualist trapped in a luxurious village with no name. Throughout the 17-episode series he was referred to as 'Number Six'.

Boasting quaintly bizarre exteriors filmed at Portmeirion, the Village presents a novel form of open-air imprisonment. Taxi drivers and public telephones offer local service only, all requests for outside routes and lines politely declined. A man-sized chessboard dominates the village square, a shamelessly blatant metaphor that works surprisingly well (games are always in progress, whether or not they relate to the main storyline). The vacant, relentlessly cheery inhabitants utter meaningless, mechanical greetings ('Be seeing you!'), their seriously impaired fashion sense highlighted by striped capes and twirling umbrellas. Tipping its novelty hat to Orwell and Kafka, the Village also offers non-stop all-round surveillance, via a device resembling a revolving seesaw. Loudspeakers broadcast a steady flow of anti-curiosity, anti-intellect propaganda, notably 'Questions are a burden to others', in cheerful holiday camp tones. Every chalet contains a two way radio transmitter that cannot be turned off.

With Number One always unavailable for comment, Number Six pitted his still considerable wits against the resident Number Two, whose identity tended to vary from week to week (more likely a comment on the nebulous, apparently transitory nature of devious establishment authority than a crude excursion into lavatorial humour). A succession of high-class offbeat British thespians took up residence in the chic semi-spherical seat of authority, including Peter Wyngarde, Kenneth Griffith, Mary Morris, Patrick Cargill and Leo McKern.

Although exhibiting a strong desire to extract information from Number Six, these cultured interrogators never became too specific about what they wanted. The early episode A, B & C reveals suspicions that Number Six had been on the verge of defecting, yet this is commonplace espionage

breaking his will, whether by drugs, hypnosis, mental torture, emotional manipulation or a supposed lobotomy

material which later instalments sharply veered away from. The big question of why the prisoner resigned often took a back seat to simply breaking his will, whether by drugs, hypnosis, mental torture, emotional manipulation or a supposed lobotomy.

Aside from Number Six, one of the few recurring characters was a diminutive butler (Angelo Muscat), short on both stature and dialogue, who served a succession of Number Twos before throwing in his

lot with Number Six. Village security came in the form of the 'Rovers', fearsome spherical flying 'guard dogs' with a passing resemblance to weather balloons and an unpleasant habit of smothering transgressors. Few episodes went by without Number Six being pursued across attractive seaside locations by either human or rubber guards. Not for nothing is the daily village newspaper called 'Tally Ho', the cry of the hunter.

Unlike Doctor Who's tetchy but ultimately good-natured time traveller and The Avengers' smooth-as-silk John Steed, The Prisoner's central character didn't offer ready audience identification a lot of the time. Sharing Number Six's understandable sense of dislocation, viewers came to admire rather than like this paranoid protagonist, who could trust no-one and made no secret of it. Frequently abrupt, sarcastic, scathing and downright ill-mannered, Number Six occasionally exhibited normal human emotions – avenging a young woman driven to suicide in Hammer into Anvil – but largely stood as a symbol for rugged integrity, an unbreakable free-thinking individual prepared to suffer countless interrogations and mind tricks in the name of humanity. Moving down the Big Theme scale, Cult TV writer John Kent suggested another reason for this perceived bad attitude. Having previously sped through the streets of swinging London in his black and amber Lotus 7, Number Six now had to make do with a Mini Moke.

Aside from the faked lobotomy featured in A Change of Mind, The Prisoner also offered a doppelganger who claims Number Six is a mere imposter (The Schizoid Man), brainwashing disguised as speed-learning (The General), a bizarre trial by a fancy dress lynch mob (Dance of the Dead) and a temporary mindswap (Do Not Forsake Me Oh My Darling), largely motivated by McGoohan's commitment to co-star in the film Ice Station Zebra (1968). Where McGoohan would have taken The Prisoner if he'd retained control over the series must remain a source of conjecture. Originally intending to produce several series in blocks of thirteen episodes, the producer-star felt the wrath of Lew Grade, who had given McGoohan virtual carte blanche in expectation of a massive ratings hit. Aside from the disappointing viewing figures, it's alleged that ITC were also unhappy with the escalating budgets and the show's too-controversial drug references.

Obliged to wrap up the series in the space of one extended season, McGoohan found himself running out of time, money and resources. Several episodes had to be made without any location work in

Portmeirion, a factor the star played to his advantage. *The Girl Who Was Death* offered an elaborate take off of the already self-mocking *Avengers*, Number Six donning frilly shirt and deerstalker as he pursues the title character through a series of high risk encounters: exploding cricket balls, poisonous candle fumes, electrified steel spikes and German hand grenades, to name but a few. Informed that his drink has been poisoned via a message on the bottom of the glass, he orders a series of spirits from a disconcerted barmaid until vomiting is induced (surely a first in British fantasy television). The real villain of the piece is revealed as a Welshman with a Napoleon complex and a rocket disguised as a lighthouse. The whole narrative turns out to be a bedtime story told by Number Six to some Village children (where did they come from?) while Number Two observes in the hope of the prisoner dropping his guard. No chance. Given that the dream-like tale is regularly punctuated by picture book illustrations, the denouement should seem far more obvious than

it actually is, a trick often pulled by *The Prisoner*. Needless to say, Number Two and his second-in-command are the villains from the story. Number Six is probably addressing the audience as much as his unseen captors when he closes the episode with a sardonic: 'Goodnight children. *Everywhere*.'

The virtual reality episode *Living in Harmony* also dispensed with the standard credit sequence. Number Six finds himself in a cut-cost Wild West frontier town called Harmony (heavy irony), cast in the problematic role of a peace-loving sheriff who refuses to carry a gun. Filled with mildly masochistic scenes of McGoohan taking a beating before deigning to fight back, the story builds towards the expected shootout, only for Harmony to be revealed as a mentally-induced environment designed to put Number Six through an emotional rollercoaster, breaking his stubborn resistance. (The premise later reappeared almost exactly in the 1977 British-Canadian science fiction film *Welcome to Blood City*, though the object of the exercise was changed to

The Prisoner (Patrick McGoohan) is persuaded to become a candidate in the Village's annual elections in Free for All. This 1967 episode was written and directed by Patrick McGoohan.

military testing; Keir Dullea, still looking adrift after 2001, played the initially reluctant gunfighter). Despite offering such interesting touches as reducing the Harmony townsfolk to cut-out figures at the climax, *Living in Harmony* didn't go down well in some quarters. The episode wasn't shown during the series's original American run, network executives fearful of total audience confusion.

Turning *The Prisoner* into a virtual one-man show, McGoohan wrote and directed several episodes himself, including the political satire *Free for All* and the linked concluding stories *Once Upon a Time* and

the election is not rigged so much as utterly meaningless

Fall Out. Though accused by some of developing a god-complex, the star proved up to the task. Scripted under the pseudonym 'Paddy Fitz', *Free for All* sees Number Six putting himself up for election to the Number Two post, his surprise victory almost immediately undercut by establishment trickery. The election is not so much rigged as utterly meaningless in a place where democracy and freedom of speech are anathema to the controlling forces. *Once Upon a Time* goes on a fantasy tour of Number Six's past,

demonstrating that his freedom and individuality had been undermined virtually from birth (the classroom scenes suggest a public school education). By the time of *Fall Out* the questions of motivation and possible side-swapping had long become irrelevant. Number Six finally makes it to the Number Two post, only to discover that the promotion was pointless. The elusive Number One is literally unmasked as Number Six himself, laughing into camera with manic glee (McGoohan was never one for understatement). This could mean that Number Six was in control of the Village all along, presumably without knowing it, or a victim of secret service loyalty tests, or a prisoner of his own mind, or simply that an embittered McGoohan really wanted to irritate people. Throwing in Kenneth Griffith's hip-talking judge, an unintelligible rebellious youth (Alexis Kanner), a jury of robed, masked figures labelled with society's ills, and a little song and dance, *Fall Out* abandons all pretence of logic, sense or intelligible plotting. Unimpressed with his new status, the prisoner formerly known as Number Six stages a breakout, accompanied by deposed Number Two Leo McKern, Kanner's spaced-out, suspiciously hippie Number 48 and the butler. While the soundtrack argues that 'All You Need Is Love',

The rebellious Number 48 (Alexis Kanner) confronted Village authority in Fall Out (1968), the final episode of The Prisoner.

machine guns and an articulated lorry also come in very useful. The circular ending places Number Six, apparently a free man, back in his London flat. That said, while McKern and Kanner are billed under their real names as their characters adjust to 'normal' life, McGoohan is still 'The Prisoner'. Whatever this playful payoff is supposed to mean, it's fairly safe to argue that the now demolished Village is a metaphor for British society: absurd, hypocritical, complacent and corrupt. Given the national reputation for pessimism, it's a little ironic that it took an American 'outsider' to add a note of cynicism to sixties television fantasy. Maybe it was all just a dream, a bad trip or a vision of purgatory. Or was it?

INVASIONS, EXPLOSIONS, CRASH LANDINGS

As a rule, anyone looking for truly adult science fiction on the television during the late 1960s had to be content with the occasional one-off drama, such

as Nigel Kneale's BBC play *The Year of the Sex Olympics* (1969), starring Leonard Rossiter and Brian Cox. Set in a near-future society where the apathetic masses are controlled by an elite body via media manipulation, *Sex Olympics* employs standard dystopian trappings, including a form of Orwellian newspeak that renders concepts such as 'despair' and 'sadness' inexpressible except as a vague sense of 'tension'. Exploring the topical fear of potentially calamitous over-population, Kneale created 'a world which was saturated with pornography'. Subjected to a non-stop diet of media sex, people have lost all interest in the actual physical act, the birth rate dropping accordingly.

Rather more subtle than Orwell, Kneale presents a group of social dropouts who are granted permission by the state to establish their own community on a remote island, providing they agree to be filmed 24 hours a day for 'The Live Life Show'. What they don't realise is that there's a murderer on

The Butler (Angelo Muscat), seen here in the closing moments of Arrival (1967), the first episode of The Prisoner. Press information issued by original distributor ITC hinted that this silent but omnipresent character may have been the mysterious Number One.

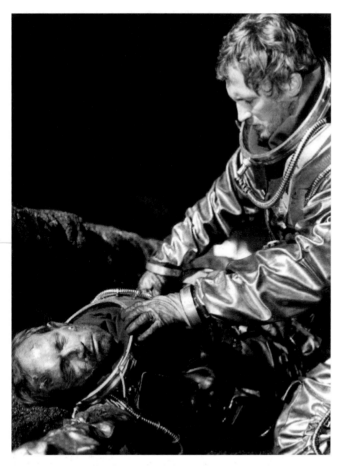

Glenn Ross (Roy Thinnes, right) struggles to revive his crew-mate John Kane (Ian Hendry) following a crash-landing on an alien planet in Doppelganger (1969).

Jason Webb (Patrick Wymark), head of the European Space Exploration Council, with the plans for a manned exploration to a newly discovered planet. Doppelganger (1969).

His switch to more heavyweight live action sf drama would lead first to UFO (1969-70), then Space: 1999 (1974-6), following a brief excursion into big screen science fiction. After two middling attempts to launch Thunderbirds as a cinema franchise, Anderson's Century 21 Productions teamed up with Hollywood studio Universal to make Doppelganger (1969), now better known under its American title Journey to the Far Side of the Sun. Co-scripted by Gerry and Sylvia Anderson with Donald James, a Century 21 regular who penned the slightly pacier Tara King Avengers episode Have Guns – Will Haggle, the film imported the American talents of director Robert Parrish. It also starred an American actor, Roy Thinnes, star of cult sf series The Invaders, then a recent victim of abrupt cancellation. A modestly intriguing tale of human duplicates, Doppelganger also drew on the services of former Avenger Ian Hendry and leading actors such as Patrick Wymark and Herbert Lom. The initial premise involves the discovery of a previously unknown planet, travelling in the same orbit as the Earth, literally hidden behind the sun. Astronaut Thinnes crashlands on the planet to find an exact mirror image duplicate of the Earth. The story is told by Thinnes as an extended flashback, the astronaut now incarcerated in a mental hospital because nobody believes him. Featuring such novel gadgets as a miniature camera concealed inside an artificial eye (double voyeurism, no less), Doppelganger is stronger on elaborate modelwork, courtesy of Anderson veteran Derek Meddings, than gripping narrative. Parrish's pedestrian handling of the cast at times renders the human element rather less interesting than Anderson's gallery of puppets. Worse, it comes as no real surprise when Thinnes's double is sent to Earth in his place.

The supporting cast for Doppelganger included Ed Bishop and George Sewell, more usefully deployed as the leads for UFO. Anderson also recycled part of regular composer Barry Gray's score for the film, played over UFO's closing credits. One of the sound-only cast for Captain Scarlet, possessing what he described as 'a wall to wall corporate voice', American-born Bishop had

the loose and no means of escape. The desensitised television audiences laugh out loud at the killings, giving the controlling powers both a handy means of eliminating dissenters and a huge ratings winner. The BBC's own live life show, Castaway 2000, looks pretty tame by comparison.

Four years earlier, Peter Watkins's harrowing docudrama The War Game (1965) demonstrated the probable consequences of a nuclear war against the backdrop of the Cuban Missile Crisis, CND rallies, the escalating Vietnam conflict and ever-present nuclear anxiety. Watkins's in-depth research resulted in a realistic, downbeat approach light years away from the expected chronicle of plucky British people pulling together in the best Blitz tradition. Soviet missiles accidentally fall on Kent, the resulting devastation leading to complete social breakdown and violent disorder. Having commissioned the film, the BBC suffered a major loss of nerve and refused to show it on television for years. (The film did receive a limited theatrical release).

By the late 1960s, Gerry Anderson's ambitions had long outstripped mere television puppet shows.

become a trusted Anderson co-worker while playing Captain Blue, 'a very good technical artist' prepared to work long hours when necessary. In the tradition of Marineville, International Rescue and Cloudbase, *UFO* has SHADO – Supreme Headquarters Alien Defence Organisation, yet another covert international outfit dedicated to protecting earth from extraterrestrial invasion. Not inclined to take any chances with global security, the London-based SHADO has established another operations centre on the moon as an early warning system. In the opening instalment, *Exposed*, top USAAF pilot Ed Straker (Bishop) is shot down by what he believes to be a Unidentified Flying Object, only to find himself under pressure from government figures who want Straker to change his story. When the saucers turn up *en masse* in episode two, cover stories seem a little redundant. Now posing as a film executive at the Harlington-Straker studios, the implausibly white-haired Straker leads the fight back as SHADO's new boss, opting out of the fetching string costumes and purple wigs adopted by some of his female co-workers.

Switching puppets for live actors, *UFO* departed from the standard Gerry Anderson format in another significant respect. Eschewing the standard one-hundred-years-on setting, the story takes place in 1980, only a decade after the show's first broadcast (the recent moonlandings, and consequent implications for lunar colonisation, may have played a part in this decision). Anderson decided to direct the pilot episode of *UFO* himself, the pressures of the job doing little for his one-hundred-a-day cigarette habit. *Exposed* features such highlights as an alien autopsy, later a regular showpiece in *The X-Files*, which initiated a tradition of mildly gruesome detail in the series. A sterile and moribund species, the humanoid alien intruders need to harvest regular supplies of human organs to survive, hence their pressing interest in Planet Earth. They also employ a noxious green liquid to cope with the Earth's atmosphere, messily spitting it out of their mouths on occasion. Straker is briefly replaced by an alien duplicate, Anderson obviously still keen on the doppelganger theme. One episode, *Reflections in the Water*, scripted by former *Prisoner* associate David Tomblin, centres on an underwater alien copy of the entire SHADO headquarters. The earth-bound stories tended to be the strongest, SHADO's film studio cover offering some offbeat details. In one pre-credits sequence, Straker shows his young son the filming of a murder scene, a woman attacked in a phonebooth, which is hardly responsible parenting (though it might explain his divorce). When a UFO

crash-lands in a forest, the SHADO vehicles sent to investigate are blasted by the still functioning ship, the battling craft rather more gripping than the somewhat token human characters. Intended as far more adult-oriented fare than the Century 21 Supermarionation series, *UFO* succeeded a little too well as far as the ITV networks were concerned, many of them consigning it to a late night 'graveyard' slot. One of the most controversial episodes, *The Long Sleep*, features an LSD-induced hallucination, a bold excursion into psychedelic drugs that delayed its initial screening.

With *Star Trek* undergoing a protracted death struggle in the late sixties, *UFO* might have been seen as a strong pretender to the television science fiction throne, yet circumstances were against it. Anderson describes his American partners on *UFO* as 'extremely difficult', a classic case of British understatement. First screened in the UK in 1970, the series didn't

Top: Commander Ed Straker (Ed Bishop), Colonel Alec Freeman (George Sewell) and Captain Peter Carlin (Peter Gordeno) in Gerry Anderson's UFO (1969).

Below: In UFO (1969), liquid-breathing aliens came to Earth in spinning flying saucers, intent on harvesting human organs to transplant into their own bodies.

Professor Victor Bergman (Barry Morse), Dr Helena Russell (Barbara Bain), Commander John Koenig (Martin Landau) and Dr Cabot Rowland (Brian Blessed) in the Space: 1999 episode Death's Other Dominion (1975).

première in the US until 1972, hardly the greatest vote of confidence (disappointing British viewing figures can't have helped matters). Nevertheless, UFO initially seemed to be an unqualified hit in the United States, proving very popular in New York and Los Angeles, where it topped the ratings for seventeen consecutive weeks. Delighted with this response, ITC boss Lew Grade commissioned a second series. Anderson had begun pre-production on season two, building a new, improved Moonbase set, when the bad news hit. Viewing figures in America had

A sterile and moribund species, the humanoid alien intruders need to harvest regular supplies of human organs to survive

suddenly dropped with episode eighteen and the US partners were cancelling the show. Stuck with a collection of unused story outlines and an expensive, now redundant set, Anderson suggested employing these resources on a new show, rapidly titled Space: 1999.

Never a great favourite with either science fiction enthusiasts or the general public, Space: 1999 remains

a real puzzle of a series, its eclectic mix of story elements never really amounting to much. The series features an exiled, tight-knit group of humans wandering the universe, strange alien worlds and creatures, and elaborate hi-tech hardware. The potential is there, yet neither executive producer Anderson nor his creative team ever gave the material a real sense of style or purpose, perhaps a reflection of the show's hasty, stop-gap conception. In the pilot episode of Space: 1999, John Koenig's first day as the new commander of Moonbase Alpha finishes badly when the moon is blasted out of its orbit round the earth, careering off into the depths of unknown space. This explosive premise came about out of sheer necessity. Still smarting from the perceived failure of UFO, ITC's American representative vetoed all proposed Earth-set episodes of the new series, forcing Anderson to back up his promise to comply by taking the Moonbase inhabitants light years away from their home planet.

A multi-million dollar undertaking, costing an average $300,000 per episode, Space: 1999 offered state of the art sets and effects and, by television standards, a star-studded cast. American husband and wife team Martin Landau and Barbara Bain, who'd both appeared in the hit spy show Mission

Impossible, were hired for the lead roles, Commander Koenig and resident medical officer Dr Helena Russell. The supporting British contingent was led by Barry Morse, cast as science officer Dr Victor Bergman. Landau and Bain were chosen by the show's American partners without Anderson's approval and it's likely Morse only got the job thanks to his co-starring role in the long-running US show *The Fugitive*.

Even at this stage, the thinking behind the show seemed reasonably sound. While UFO offered sinister visions of alien invasion, *Space: 1999* could combine its spectacular monstrous creations with some serious deep-space exploration, led by the intrepid top-billed trio. Yet the formula failed to win either American or British hearts and minds. Unlike the Kirk-Spock-McCoy triumvirate of *Star Trek*, whose differing outlooks and frequent personality clashes masked an underlying affection, the *Space: 1999* leads often seemed to be inhabiting different galaxies for all the chemistry they generated. Though obviously patterned on the Gene Roddenberry series, the Moonbase saga appears to have taken its stylistic cues from *2001*, with clinical white-on-white sets, banal dialogue spoken in varieties of monotone and a pace best described as somnambulistic. The ersatz Kubrick approach just doesn't work, no matter how much the directors cut to lingering soft focus close-ups of Barbara Bain. The crew of Moonbase Alpha is made up of bland, ill-defined characters whose blank-faced interaction creates little sense of warmth or even professional camaraderie. The varied alien lifeforms encountered are strange and inscrutable at best, overtly hostile at worst. With or without the prospect of immanent disaster, the mood is relentlessly sombre, down to the dreary pale beige uniforms with their flared trousers and colour-coded left arms.

This depressing atmosphere seems to have extended to behind the cameras, gifted directors such as Charles Crichton, Val Guest and Peter Medak succumbing to the ponderous, plodding environment. Each episode opens with a rapid-fire montage of the story's supposed highlights, an approach Gerry Anderson deployed more successfully for *Thunderbirds*, which at least kept moving. The scripts tend to offer a promising initial situation, sometimes quite intriguing, but rarely develop ideas into strong storylines. Given Landau and Bain's terminal glumness, audience sympathies have nowhere to go but Victor Bergman, who seldom seems bothered by anything. Rendered largely immune to panic by his artificial heart, Dr Bergman reacts to even the most

terrifying situations with mild curiosity. Given Gerry Anderson's extensive experience with special effects, it comes as no surprise that *Space: 1999* scores reasonably well in the modelwork department, supervised by *2001* veteran Brian Johnson. The distinctive Eagle spacecraft, presumably named after the Dan Dare comic, are interestingly designed but appear to move almost as slowly as the plots.

Occasionally, by some mysterious cosmic alchemy, the show got something right, notably with the

Space: 1999 could combine its spectacular monstrous creations with some serious deep-space exploration

episode *Dragon's Lair*, which features a hell-mouthed, glowing eyed, multi-tentacled alien that materialises out of nowhere to drag hapless humans into its infernal orifice, spitting out the desiccated remains. The standard issue ray guns used by the Moonbase crew have no effect on the monster, which is finally vanquished with a good old fashioned hatchet in the eye. This is efficient, effective horror. Other than this, the audience is treated to a hackneyed retread of the familiar man's-innate-capacity-for-self destruction theme. The moonbase was originally a dumping ground for nuclear waste – the cause of the big explosion.

Given Martin Landau's impressive performances both before and after *Space: 1999*, notably his implicitly gay spy in Hitchcock's *North by Northwest* (1959) and an Academy Award winning turn as Bela Lugosi in Tim Burton's *Ed Wood* (1994), the failure of his central character is all the more frustrating. Commander John Koenig is a man of integrity, intellect and, sometimes, action, but never succeeds in drawing audience sympathy or even involvement. Faced with an uncertain, often dangerous new life for himself and his 300-strong crew, Koenig is entitled to a little anxiety and self-doubt, yet he seems simply cold and uninterested much of the time. It's arguable that Landau, an American actor in a British-made series, paved the way for Patrick Stewart, a British actor who came to international prominence in the American show *Star Trek: The Next Generation* (1987-94). Captain Jean-Luc Picard, an intelligent, mature, rational leader of men is not a million miles away from Commander Koenig, but could surely teach him a thing or two about the quality of humanity (and a decent script). As with Picard's libidinous second-in-command William Riker, the more conventional action man duties in *Space: 1999* are left to Chief Eagle pilot Alan Carter (Nick Tate), a rugged Australian with an eye for the ladies.

For all the expense, time, effort and compromise, *Space: 1999* pretty much crashed on take-off during its first season. Despite the American leads, the show failed to win a regular network slot on either side of the Atlantic, which doomed it to ratings limbo. When the go-ahead came for a second season, produced on a reduced schedule and budget, Gerry Anderson found himself more or less marginalized. The first series had been produced by Sylvia Anderson, his longtime marital and creative partner. Their dual relationship came to an end before the second run of *Space: 1999* began production, leaving Anderson with a major gap in his key personnel. Hands-on control of the show fell to American producer Fred Freiberger, who'd acquired a reputation as a science fiction series troubleshooter when he took over the insufficiently popular *Star Trek* from Gene Roddenberry during its third and final season. Whether or not this was a good reputation is open to question, given the extremely variable quality of the Freiberger-produced episodes and the series's subsequent cancellation.

Freiberger, who'd previously worked as a writer on such no-nonsense Western shows as *Rawhide*, felt that *Space: 1999* needed more action and a major cast shake-up. Several lead characters were dropped, notably Victor Bergman and Paul Morrow, Koenig's unmemorable second-in-command. Though supposedly hired by Anderson himself, Freiberger's more gung ho approach suggested little empathy with his nominal boss. Still a firm believer in the

Aside from some bizarre hairstyling, Maya looked reassuringly humanoid

basics of Western-style storytelling, the new producer drew on his former profession, scripting several episodes under the pseudonym 'Charles Woodgrove'.

Under Freiberger's supervision, *Space: 1999* acquired a racier, less portentous theme tune, composer Derek Wadsworth taking over from Barry Gray, more colourful space jackets and a new main character. Played by Catherine Schell, Maya was a Metamorph from the planet Psychon, capable of transforming into any life form (often represented by a large stunt man in a hairy suit). Aside from some bizarre hairstyling, Maya looked reassuringly humanoid most of the time, though her outsized

eyebrows seemed needlessly elaborate. Intended as an offbeat love interest, Maya was tentatively paired off with new second in command Tony Verdeschi (Tony Anholt), a decidedly spark-free romance. Schell's previous science fiction credits included the equally ill-conceived 'space western' *Moon Zero Two* (1969), conclusive proof that Hammer's sf success largely began and ended with the *Quatermass* series. An unusually lavish project for the studio, produced and scripted by Hammer stalwart Michael Carreras, this 2021 saga of crooked moon prospectors illegally mining an asteroid made of sapphire proved a total flop, completely misjudging the public mood. Soon to be glued to their television screens by the real-life moon landings, paying audiences had little time for such novelties as 'Moonopoly', not to mention a truly awful theme song. For all its faults, *Space: 1999* at least tried to operate on a slightly higher intellectual plane.

Having recently scored with *Quatermass and the Pit*, *Moon Zero Two* director Roy Ward Baker found this facile science fiction follow-up a sad comedown: 'It wasn't a very good script. It fell between several different stools, between comedy and satire and also the western, which was really going a bit far … Perhaps it wasn't my metier, I don't know.' During production at Elstree Studios, Baker encountered fellow sf director Stanley Kubrick, then finishing up 2001 at the nearby MGM complex. Kubrick offered handy tips on how to film weightless sequences, which Baker had to stage with his cast strung up on piano wire: 'We were up against some problems which were insuperable'. Billed as Catherina Von Schell, the future *Space: 1999* co-star had little to do but pout as rugged space pilot James Olson attempts to thwart the bad guys. Aside from some entertaining, if low-tech, special effects, the film's nicest touch is female lunar sheriff Adrienne Corri, who nobly expires in the course of duty.

Season two of *Space: 1999* was originally intended to finish with the relatively cerebral *Children of the Gods*, where the Moonbase crew, known by those who care as Alphans, are visited by their own descendants from 300 years in the future. Endowed with amazing powers, these children are being tested by an advanced alien species to determine whether or not the human race, as represented by the inhabitants of Moonbase Alpha, is fit to survive. A poor result means a permanent shutdown of operations. While *Star Trek* had already covered similar ground more than once, the *Space: 1999* producers lost faith in the idea, opting for a more action-oriented showdown with *The Dorcons*, a hostile alien race seeking to render

themselves immortal by stealing Maya's brainstem. The switch made little difference, the series folding for good after 48 episodes.

The high profile, not to say expensive, failure of Gerry Anderson's two live action science fiction series left his career with nowhere much to go. In 1976, Anderson teamed up with the BBC for the first time to make the one-off space drama *Into Infinity*, starring Brian Blessed, who'd played Maya's less than trustworthy father in *Space: 1999*. While the model-work was well up to standard, this pilot didn't attract enough interest to generate a full-fledged series. The 1980s brought a return to puppets with *Terrahawks*, a largely forgettable effort that bore little trace of Anderson's groundbreaking 1960s shows.

NEW LOOK FOR DOCTOR WHO

While Gerry Anderson struggled to maintain his position as a science fiction trendsetter in the early 1970s, *Doctor Who* seemed to take on a new lease of life, moving into the colour era with a dynamic lead actor and a pacier style. Favouring velvet smoking

jackets, frilled shirts, opera cloaks and increasingly bouffant hair, Jon Pertwee's Doctor number three cut a dandyish figure of a space-time traveller, though budget constraints meant that he didn't get to check out an alien planet until his eighth story. The series would, by and large, remain fresh and inventive throughout the next ten years, peaking, for many, with the arrival of Doctor number four, Tom Baker.

Four years prior to Pertwee's debut, William Hartnell's decision to quit the series in 1966 had caused undeniable consternation, until someone hit upon the inspired narrative device of bodily regeneration. The official reason for Hartnell's departure was ill health, yet there appear to have been other factors. Original producer Verity Lambert had left the show two stories into season three, shortly before the twelve part epic *The Daleks' Master Plan* (1965/66). Her successor, John Wiles, proved unhappy in the post, making way for Innes Lloyd midway through the season. Debuting with the memorably surreal story *The Celestial Toymaker*, Lloyd had a much stronger rapport with *Doctor Who* than

On the Elstree Studios set of Moon Zero Two *(1969), Catherina Von Schell and James Olson browse a* Film Review *report on* 2001: A Space Odyssey. *Hammer's science fiction spoof proved to be no match for Kubrick's blockbuster.*

Patrick Troughton replaced William Hartnell in the title role of Doctor Who.

Wiles and clear ideas about where to take the series. Hartnell didn't agree, regarding creations such as the Cybermen as much too violent for a family show. (The actor's own ideas for the show apparently included a spin-off called Son of Doctor Who, which would feature Hartnell as the Doctor's less benevolent offspring.)

Faced with the stark choices of either scrapping Doctor Who or carrying on with a new star, the BBC opted for the latter, casting Patrick Troughton in the role. Described by series director David Maloney as 'a bit of an oddball', Troughton felt his Doctor should be radically different from the Hartnell incarnation, whimsical instead of authoritarian. Sydney Newman, still heading up the drama department, suggested making the character almost Chaplinesque, hence the much-quoted 'cosmic hobo' tag. The second Doctor's debut story, The Power of the Daleks, proved that, underneath the new exterior, he'd not lost any of his old skill at outmanoeuvring devious alien plots. In The Moonbase (1967), Troughton's first encounter with the Cybermen, the Doctor makes his philosophy of intervention clear: 'There are some corners of the universe which have bred the most terrible things. Things which act against everything we believe in. They must be fought.'

The Troughton era brought memorable encounters with Cybermen, giant Macra crabs, a seaweed creature, Ice Warriors and robotic Yeti, but after *The Evil of the Daleks* (1967) it looked as if the show would have to survive without its best-known and best-loved villains. Terry Nation, whose involvement with the show had been minimal since *The Daleks' Master Plan* (which was extensively rewritten by Dennis Spooner) wanted to launch his creations in a series of their own. Given the Daleks' spin-off success as toys, board games, comic strips and film stars – the two 1960s *Doctor Who* movies were sold on the strength of the Daleks rather than the Doctor himself – Nation's decision made commercial sense. Aside from a brief cameo appearance in *The War Games*, Troughton's last story, the Daleks would not be seen on television again for five years. Still well supplied with BBC monsters, Troughton himself regretted the fact that, unlike the more balanced mix of the Hartnell era, most of his alien co-stars were hostile.

Troughton's third season as *Doctor Who* (1968-69) seemed a little stale to some, the show reaching the end of the 1960s guided by solid professionalism rather than any great inspiration. Repeat meetings with the Cybermen and Ice Warriors didn't quite live up to earlier adventures and new monsters such as the Quarks and the Krotons failed to set the sf world on fire. The opening story, *The Dominators*, seemed peculiarly lacklustre at times, with an uninspired script and variable acting. Even future *Play Away* star Brian Cant appeared unenthusiastic, clad in an unbecoming white space smock. Previously cast as special agent Kert Gantry in *The Daleks' Masterplan*, Cant had delivered a forceful performance before suffering agonising extermination. Faced with the Quark death rays, he just didn't seem to care. Only *The Mind Robber*, which deposited the Doctor and his companions in a shifting, fiction-based dimension, showed *Doctor Who* at peak form.

With viewing figures on the slide, the BBC actively considered dumping the ailing series after six seasons in favour of a new *Quatermass* serial. The outline for what became the first Pertwee story, Robert Holmes's *Spearhead from Space* (1970), was conceived in late 1968 just in case *Doctor Who* continued. Unable to negotiate terms with Nigel Kneale, the corporation grudgingly agreed to reprieve the Doctor, largely because there was no obvious replacement waiting in the wings. The stay of execution came at a price, the ever

cost-conscious BBC dictating that the new season of *Doctor Who* would remain earthbound. Even the most bargain basement alien worlds put a strain on the show's less-than-generous budget.

Forced to call for help from his own race, the aloof Time Lords, at the end of *The War Games*, Troughton's Doctor found himself on trial for interfering in other worlds' affairs. To this serious breach of Time Lord policy was added the offence of taking a TARDIS without permission. Running at ten episodes, this story had been something of a long haul, yet the trial sequence proved quite powerful. The gloomy, functional settings and uptight, humourless Time Lords demonstrated very clearly why the Doctor had fled his home planet in the first place. Mounting his own defence, the Doctor cited such aggressive species as the Daleks, the Cybermen, the Ice Warriors and the Quarks (hmm) as prime reasons for intervening in a big, often very bad universe. Partially convinced, the Time Lords altered

'There are some corners of the universe which have bred the most terrible things'

the Doctor's appearance for a second time and exiled him to Earth, confiscating the TARDIS's all-important dematerialization circuit. Unable to decide on his new appearance, the Doctor materialised on his new 'home' planet with no idea of what he looked like. Uniquely, the Troughton-Pertwee switchover was not justified by the Doctor being close to death, merely Time Lord vindictiveness. Like Prospero before him, the Doctor was a man of secret learning banished to a remote outpost by his cultured yet devious civilisation, defending the primitive inhabitants of Earth against the technological 'magic' of hostile forces, both external and internal.

Slightly more adult in tone than his later stories, Jon Pertwee's first season as the Doctor borrowed from both *Quatermass* and *The Avengers*. His debut appearance, *Spearhead from Space*, is best known for the Autons, animated mannequins controlled by the Nestines, intelligent disembodied alien lifeforms with an affinity for plastic and a preference for physically manifesting themselves as tentacled mollusc-style creatures. Usually dressed in casual blue overalls, the mindless, largely featureless Autons were the teatime sf equivalent of soulless zombies, blindly obedient to their controlling masters. Unlike most *Doctor Who* creatures, the Autons could move at a fair speed, impressively sprinting through the sedate English countryside, which boosted the menace factor by a considerable degree. They also came equipped with formidable disintegrator guns, cunningly concealed within their hinged right hands. Like *Quatermass II*, *Spearhead* opens with an unusual meteorite shower that turns out to be an alien invasion. Rather than risk a full-on assault, the Nestenes employ their amazing plastics technology to duplicate key members of the British cabinet, an establishment take-over also reminiscent of the Nigel Kneale storyline. For anyone still convinced that ugly, shiny man-made plastics had brutally usurped the finer, traditional materials, *Spearhead* confirmed their worst fears.

The third Pertwee story, *The Ambassadors of Death*, replays elements of the original *Quatermass Experiment*. A manned space expedition returns to earth with

the Nestenes employ their amazing plastics technology to duplicate key members of the cabinet

Martians on board instead of the original astronauts. This time around, at least, the aliens are not aggressors, merely diplomats confronted with human xenophobia. *Inferno*, the season's grand finale, centres on a well-intentioned but inevitably foolhardy attempt to drill into the Earth's crust and release a new source of energy, Stahlman's Gas. The pipelines housing the drill have started to leak a strange liquid that reacts with human tissue to transform anyone who gets splashed into a savage apeman called a Primord. In a very Kneale-esque plot twist, the Doctor is transported to a parallel Earth where England is controlled by a fascist regime. Unable to prevent the completion of Project Inferno in this unlovely universe, the Doctor is forced to make a run for it as the Earth goes up in flames: 'Listen to that! That's the sound of this planet screaming out its rage.'

The *Avengers* parallels, notably Pertwee's dandyish dress sense, vintage car and strongwilled female assistant, may have come about thanks to the input of *Doctor Who* script editor Terrance Dicks and regular series writer Malcolm Hulke, who co-authored *The War Games* to set the scene for the first Pertwee season. An established writing team, Dicks and Hulke had provided a number of *Avengers* scripts, including the early Cathy Gale episodes *The Mauritius Penny*, screened in November 1962, *Intercrime* and *Concerto*. On his own, Hulke scripted a further four Steed-Gale stories, *The White Dwarf*, *The Undertakers*,

The Medicine Men, *Trojan Horse*, and the season four Emma Peel episode *The Gravediggers*. After a period away from the show, the Dicks-Hulke duo returned to co-write the much re-edited season six episode *Homicide and Old Lace*, which began life as 'The Great Great Britain Crime'. Terrance Dicks first worked as a *Doctor Who* script editor on the 1968 Patrick Troughton story *The Invasion*, which introduced the United Nations Intelligence Taskforce (UNIT), a military outfit that would play a central role during the Pertwee era. Briefly giving way to Derrick Sherwin for *The Space Pirates*, a decidedly minor Troughton story, Dicks stayed with *Doctor Who* for all five Pertwee seasons, returning during the Baker era as an occasional writer. (Dicks spent much of his time during this period writing the popular series of *Doctor Who* 'novelizations' for Target books, an essential purchase for diehard fans before the advent of home video).

Dicks denies ever trying to revamp *Doctor Who* as a junior league *Avengers* and it is fair to say that most of his work for the latter show came before it shifted into outright sf-flavoured fantasy. In fact, there was always a fair amount of crossover between the two shows in the writing department. Dennis Spooner (*The Reign of Terror*), Bill Strutton (*The Web Planet*) and John Lucarotti (*Marco Polo*) all worked on *The Avengers* during its first season before moving over to *Doctor Who*, Lucarotti switching back during the Diana Rigg era to script *Castle De'ath*. Robert Banks Stewart, writer of *The Quick-Quick Slow Death*, later penned two top-drawer Tom Baker stories, *Terror of the Zygons* and *The Seeds of Doom*. Terry Nation, who would return to the *Doctor Who* fold in 1973 with *The Planet of the Daleks*, wrote a good half dozen of the season six *Avengers* episodes, including the science fiction themed *Invasion of the Earthmen* and *Thingumajig*, which features mysteriously animated black boxes with the power to kill. Whatever Dicks's views on the subject, the similarities are fairly blatant. Like John Steed, Pertwee showed a preference for rakish, vaguely Edwardian attire and vintage automobiles, stealing both from a visiting dignitary during his hospital stay in *Spearhead from Space*. According to the actor, the 'dandy' wardrobe came about largely by chance. Summoned to a *Radio Times* photo session, Pertwee provided his own costume, drawn from his grandfather's wardrobe, assuming that the BBC would subsequently fit him out with something a little sleeker. Forced to give up his purloined motor vehicle at the end of *Spearhead from Space*, the Doctor settled for another classic car, 'Bessie', fetchingly decked out in shades of yellow and black.

Jon Pertwee met a friendly Yeti at the 1969 photo call to announce his casting as the third Doctor Who.

The end of the Patrick Troughton era marked a complete changeover in the regular *Doctor Who* cast line-up, though actor Nicholas Courtney agreed to reprise his *Invasion* role, Brigadier Lethbridge-Stewart of UNIT, as a recurring character. Sharing Troughton's concerns over possible typecasting, co-stars Frazer Hines, who played the eighteenth-century Highlander Jamie, and Wendy Padbury, cast as genius teen scientist Zoe, opted to leave. Their replacement came in the form of Liz Shaw (Caroline John), a rather more sussed female 'companion' than most of her predecessors. A fellow of Cambridge University with a handful of doctorates, Shaw offered intelligence, independence and an inquiring mind, not to mention an occasional flash of leg. The mini-skirt era was still going strong and even respectable scientists were proud to be seen in them. Though never one for physical combat, Liz Shaw didn't lack for courage, refusing to be intimidated by snide company executives, pompous government officials or reptilian humanoids.

Often regarded as the crucial period that saved *Doctor Who* from cancellation, Jon Pertwee's first season ran into severe production problems. Originally intended to be shot using the BBC's new, full-colour videotape system, *Spearhead* found itself banished from the studios by a scene-shifter's strike. Shot on low tech sixteen millimetre colour film, the end result had a low key, near-documentary quality – slightly grainy visuals, occasionally echoing sound – at odds with the later *Doctor Who* house style, which favoured a sharp, bright look (overly bright, in some people's opinion) and flawless acoustics. *Doctor Who*

snide company executives, pompous government officials or reptilian humanoids

and the Silurians, Pertwee's second story, suffered from cramped, flimsy cave sets and those still troublesome scene-shifters. *Ambassadors of Death*, based on a script written back in the late Troughton era, underwent multiple rewrites without ever reaching a satisfactory form. Dicks and Hulke were forced to fashion a final draft, the story blatantly padded out to fill seven episodes instead of the intended four.

After a long period of prevarication, the BBC eventually agreed to a second season of full-colour *Doctor Who*, largely thanks to Jon Pertwee's fast-growing popularity in the role. Feeling that Liz Shaw seemed too intellectual to serve as an effective foil to the genius Doctor, producer Barry Letts dropped her from the show. Pertwee argued that the Doctor should be a father figure or 'mother hen' to his companion, a relationship that couldn't really work with an whiz-kid academic. Pertwee's second season set the tone for the rest of his reign. The slightly harder edge of stories like *Doctor Who and the Silurians* and *Inferno* largely disappeared, though on occasion the series still provoked controversy. The 1971 story *Terror of the Autons*, a sequel to *Spearhead from Space*, featured an impressive array of plastic 'monsters': an ugly troll doll that strangles its owner, policemen revealed to be faceless Auton killers, an inflatable chair that smothers the occupant, a throttling telephone wire and artificial daffodils that spray suffocating film over the nose and mouth of their victims. Using everyday objects as sources of terror in a family show was deemed to be not playing fair by the authorities, who probably didn't care for the bogus police officers, either. Suitably chastened, the *Doctor Who* production team steered clear of risky material, by and large, until the Tom Baker era.

Far more of an action man than his previous incarnations, the third Doctor developed an expertise in Venusian aikido, a defensive, if often imprecise form of martial arts that brought many an aggressor to his knees, alien or human. Thanks to Bruce Lee's fashionable fists of fury, no self-respecting early 1970s television hero could be without a few nifty moves when the going got rough. While *Who* producer Barry Letts liked the idea of the Doctor fighting back without recourse to weapons, actual kung fu or karate would have been too violent for a family show, difficult to stage believably on a tight recording schedule and open to accusations of inspiring harmful imitation. This aside, Pertwee had a history of chronic back trouble, and was in his early fifties – not the best time of life to engage in vigorous punch-up routines. In the event, these action scenes tended to consist of Pertwee uttering strange cries and waving his arms while members of the Havoc stunt team gamely threw themselves around studio floors or quarry pits. While this worked pretty well in *The Mind of Evil*, by the time of *The Time Warrior* and *Planet of the Spiders*, the last Pertwee story, there was a definite impression of going through the motions.

Early 1970s *Doctor Who* featured a virtual repertory company of regular supporting characters. The Doctor acquired a new super-adversary, fellow renegade Time Lord The Master (Roger Delgado), whose stylish dark attire and pointed beard gave the character unmistakably devilish connotations. This arch-enemy had originally been conceived as a woman (The Mistress?), clad in black leather, until the BBC became nervous about the 'kinky' overtones of an evil Mrs Peel figure. On the side of right was the Brigadier, first seen fighting off robot Yeti in the 1968 Troughton story *The Web of Fear*. Moulded into a good-natured, if hidebound paternal figure, Lethbridge-Stewart's relationship with the third Doctor veered towards the antagonistic during the early days. In *The Silurians*, he assures his anxious scientific advisor that the humanoid reptiles will not be harmed once they return to suspended animation, only to blow up their cavernous lair when the Doctor's back is turned. One of the Brigadier's most memorable scenes occurred in *The Daemons* (1971), where, faced with a living church gargoyle bent on grievous bodily harm, the unflappable Lethbridge-Stewart calls out 'Sergeant Benton. Chap with wings. Eight rounds rapid.' It doesn't work, the fragmented stone monster reassembling itself seconds later.

If the third Doctor was an extraterrestrial Prospero, he found a worthy Miranda in the form of Josephine Grant (Katy Manning). Naive, childlike and usually clad in an impractical miniskirt, Jo never looked likely to shape into a feminist icon, though her scream-and-run tendencies have been exaggerated. Jo Grant did have a fierce sense of loyalty to the Doctor, boldly defying the 'horned god' alien Azal when the latter proposes to eliminate the Time Lord (unable to handle this 'illogical' act of selflessness, Azal self-destructs, which is fortunate). *The Green Death* (1973), the last Jo Grant story, ventured into *Doomwatch* territory, offering a family version of the latter's dire environmental warnings. Global Chemicals' reckless, not to say illegal, waste disposal into the Welsh countryside has created something very nasty down in the local mineshaft. Contending with infectious green slime, giant maggots and corrupt corporate figures, Jo gets her platform shoes well and truly soiled. Producer Barry Letts, who also co-wrote the script, hoped to stir up a little controversy with the blatant anti-pollution theme, only to encounter a wave of indifference. Having been hero-worshipped by Jo for three seasons, the Doctor was faced with some serious competition in the form of the hippie-ish Professor Cliff Jones, whose scientific curiosity was balanced by a commendable concern for the earth's ecology. Losing Jo to a more earthbound man of knowledge, 'So ... the fledgling flies the coop', the Doctor departed alone in Bessie, driving off into the night. (Manning later took *Doctor Who* to places undreamed of in Sydney Newman's philosophy when she posed naked with a Dalek for a men's magazine.)

Pertwee's *Doctor Who* episodes have their faults, including some irritatingly tinkly incidental music

and very variable supporting performances. But at the time his intellectual space swashbuckler reigned more or less supreme in television science fiction. The best ITV could manage by way of competition was *The Tomorrow People*, offering telepathic teens and intergalactic chicanery on a sub-*Who* budget (Nietzsche might well have approved of the Homo Superior concept). Pertwee's replacement, the little known ex-National Theatre actor Tom Baker, brought the show back to a level of success it hadn't enjoyed since the Daleks first appeared a decade earlier. Not so much eccentric as genially demented, Baker's Doctor made floppy hats, long curly hair and oversized scarves seem not only acceptable but stylish, his beaming grin and piercing eyes suggesting a mind so sharp that exposure to its full force

his beaming grin and piercing eyes suggesting a mind so sharp that exposure to its full force could be fatal

could be fatal. (Baker's prior credits included a memorable Gregori Rasputin in the extremely downbeat epic *Nicholas and Alexandra* 1971).

Baker had previously been offered a chance to play another of British science fiction's great icons, testing for the role of the monster in *Frankenstein: The True Story*. Having lost out to Universal contract actor Michael Sarrazin, Baker was compensated with a bit part as the ship's captain who transports creator and creature to their Arctic resting place. His other pre-*Who* science fiction credits include a role as a deformed freakshow owner in *The Mutations* (1973), a highly dubious piece of horror exploitation that mixed hybrid human-vegetable creatures with genuinely deformed carnival performers.

Produced by the departing Barry Letts, Tom Baker's debut appearance as the Doctor in *Robot* (1974) felt like a hangover from the Pertwee era, the newly regenerated Time Lord joining forces with UNIT to combat a group of megalomaniac scientists bent on provoking World War Three. Baker found a worthy companion in his quest to reshape *Doctor Who* in the form of producer Philip Hinchcliffe, who would guide the show for three outstanding seasons. Taking the Doctor away from present day earth and the Brigadier's clutches, Hinchcliffe inaugurated what is best described as the series' 'Gothic' era, eschewing straightforward sf adventure and space opera in favour of something a little darker. *Doctor Who* had played with horror-tinged ideas in the past, offering variations on the vampire myth in the 1967 Patrick Troughton favourite *The Tomb of the Cybermen* and the Pertwee space parasite story *The Claws of Axos* (1971). *The Daemons* explored the idea of rural village devil worship as comprehensively as the show's teatime fixture would allow, the followers of the horned, goatlegged alien Azal led by the Master's bogus vicar.

Hinchcliffe set out to invest every *Doctor Who* story with a sense of genuine menace, each triumph over alien aggression a hard-won victory with serious casualties. Baker's second story, *The Ark in Space*, sees the entire human race stored in suspended animation on an orbiting space station. Unfortunately, the nomadic Wirrn, a parasitical giant insect, has laid its eggs in one of the chambers. The infected human, his body gradually eaten away by green slime, is a disturbing sight, even if the effect is partly achieved with coloured plastic bubble-wrap.

Genesis of the Daleks (1975) takes the Doctor back to the creation of his arch enemies, which he has been instructed to prevent by the Time Lords. Opening with grim scenes of trench warfare, the story catches the Thal-Kaled conflict several

centuries after kick-off, both races now victim to radioactive poisoning. The Kaleds have given their chief scientist Davros a free rein in his attempts to preserve the mutated species they are destined to become. What they don't realise is that Davros, whose custom-built wheelchair looks strangely familiar, is demented enough to destroy both sides in his quest to develop a new, 'superior' race. Reasoning that the universe may actually be a better place with the Daleks – potentially antagonistic species uniting out of fear of this common enemy – the Doctor declines to destroy them.

Set in turn-of-the-century England, *Pyramids of Mars* reworks the standard living Mummy cliches, the walking dead transformed into thuggish robot slaves. Centuries earlier, the long extinct Osirian race dumped their worst criminal, the ultra-evil Sutekh, on earth, holding him in his purpose-built prison with a beam projected from the Red Planet. Mankind did gain the Egyptian civilisation as a by-product of this move but it still smacks of gross presumption. Sutekh's escape means the end of all life in the galaxy, his Destroyer tag well earned. Informing Sutekh that 'all sapient lifeforms are our kith', the Doctor's own non-human nature shows through in this story, his apparent indifference to the murder of one ally riling companion Sarah Jane Smith (Elizabeth Sladen). In *The Planet of*

Leela (Louise Jameson), K9 and the fourth Doctor, (Tom Baker).

Evil, a retelling of the Jekyll and Hyde story, the Doctor informs fellow scientist Professor Sorenson (Frederick Jaeger) that the price of their search for knowledge can be very high and should be met without complaint. Oddly, Sorenson survives his reckless tampering with the anti-matter universe, despite having caused the deaths of many colleagues. The Brain of Morbius (1976) is a shameless Frankenstein retread, disowned by original writer Terrance Dicks after the BBC rejected his monster-creates-man concept, a cunning reversal of the original. Despite being credited to 'Robin Bland' the end result is anything but, featuring decapitation, a vicious telepathic duel, strangulation, bloody gunshot wounds and a near burning at the stake. Set on the desolate planet Karn, where the discredited surgeon Solon (Philip Madoc) is up to something very sinister, Morbius is sf Hammer horror, complete with a storm-swept gothic castle, severed limbs, a strange religious cult and not one but two mad geniuses (not including the Doctor). In one memorable episode finale, Sarah Jane Smith is confronted by a headless monstrosity fitted out with a giant crustacean claw and a human forearm. Star Trek never went this far, no matter how much Captain Kirk got his uniform ripped.

Though strictly on the PG level, the violence in Doctor Who attracted the attention of Mary Whitehouse's ever-watchful National Viewers and Listeners' Association. The most notorious moment came in The Deadly Assassin, a rare solo venture for the Doctor set on his homeworld of Gallifrey. Having entered a surreally unpleasant virtual reality environment in pursuit of traitorous Time Lord elements, the Doctor is set upon by a mystery attacker, who tries to drown him. The episode ends with a lingering shot of Baker's head being held under water, his anguished face clearly visible, and the show's critics cried foul. (When producer Graham Williams took over Doctor Who from Philip Hinchcliffe, he was shown this clip and instructed never to attempt anything similar).

The controversy over Doctor Who didn't let up when Hinchcliffe introduced a new companion, the knife wielding retro-primitive Leela, whose Sevateem tribe were descended from an interplanetary survey team that strayed well off the beaten track. Portrayed by Louise Jameson, who'd previously auditioned for the role of Purdey in the less than sparkling The New Avengers, Leela might have lacked Sarah Jane Smith's enlightened feminist credentials, but wielded a mean hunting knife. Usually clad in a brief, if entirely decent leather outfit, Leela proved loyal, courageous and resourceful. Lacking the finely honed wit of

Emma Peel, her down to earth view of things provided a useful counterpoint to the Doctor's often bizarre flights of fancy. As sometimes happened with the show, stories intended for one companion were reworked with only token changes for their successor and Jameson found herself being lumbered with scream-and-run scripts written for Sarah Jane Smith. 'I had to fight tooth and nail to hold on to my principles.'

Her first three stories, all produced by Hinchcliffe, were full-strength Doctor Who, The Robots of Death (1977) coolly pointing out that an android masseur could quite unintentionally pull a human

a stormswept gothic castle, severed limbs, a strange religious cult and not one but two mad geniuses (not including the Doctor)

arm from its socket. Discovering to her near fatal cost that knives and poisoned thorns don't work against homicidal robots, Leela is forced to tailor her natural fighting instincts to the Doctor's more subtle battle plan. In The Talons of Weng-Chiang, the last Hinchcliffe story, Leela is pursued through the less desirable areas of Victorian London by a giant rat, a homicidal ventriloquist's doll and a fugitive future war criminal with terminal cellular decay. Throwing in elements of Sherlock Holmes, the Phantom of the Opera and Fu Manchu, Weng-Chiang remains impressive viewing, though the use of 'Yellow Peril' Chinese stereotypes is regrettable, not helped by the casting of an obviously caucasian actor in the lead oriental role. Rakishly attired in Victorian 'pageboy' costume, Leela requires a little more rescuing than usual but holds her own in the bravery stakes, leaping through a plate glass window at one point. Even in a later, watered down effort such as The Horror of Fang Rock, Leela is still given some choice lines, notably 'Obey the Doctor or I will cut your heart out.'

Leela debuted towards the tail end of Doctor Who's Gothic period, when the aliens were especially mean, the mortality rate high, and the death scenes unsanitised. Still faced with complaints from the Mary Whitehouse quarter, new producer Graham Williams was pressured to lighten the show's tone, allowing Tom Baker's whimsical sense of humour more or less full sway. Williams's first season in charge of Doctor Who featured some good stories, notably the borderline horrific The Image of the Fendahl and the fiscal satire The Sunmakers, but times had changed.

The camp costumes of Terry Nation's Blake's 7 (1978) belied the series' cynical overtones. The show's original cast, from left to right: Vila Restal (Michael Keating), Cally (Jan Chappell), Roj Blake (Gareth Thomas), Jenna Stannis (Sally Knyvette), Kerr Avon (Paul Darrow) and Olag Gan (David Jackson).

BLAKE'S 7: 'IT WAS A GREAT ADVENTURE'

While the Doctor continued his intergalactic struggles against evil, *Who* veteran Terry Nation explored new, earthbound dystopian visions with the more low key BBC series *Survivors* (1975-77), which followed the usual disparate group after a near apocalyptic plague wipes out most of the civilised world. Against a backdrop of disease and anarchy, one small band, led by Abby Grant (Carolyn Seymour), attempts to rebuild some form of civilisation, more or less from scratch. Aside from its female lead, still a rarity in sf 25 years later, one of show's strongest points was its emphasis on how everyday resources largely taken for granted would suddenly become very precious, the object of violent conflict. One character, still clinging to her religious faith in the face of Old Testament-style destruction, sacrifices some of her most prized dresses to make new clothes for a priest (who subsequently gets killed). If nothing else, *Survivors* continued the BBC's occasional post-nuclear wasteland genre first seen in Peter Watkins's harder-edged *The War Game*.

The low budget docudrama *Threads* (1983) came closer to Watkins's original concept, depicting a nuclear attack on Sheffield and its nightmare aftermath in harrowing graphic detail. As a vast mushroom cloud appears on the horizon, a woman drops her ice cream cone into the spreading puddle of her urine. The entire city centre vaporises approximately 20 seconds later. After nuclear winter sets in, the radiation-sick survivors revert to a near feudal society. Made at a time when nuclear war seemed a distinct possibility, *Threads* concludes with the screams of a young woman as she gives birth to a mutant baby, a finale all the more chilling for the 'child' remaining unseen.

Terry Nation's biggest post-*Doctor Who* success was the less doomladen space opera *Blake's 7*, the saga of a small band of intergalactic rebels taking on the might of the tyrannical Terran Federation in a mysterious purloined spacecraft. Once rather tastelessly described as 'Star Trek for the educationally sub-normal', *Blake's 7* has tended to be dismissed as something of a running joke even by diehard science fiction fans. The later episodes, made without most of the original cast, are certainly underwhelming, with cheap sets, shaky effects, discard space costumes, ham acting and *Blue Peter*-style hardware. At the start, however, *Blake's 7* had a narrative strength and sense of integrity that the cut-cost production values couldn't undermine. First broadcast in January 1978, when *Stars Wars* was wiping the floor with all film rivals, the series opens on a less than idyllic Earth, where model citizen Roj Blake (Gareth Thomas) discovers that he was once a leading freedom fighter, captured and brainwashed by the state to serve as a meek political stooge.

The tone is unrelentingly downbeat and cynical, Blake framed by his former puppet masters with a child abuse charge when his memory begins to return. Largely recruited on board a prison ship, Blake's somewhat unwilling band of outlaws consists of five humans, one telepathic alien and one supercomputer, the tensions within the group suggesting that moral crusades against vastly overwhelming forces are not everyone's idea of a good time. The first season of *Blake's 7* was firmly character driven, the actors hampered only a little by instantly dated hairstyles and less than flattering wardrobes. The performances tended towards the stiff at times, Gareth Thomas evidently convinced that the material required a dead straight Serious Actor approach to work. Blake's earnest idealism contrasted with the sneering cynicism of suave genius computer hacker Kerr Avon (Paul Darrow), with embittered but humane smuggler Jenna Stannis (Sally Knyvette) acting as a reluctant, if carefully made-up mediator. Despite the large number of shootouts with the black-clad Federation stormtroopers, the series didn't always score so well in the action stakes. A confusingly staged and edited fight scene in the third episode, *Cygnus Alpha*, makes a bewildering number of jumps from videotape to film and back, suggesting some hurried re-shoots. Depicted as a largely faceless entity for the first few episodes, the Federation came to be embodied in *Blake's 7*'s two chief villains. Commander Travis was a fairly conventional bad guy, a ruthless, black-clad thug with a scary moulded eyepatch and a laser gun concealed in his artificial left hand. The crop-headed, lethally ambitious Servalan (Jacqueline Pearce) seemed a little more offbeat, a coolly poised young woman with a strong dose of charisma and no scruples whatsoever. The political element in the show touched on some intriguing grey areas at times, Blake's not-so-merry band of freedom fighters engaged in acts verging on terrorism.

At its peak, *Blake's 7* attracted an extremely healthy ten million viewers, including a few who would go on to make their own mark in science fiction. Justina Robson, author of the acclaimed sf novel *Silver*

Screen (1999), regards *Blake's 7* as one of her key television influences during childhood: 'It was the most fantastic thing I'd ever seen. I completely lived for it and adored it…'. A recent repeat of the first season dissipated any lingering nostalgic haze around the show, cruelly revealing its shortcomings, yet Robson remains impressed by the underlying ideas: 'It was a great adventure.'

Just how long *Blake's 7* could have lasted with its original crew on board will remain a cult science fiction mystery. Lured away by the call of the Royal

Blake's somewhat unwilling band of helpers consists of five humans, one telepathic alien and one super-computer

Shakespeare Company, Gareth Thomas quit the show after two seasons, along with Sally Knyvette. David Jackson, a useful presence as the not always so gentle giant Gan, left a few episodes earlier after the character was killed off. The vacant lead slot fell to Avon, whose line in sarcastic putdowns soon became the show's main selling point. Paul Darrow felt that Avon was originally conceived as a variation on the Mr Spock-style sidekick and decided to take the character in a different direction, encouraged by Terry Nation. Adopting the leadership mantle with relative ease, Avon never really overcame the brutal fact that he was fielding a second division crew. By the time the show reached its fourth season, both the storylines and costumes were showing signs of creative exhaustion, typified by the shabby reuse of a monster outfit from the 1972 *Doctor Who* story *The Sea Devils*. The final episode, *Blake*, reintroduced the original leader,

The villains of *Blake's 7* – Federation official Servalan (Jacqueline Pearce) and the psychopathic Travis (Brian Croucher) – in the 1979 episode *Weapon*.

Halo Jones: Alan Moore's ordinary young woman who quits Earth in search of adventure.

only for Avon to bloodily gun him down just before the Federation launches an all-out massacre. After years confined to BBC Video reissues, a handful of the original Mark II cast recently reunited for a pair of disappointing Radio 4 dramas, scripted by *Doctor Who* veteran Barry Letts.

1977 proved a significant year in the history of British-produced science fiction. With *Doctor Who* still going strong on the television and the made-in-England *Star Wars* rewriting the movie rulebook, sf comics came up to strength with an injection of new blood. While Frank Hampson's *Dan Dare* had blazed the trail back in the 1950s, offering the green-skinned flying Mekon and ever-handy translator wig, 2000 AD brought sf graphic art bang up to date.

'the thing that authority disliked about it was that it was so anti-authoritarian

Dominated by the infamous, and soon well-nigh legendary *Judge Dredd*, 2000 AD had both guts and wit, offering a subversive British reworking of the American comicbook superhero genre. Twenty three years on from the first issue, 2000 AD is still regarded

by many as the premiere British science fiction comic, weekly or otherwise.

2000 AD was intended as a cleaned-up successor to the controversial *Action* comic, described by current editor David Bishop as 'the comic that dripped blood from every page'. More than living up to its name, *Action* contained a certain amount of science fiction-related fantasy, notably *Death Game 1999*, an extra-brutal motorbike version (or rip off) of *Rollerball*, where the contestants were regularly crushed, flattened, amputated and pulped by their opponents' vehicles in loving graphic detail. Editor Pat Mills, who later co-launched 2000 AD, continually pressed the writers and artists for stronger violence, his eye on the comic's ever-rising circulation. Occasionally granted the premiere front cover slot, *Death Game 1999* made few pretensions to deep philosophical musings: 'They call it a sport ... It's more like plain murder!'

Nevertheless, the premise behind the innocuously named 'Spinball' tournament offered a fair dose of cynical social comment. The teams are made up of hardened convicts who can supposedly win commuted sentences if their side does well. Those who get crunched in the process are no great loss to society and the game is rigged to prevent any players from actually earning parole (a classic case of killing two birds with one stone). The conscience and the bloodlust of the spectators are appeased at the same time, audiences secure in the knowledge that the players literally dying to entertain them are both paying their debt to society and earning their freedom. Based, like most of the *Action* strips, on a high profile movie its target readership was too young to see legally, this bloody biker mayhem proved a hit with the kids but quickly incurred establishment wrath. Worried parents also voiced concern about strips such as *Hookjaw*, where a particularly aggressive shark regularly bit people in half, and *Look Out For Lefty*, a no holds barred chronicle of violence in the football terraces. While 2000 AD would largely confine itself to the world of fantasy, its characters wielding implausibly high-tech firepower in futuristic settings, *Action* preferred much more realistic, contemporary backdrops. With real-life football violence seen as a serious social problem, comic strip hooliganism was attacked for gross irresponsibility. One particular image, a bottle thrown onto a football pitch, was held up as a virtual incitement to riot. Current affairs programmes such as the BBC's *Nationwide* ran concerned reports and questions were asked in Parliament.

David Bishop feels that the strong violence in *Action* was only the most obvious source of contention: 'The thing that authority disliked about it was that it was so anti-authoritarian. Most of the stories were basically on the side of the disenfranchised.' The final straw came in the shape of Kids Rule OK, described by Bishop as 'a bit like The Lord of the Flies, but with the violence turned up to eleven' (a reference to This Is Spinal Tap's legendary amplifier). Set in a future society where all law and order has broken down, Kids offered a vision of abandoned, alienated youth who survive by forming gangs and taking on all comers. One cover showed a long-haired adolescent looming menacingly over a prone adult, a discarded policeman's helmet lying on the waste ground nearby.

Appearing at a time when the nihilist punk rock movement was making headlines, the trend-setting Sex Pistols shocking the nation by swearing on early evening regional television, this junior league Clockwork Orange went down with the establishment like a bucket of cold vomit. David Bishop's own attitude to the violence in 2000 AD suggests that some hard lessons were learned: 'You do have to be careful about the way that you present violence... There's a degree of responsibility. You have to be aware that there are young readers reading this material.' Firmly pinned down as an irresponsible, if not actively corrupting influence, Action disappeared from the news stands in October 1976, to be re-launched in December with its violence toned down and its subversion cut out. The comic struggled on for another year in this watered-down form, then bit the dust.

Filling the gaping, gore-filled void left by Action's demise, 2000 AD had a difficult brief, required to placate lingering parental hostility without disappointing the kids in the violence stakes. Hot rumours circulating around the as-yet unseen films Star Wars and Close Encounters of the Third Kind suggested that science fiction could be the next big thing. If nothing else, Close Encounters came from the same director as the megahit Jaws (1975), whose marauding great white shark had provided some useful inspiration for Action. Launched in February 1977, when the punk 'era' was still going strong, the comic's creators expressed the same Do It Yourself attitude, a sense of rules being rewritten. As David Bishop explains: 'It used young British artists [many still in their teens]... it jumped up and down on the toes of the established boy's adventure comic marketplace.' Pilfering ideas and images from popular television and cinema, much as Action had done, 2000 AD reworked them comic book style, 'gobbing in the face of tradition... like dropping a nuclear bomb in an old lady's tea party'. Ex-Action editor Pat Mills aimed to create 'a twisted sci-fi vision of contemporary pop culture'. Editorial responsibilities were supposedly handled by 'Tharg', a green alien with telepathic powers who bossed around his subservient droids. Whatever his intergalactic wisdom, Tharg's choice of free gifts would probably underwhelm even the youngest contemporary readers (aged seven and up). Issue one of 2000 AD came with

'a twisted sci-fi vision of contemporary pop culture'

a 'Space Spinner', a plastic frisbee-style disc now worth around £30 to diehard collectors. Tharg's face stared out from the middle of the disc, inviting potential customers to 'Enjoy Your Space Spinner Earthlet!', a term some might regard as a little patronising.

In keeping with the classic British science fiction tradition, 2000 AD offers a largely dystopian worldview, as Bishop readily admits. 'It's quite pessimistic. I think almost every story we've ever published has been basically predicting a bad future.' Tempering the gloom with a strong dose of black humour, the comic has never pandered to readers in search of a reassuring, feelgood story. 'It's saying essentially the world's getting worse, things are going downhill.' While this viewpoint is not unknown to American comic strips, the Land of the Free prefers to accentuate the positive. 'An awful lot of American comics are basically optimistic... if somebody has incredible powers, like Superman, they will use them for good, they will go round saving their fellow man, stopping crime and generally being nice guys... that almost never happens in 2000 AD.'

Early 2000 AD strips included the Jurassic Park prototype Flesh, where twenty-third century man travels back in time to the prehistoric age to hunt dinosaurs, reducing the once terrible lizards to supermarket fodder. Maybe not as plausible as the crashing meteor theory of dinosaur extinction, but a little more exciting. Looking to American popular culture for some ready-made action genres to subvert, 2000 AD offered Harlem Heroes, a British spin on blaxploitation, and the hit Mach 1, inspired by The Six Million Dollar Man television series. The latter strip was launched with a free gift of 'biotronic' stickers, designed to be placed on readers' arms for that sinister, spookily realistic cyborg effect. (According to David Bishop, the stickers tended to cause skin rashes). While the adventures of special agent Colonel Steve Austin were unrelentingly upbeat,

Mach 1 hero John Probe was depicted as the pawn of a shady government operative, a manipulated, tragic loner. Austin's bionic powers, contained in his legs, right arm and left eye, are shown as unconditionally positive forces for good. Probe's cybernetically altered body is a covert weapon serving the dubious interests of the state. As with so many *Action* and *2000 AD* strips, the underlying message stayed cynical: 'Authority is bad'. Needless to say, the readers lapped it up. *Invasion* offered a scary vision of near-future Britain where top 1970s newsreader Angela Rippon has to announce a nuclear attack on the Midlands and an implausibly mustachioed King Charles III is forced to escape to Canada (the invaders were originally going to be the Russians before the editors lost their nerve and switched to safer aliens).

Standing out like a beacon of righteousness amid the gleeful carnage stood *Dan Dare, Pilot of the Future*, formerly of *The Eagle*. Founding *2000 AD* editor Pat Mills was not keen on using the strip but felt that the character might be useful for public relations, marketing and instant reader recognition. Realising that the original *Dan Dare* artwork would look hopelessly at odds with the overall style, Mills had the character redrawn to resemble what David Bishop describes as a David Bowie lookalike from the latter's 'Aladdin Sane' era, lacking the distinctive square jaw. Even with a touch of the original Space Oddity, Dan Dare was out of place, a noble relic from another era.

Other *2000 AD* strips included the Mars-set *ABC Warriors*, a tale of combat robots, *Ant Wars*, a Brazilian saga of man versus giant ant, *Johnny Alpha, Strontium Dog, Rogue Trooper* and *Rojaws. Strontium Dog*, the saga of a mutant bounty hunter, started life in the *2000 AD* spinoff comic *Starlord*, before switching to the

Although Judge Dredd is the good guy, he's also the fascist cop of the future

mother ship. Amid the carnage highlights, more discerning readers could pick out a racism allegory, *Dog*'s fellow mutants herded up and forced to live in the horrendous ghetto that is Milton Keynes. A genetically modified warrior from 200 years into the future, *Rogue Trooper* keeps his slaughtered comrades 'alive' by storing their memories on the bio chips he carries with him. If he gets lonely out in the field, his intelligent, self-operating rifle has a good line in conversation. *Rojaws*, a garbage-eating, cigar smoking android with a penchant for witty one-liners, later signed on with the ABC Warriors, serving as a

Ro-Buster. More recent strips include *Nicolai Dante*, set a mere 700 years in the future, and *Tsar Wars*, a pun so terrible it's rather fine. Recently celebrating its third birthday, the *Nicolai Dante* strip is *2000 AD*'s big hit of the late 1990s, its cocky swashbuckling protagonist proving that there is life in the anti-hero yet. In the political satire department, *Glimmer Rats* depicts the future European Union as a fascist trade federation state, where political dissenters and other assorted undesirables are dispatched to a parallel dimension to combat an unbeatable alien foe. *Pussyfoot Five* features a covert team of operatives employed by the Vatican in outer space, aggressively quelling anti-Catholic rebellion in all corners of the universe.

Though a notch down from the perceived excesses of *Action*, *2000 AD* was still fairly brutal at the beginning. David Bishop feels there was often little to distinguish the new comic from its predecessor in terms of gore quotient: 'It was really ultraviolent in the early days'. One particular strip intended for the first issue proved so problematic that its introduction was delayed. Glimpsed only as a preview in *2000 AD* number one, *Judge Dredd* didn't make his official debut until issue two. Still the comic's flagship character, *Dredd*'s enduring appeal sums up the whole *2000 AD* ethos, as Bishop explains: 'You tend to find in British comics it's about anti-heroes, not heroes. Although Judge Dredd is the good guy, he's also a fascist cop of the future, and he will punish you for almost any crime imaginable …that's something British readers can relate to'.

Drawing inspiration from Clint Eastwood's *Dirty Harry* series, *Dredd* took the figure of the maverick loner cop to new extremes, the masked lawman gunning down passers by for shouting. Conceived as a blackly humorous story centring on a taciturn near future supercop, *Dredd*'s darker side caused anxiety with the *2000 AD* management, who wanted a more conventionally heroic figure in the best American style. All too aware of *Action*'s problems, the editors found it difficult to establish the right tone for the strip. John Wagner, still the main writer for Dredd, placed the Judge firmly in the anti-hero camp, creating a character and a world that others regarded as too bleak and dystopian. Bishop feels that British readers would have rejected a clean cut, unconditionally benevolent Judge Dredd out of hand: 'Superheroes have never worked in British comics. People have tried and failed many times.' Bishop is presumably referring to the post *Dan Dare* era, given that *The Eagle*'s Pilot of the Future drew well over a million weekly readers before the comic's demise in 1969 (shortly before the Apollo moon landing, in fact). Certainly, Marvel Comics' 1970s attempt to create a US-style hero with *Captain Britain* met with only qualified success. Promoted as 'All New! All British!', this Union Jack-adorned Adonis, with saucy face mask and wavy blonde hair, resembled nothing so much as a poster boy for the British National Party. Not even a guest appearance from a badly drawn H.M. the Queen could save the comic (though the character himself subsequently prospered as part of Marvel's *X-Men* franchise). Finding an acceptable level of violence for Dredd proved less taxing. Then working predominantly in black and white, with only the cover art in colour, the 2000 AD staff eventually decided that gouts of blood were okay as long as they were carefully placed.

Judge Dredd is set in the aftermath of the 2070 atomic war, which reduced middle America to a radioactive wasteland, dubbed 'The Cursed Earth'. The not-so-good Judge operates in Megacity 1, basically a conglomeration of North America's Eastern Seaboard, where radiation has spawned a high level of mutation among the inhabitants. Rating *Dredd* as his personal favourite, Bishop argues that the vast Megacity is the strip's real character, Judge Dredd himself remaining obstinately two dimensional. Notoriously intolerant of even minor offenders, Dredd will turn his terrible, often fatal wrath on drivers with faulty exhausts and outdoor smokers, dismissing all protest with the proclamation 'I am the Law!' The archetypal all-in-one judge, jury and executioner, Dredd shoots the hands off litterbugs rather than waste valuable state resources on offender reconditioning programmes.

Somewhat alarmingly, David Bishop feels that real life is getting closer to the Dredd universe every day: 'It's the world that's coming true around us.' Dredd's oft-used weapon of choice, the Lawgiver handgun, offers a selection of six different kinds of bullet. Ricochet bullets bounce off and around innumerable surfaces until the desired target is hit, preferably right between the eyes (the 1987 American sf hit *Robocop* paid graphic 'homage' to these ingenious projectiles). The less tricksy armour-piercing bullets are equally effective on walls and robot plating. Heat-seeking bullets lock on to and track a given heat signature, travelling around corners where necessary. Dredd's high explosive bullets render even the most aggressive transgressor into easily-disposed-of raw meaty chunks. The character's use of slang language, private and exclusive, is similarly appealing to the largely male teenage readership.

Judge Dredd's successful launch didn't end the strip's controversy by any means. One proposed story

featured Dredd trying a group of prisoners, whom he casually electrocutes one by one as the inevitable 'guilty' verdict is reached. The editors rejected the idea out of hand and it never even made the preliminary drawing stage. Despite this vetting process, several *Dredd* stories did fall foul of the authorities, though not entirely for reasons of graphic violence. One memorable episode featured the bloody

'I am the Law!'

burger franchise war, where Ronald McDonald and the Burger King beat each other to a pulp in the name of fast food supremacy. This mischievous, not to say downright malicious use of copyrighted characters owned by vast American corporations drew serious legal trouble. As David Bishop puts it: 'they just got sued to high heaven'. Dredd's tangle with a not-so-Jolly Green Giant provoked similar outrage, though the dispute was settled a little more amicably. Without a leg to stand on, green or otherwise, 2000 AD agreed to print a half page 'retraction' strip where the real Jolly Green Giant turns up to present Dredd with a tin of sweetcorn, advising the Judge to keep a sharp look out for the evil imposter giant.

After years of strong rumours and false starts, *Judge Dredd* finally made it to the big screen in 1995 in the form of ageing action man Sylvester Stallone. David Bishop describes the transition as 'a very painful experience... a bit like watching a very slow car accident'. The film rights had been optioned back in the early 1980s, long before Bishop took over as editor, the deal ceding all creative control to the movie makers. While a big American name made the project viable with the Hollywood studios, casting the *Rocky* star compromised the film in terms of fidelity to the original comic strip. Unwilling to obscure his distinctive, money-making visage, Stallone got rid of the famous Dredd helmet at the first opportunity, instantly alienating the 2000 AD fans most likely to support the movie. Bishop now feels that any 1990s *Dredd* film project was probably ill-fated from the start, beaten to

Judge Dredd lays down the law – as only he can.

THE STREET GANGS HAVE LOST THEIR **FEAR** OF US. IT'S TIME WE GAVE IT **BACK** TO THEM...

LET'S SHOW THEM **ONE** JUDGE IS WORTH A **HUNDRED** PUNKS – COSMIC OR OTHERWISE !

Sylvester Stallone starred as Judge Dredd (1995) in Danny Cannon's controversial film based on the 2000AD character.

the punch by *Robocop*, which located its similarly masked, armour-plated law enforcer hero in a crumbling, dystopian American city (Detroit), the gory action complemented by jet black humour and satirical commercial breaks. Unwilling to retread the same ground, the *Judge Dredd* makers were left with very few options. As directed by Danny Cannon, self-proclaimed Messiah of the British film industry, *Judge Dredd* the Movie is a competently assembled but utterly unmemorable sf romp, unsuccessfully pitched at a mass American audience who had never heard of the main character. Even those familiar with 2000 AD tended to feel that their culture was being sent up, hardly the best way to fete goodwill. Ironically, Cannon had been a longtime fan of 2000 AD, once writing in to the comic to suggest *Bladerunner* star Harrison Ford as the ideal Dredd. Cannon announced that he wanted the film to look like 'Ben Hur meets *Star Wars*', an sf gladiatorial epic far removed from the original strip. For all his questionable casting, Stallone at least tried to retain some of the true Dredd feel. When Gianni Versace produced a Judge costume that resembled, in Bishop's words, a 'limpwristed excuse for a police outfit', the star rejected it out of hand. Stallone later trashed both the film and the director, claiming to

have known from the start that the whole enterprise was doomed. 2000 AD learned from the experience, at least, forming Fleetway Films and Television to retain full involvement in any future deals. At the time of writing, the Showtime cable network has an option on the *Strontium Dog* character.

2000 AD maintains a strong sense of continuity with the past. Founding editor Pat Mills now works for the comic as a writer, one of the scattered freelance team largely responsible for the content of each issue. David Bishop feels 2000 AD has survived by staying true to the original formula of action adventure, contemporary satire and future speculation: 'Unlike *Doctor Who* or *Blake's 7*, which always ended up being slightly kitsch and campy, and lapsed into self-parody all too often, 2000 AD has actually played it pretty straight over the years.' The readership for the comic starts around the age of ten, peaks at fifteen, then steadily declines until a second peak at the thirty mark, the more mature following almost certainly made up of fans who got hooked back in 1977. (Bishop regards 2000 AD as 'a passage of male adolescence'). A number of the predictions first mooted on its pages have come to pass, more or less: cigarette smokers consigned to special rooms; guns equipped with a palm reader to ensure legitimate owner identification. Celebrity fans include pop groups ranging in style and vintage from Madness, The Human League and The Cure to The Prodigy and Anthrax. References are scattered through their songs. Another measure of 2000 AD's international standing is *Judge Dredd*'s repeated teaming with Batman – a different kind of iconic vigilante. For 2000 AD's 21st anniversary issue, the comic reworked some of its early characters in contemporary form. *Mach 1*, for example, became *Blair 1*, prime minister Tony Blair transformed into a super-powered politician equipped with a computerised brain for easy spin-doctoring (some might say he hardly needed the enhancement).

The rapidly dating title of the comic remains a source of contention, its strong brand-name status undermined by impending obsolescence. Back in 1977, the year 2000 seemed a reasonably distant prospect and, in truth, no-one expected 2000 AD to last so long. A futuristic comic dated in the ever-receding past may raise problems, yet it's hard to imagine the likes of *Dredd* being put out to pasture. As the saying goes, there's life in the old judge yet. Working to the motto: 'Reality is the only Alternative', 2000 AD is certainly not afraid to send up its most famous character's ultra-macho image, the cover of Issue 1194 featuring Judge Dredd on the lavatory, trousers around ankles but helmet safely in place. Sylvester Stallone take note.

WHO WATCHES THE WATCHMEN?

In addition to its two decades of thought-provoking mayhem, 2000 AD has provided a useful vehicle for a number of science fiction writers who moved on to bigger, if not necessarily better, venues. Grant Morrison honed his hallucinogenic, conspiratorial style with stories for 2000 AD before being co-opted by American comics. The rise of the graphic novel saw the emergence of Alan Moore, acclaimed author of *V for Vendetta* and *Watchmen*, a regular contributor to both 2000 AD and *Doctor Who Weekly* from 1980 onwards. Rated by David Bishop as 'one of the most warped and fertile imaginations in Britain', Moore spent most of his 2000 AD phase working on stories for the one-off slots *Tharg's Future Shocks* and *Time Twisters*. His greatest hit for the comic is generally agreed to be *The Ballad of Halo Jones*, the future-set allegorical story of an ordinary young woman who quits the earth in search of galactic adventures. Far from being mere well-endowed eye candy for the boys, Jones is a fully drawn character, devoid of special powers or unlimited wealth, who decides that

there must be more to life than 'The Hoop', her home territory just outside Manhattan.

Set in 1997, *V for Vendetta* (1982-89), drawn by David Lloyd, depicts a post-nuclear British society where the masses have given in to rule by fascist tyranny and the few remaining dissenters are herded into quarantine zones or concentration camps. The central character, V, spent his own period of internment honing his deadly skills, emerging to serve as a hate-filled vigilante undercover agent.

'one of the most warped and fertile minds in Britain'

Dressed in a Guy Fawkes costume, complete with sinister grinning mask, V is contemptuous of both the abusers and the abused, feeling that the latter are complicit in their own oppression, meekly submitting to media control. Like the original Fawkes, he aims to bring down the totalitarian order, using the all-pervasive media as his chief weapon.

Moore consolidated his reputation with *Watchmen* (1986-87), drawn by fellow 2000 AD and *Doctor Who Weekly* veteran Dave Gibbons. Revisionist, ironic, cynical, satirical and heavily self-referential, this reworking of the entire comic book superhero tradition operates on the genre's home territory, the United States of America. The series was originally written for the giant US publisher DC Comics, home of Superman and Batman, which revived its flagging circulation in the mid 1980s by initiating a boom in more adult-oriented material that included Batman's gothic comeback in Frank Miller's *The Dark Knight Returns*. Moore later penned the acclaimed Batman tale *The Killing Joke* (1988), illustrated by Brian Bolland, which largely relegates the Caped Crusader to a supporting role in favour of his old arch enemy The Joker. DC Comics first published *Watchmen* in twelve monthly instalments, from October 1986 to September 1987, before the entire series was reissued in its current 'upmarket' graphic novel form.

Eschewing the futuristic settings of many sf comic strips, *Watchmen* takes place in the then very recent past, 1985, in a parallel America, specifically New York, favoured playground of the costumed crimefighter. Richard Nixon is still president,

Watchmen. The low-key covers of the original, 12-part series made only indirect references to the stories within.

having amended the US Constitution to gain a fifth term in office, and vigilante superheroes have been around for decades, co-opted by politics and big business to exploit their mass appeal. No longer popular with either the public or the regular police force, the vigilantes have been largely outlawed since 1977, only a select few still permitted to operate. These super 'heroes' are not the most prepossessing or enlightened bunch. The Comedian, whose mysterious death sets the story in motion, is an ultra-right-wing patriot, whose public endorsement of the American Dream is tinged with inner cynicism. Dollar Bill, one of the earlier generation of masked heroes, was sponsored by a large American bank, which dictated the impractical crime-fighting costume that eventually got him killed while thwarting a robbery. Like the Comedian, Doctor Manhattan, a blue skinned, bald headed titan, is one of the few superheroes still allowed to work with government approval. In the best Nietzschean *ubermensch* tradition, Manhattan is a genuinely all-powerful superbeing, accidentally created by the Americans during nuclear experimentation. Employed by Nixon to win the Vietnam War, Manhattan's virtual omnipotence has rendered the Soviet Union effectively impotent, the USSR edging towards launching a pre-emptive nuclear strike as a last gesture of defiance.

In the best Batman tradition, most of the other characters display a conspicuous lack of superpowers, relying instead on physical fitness and state of the art gadgetry. Reluctantly brought out of forced retirement by the Comedian's death, Nite Owl and the Silk Spectre are reassuringly ordinary beneath the costumes, ageing and a little overweight in the former's case. The masked vigilante Rorschach is a card-carrying psychotic who continues to fight

depicting the superhero costume as a sexual fetish object

crime in defiance of the superhero ban. Clad largely in scruffy 'civilian' clothes, Rorschach inhabits a squalid apartment and grosses out his fellow avengers with his vulgar eating habits and potent body odour. Even the angst-ridden Spiderman washes regularly. Having intended Rorschach to illustrate the depressing, if logical consequences of being a rogue crime fighter with a damaged past, Moore felt a little disconcerted at the character's huge, non-ironic popularity. Offering some pointed satirical digs at the print media, *Watchmen* delves into areas most comic strips prefer to leave as an undisturbed subtext, depicting the superhero

costume as a sexual fetish object. One of Nite Owl's biggest fans is a leather-clad dominatrix, 'The Twilight Lady', he once arrested on vice charges.

Given its meticulously detailed downbeat tone, *Watchmen* concludes on a surprisingly sort of-optimistic note. The superpowers are united, and nuclear warfare averted, through the arrival of an alien menace that wipes out part of Manhattan. In fact, the extraterrestrial aggressor is an ingenious fake concocted by Adrian Veidt, formerly known as the costumed crime fighter Ozymandias. Reasoning that mankind's internal dissensions can only be overcome by mutual fear of an external threat, Veidt kidnapped comic book writers and artists to devise the perfect hideous alien. The destruction in Manhattan, presumably a sly reference to Veidt's former colleague, is surely a small price to pay for global harmony.

An instant bestseller, *Watchmen* remains a landmark in the graphic novel genre, Alan Moore's dark and complex narrative style influencing subsequent works such as Neil Gaiman's highly acclaimed *Sandman* series, also published by DC Comics. The comic also attracted considerable interest as potential film material, director Terry Gilliam, creator of the baroque science fiction satire *Brazil* (1985), buying up the rights, only to admit defeat. To date, there's been no word from Sylvester Stallone.

'PERHAPS YOU'RE NOT SO DIFFERENT...'

While contemporary cinema is well-supplied with science fiction releases — mostly of the action-adventure variety — during the pre *Star Wars* 1970s, there was comparatively little on offer. British sf barely existed as a movie genre, though the handful of films that did emerge were usually both thoughtful and intriguing.

Nicolas Roeg's *The Man Who Fell to Earth* (1976) depicts the flipside to the sterile, yet ultimately optimistic vision of 2001, with David Bowie's fragile, vulnerable alien visitor unable to save himself, let alone ignorant, aggressive humanity. Very loosely based on a novel by American writer Walter Tevis (best known for *The Hustler*), *The Man Who Fell to Earth* was a British-financed production filmed on location in America, largely New Mexico, an unusual reversal of the Hollywood norm. A hairless, cat's-eyed alien humanoid journeys to Earth, disguised as a passable, if androgynous native human. His mission – apparently – is to save his home world from drought (his first action is to head for a lake to take a long drink of water). This mysterious visitor, soon under covert surveillance from the CIA, assumes the identity of

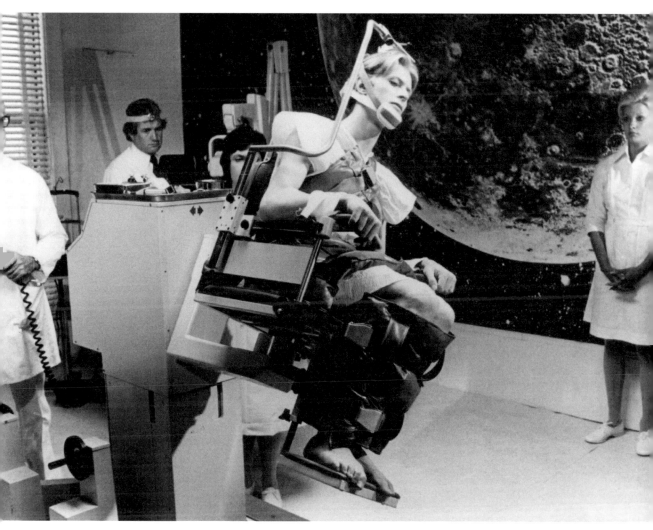

English electronics entrepreneur Thomas Jerome Newton (any relation to Isaac?), rapidly amassing a vast fortune through a series of industry-shaking patents. His vast company, World Enterprises, seems certain to wipe out much of American big business, which naturally seals his doom.

Newton's first contact with humanity is a taste of things to come, an aged pawnbroker offering him an insultingly low sum for his fake wedding ring (one of many). Despite finding a near kindred spirit in the touchingly awkward form of lonely hotel maid Mary Lou (Candy Clark), this visitor stands no chance of adapting to life on earth. In a neat reversal of the usual alien body snatchers theme, Newton has his identity taken away by the humans, both by accident and design, the alien visitor corrupted by sex, booze, television and the empty trappings of unspendable wealth. Unfolding in Roeg's usual fragmented, hallucinatory visual style, The Man Who Fell to Earth is

often more stimulating than coherent, Newton's apparent psychic time-travelling ability accounting for some, but by no means all of the spacial-temporal shifts. Displaying a penchant for lingering shots of nubile young women's exposed bodies, whether writhing in sexual ecstasy or pissing themselves with fright, Roeg does better with less voyeuristic material. Glimpsed in flashback, Newton's alien homeworld is an arid wasteland, his wife and children first seen waving him off on his journey, then crawling on the barren ground as they slowly die of thirst. Recruited by Newton, patents lawyer Oliver Farnsworth (Buck Henry) is offered a complete upgrade of his stereo system courtesy of World Enterprises, at cost price, naturally. 'Perhaps you're not so different', Farnsworth muses. As the title suggests, Newton's dream of beating corporate America at its own game is brought down to earth with a violent bump. Like Icarus before him, Newton

David Bowie as Thomas Jerome Newton – a water-seeking alien in Nicolas Roeg's dark fantasy The Man Who Fell To Earth (1976).

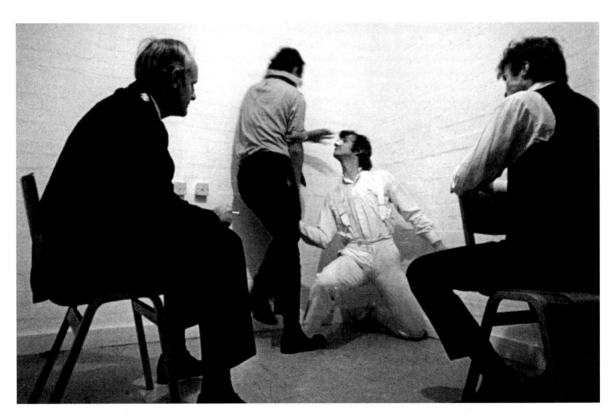

Murderer and rapist Alex (Malcolm McDowell) proves unco-operative in Stanley Kubrick's disturbing A Clockwork Orange (1971).

falls from grace with the elements and drowns, though in alcohol rather than salt water. Recalling Howard Hughes, another brilliant young inventor who ended up as a stunted, self-pitying recluse, Newton is also reminiscent of David Bowie's own musical persona, ending the film as a substance-abusing pop star.

The image of the sf Messiah redeemer as a lonely, rejected outsider and victim is also central to Ken Russell's rock musical *Tommy* (1975), where man must fuse with (pin)ball machine to become a functioning, if non-productive whole. Inspired by The Who's groundbreaking concept album, impressive, bombastic and pretentious by turns, the film version plays on various science fiction riffs with more visual aplomb than conceptual thought. Rendered deaf, dumb and blind by the childhood trauma of witnessing his father's murder, young Tommy (Roger Daltrey), is taken on a tour of various potential cures, including a session with the drug-peddling Acid Queen (Tina Turner). Encased inside a device that resembles a futuristic combination suit of armour and iron maiden, Tommy is pierced not with spikes but syringes, emerging unscathed but still insensate. Throwing in such additional sf images as a brain-scanning machine attached to Tommy's head and a rock star Frankenstein monster, Russell's

all-out assault on the senses has no particular message, other than the perils of disappointing the fickle paying public. Unhappy with *Tommy's* message of enlightenment through sensory depriva-tion and pinball, his previously devoted followers turn violently nasty, their discontent forcibly expressed in Pete Townshend's lyrics: 'We forsake you/Gonna rape you/Let's forget you better still'. Probably not as partial to the original album as the film's pressbook claimed, Russell appears to have mixed feelings about *Tommy* the movie, which provided a useful box-office boost for his career but lacks the sense of committed passion that drives his best work.

The climactic scene of *Tommy's* rebellious disci-ples running riot echoes the delinquent youth of Anthony Burgess's 1962 novel *A Clockwork Orange*, brought to the screen by Stanley Kubrick a decade later. Fairly or not, the Kubrick film has largely eclipsed its literary inspiration, Penguin Books' much reprinted paperback edition of the Burgess original not appearing until the movie's high profile premiere in 1972. Having written the book as a hoped-for moneyspinner, Burgess felt disappointed by the initial public response, though writing the entire narrative in the specially devised youth slang language of Nadsat did little for its mass appeal. Consider the novel's opening paragraph, where adolescent gang leader Alex describes the effects of drinking 'the old moloko', hallucinogen-spiked milk guaranteed to induce 'a nice quiet horrorshow fifteen minutes admiring Bog And All His Holy Angels and Saints in your left shoe with lights bursting all over your mozg'. Not to mention a taste for an evening of the old ultraviolence and in-out in-out. Developing a serious cult following during the increasingly swinging sixties, this moral parable nearly made it to the screen with the Rolling Stones on board, though Mick Jagger's subsequent thespian efforts suggest that the Dark, if spindly Prince of Rock and Roll was never destined for celluloid glory. One of the most debated, criticised and analysed films of all time, much like 2001, Kubrick's *Clockwork Orange* plays with some potent themes – social breakdown, drug-fuelled teen killers and state-sanctioned brainwashing – without reaching any discernible conclusions. Like Roeg and Russell, Kubrick dazzles with his visual flair, seducing the audience into accepting the film's exquisitely composed series of tableaux as some kind of profound statement.

Set in a near future Britain that proved uncomfortably close to the present for many, *Clockwork Orange* is quite literally the story of Alex (Malcolm McDowell), the 'Humble Narrator', a charismatic teen thug whose gleefully nihilistic back catalogue of assault, rape, torture, theft and murder is mitigated – in Kubrick's view – by a sense of style and an appreciation of high art. Complementing his nifty white shirt and jeans ensemble with a bowler hat and combat boots, Alex also sports a single fake eyelash and cuff links shaped like severed eyeballs (possibly a homage to Hammer's *The Curse of Frankenstein*, which appears as a drive-in movie in Kubrick's *Lolita* 1962). Despite a succession of truly appalling acts, Alex remains a loveable rogue in the best Artful Dodger tradition, dominating every scene with his dynamic presence. After a hard night's thuggery, he likes nothing better than masturbating to Beethoven's 'glorious' Ninth Symphony, especially the Ode to Joy. Good looking, charming, witty and intelligent, Alex runs the gamut of thrill criminal, model prisoner, voluntary laboratory specimen, victimised outcast, tabloid *cause celebre* and compliant government stooge, his last line of dialogue reassuring audiences that he's back to his old self: 'I was cured all right'.

As with Jack Nicholson's gibbering loon of a writer in *The Shining* (1980), Kubrick seems too much in love with his lead actor's performance, throwing the surrounding film off balance. Burgess argued that the state-sponsored brainwashing of Alex, a harrowing aversion therapy process involving drugs

and forced sado-voyeurism, is as fundamentally amoral as his earlier acts of violence. Man cannot function without free will, the choice between good and bad. This is a legitimate, if contentious point of view, yet Kubrick stacks the deck so much in Alex's favour that the theme loses all validity. The society Alex inhabits, all empty decadence and rundown industrial estates, is so drab and lifeless that any show of verve and enthusiasm seems welcome,

social breakdown, drug-fuelled teen killers and state-sanctioned brainwashing

whatever its nature. Most of the supporting characters are either mannered grotesques or anonymous flashes of female flesh, only our humble narrator registering as a living, breathing individual. The scenes of extreme brutality are staged and edited as fiendishly exhilarating musical numbers, choreographed to Rossini's 'The Thieving Magpie' and 'Singin' in the Rain', the ultra stylisation rendering the ultraviolence not only watchable but inconsequential. When it's Alex's turn to suffer, however, whether attacked by his own droogs or beaten by the police, the blows to the face and body are suddenly much more realistic. This, after all, is a real victim. Where Burgess has Alex drug and rape two ten year old girls, Kubrick offers the jokey seduction of two airhead young women, their speeded-up threesome with Alex accompanied by a synthesised version of Rossini's 'William Tell' overture.

British science fiction at its best does not flinch from tackling its ideas full on, however dark or unpalatable. Anthony Burgess' *Clockwork Orange* is a work of both imagination and integrity. Obsessed with its narrative tricks and visual audacity, Kubrick's film has been seen by some as a symptom of the brutality it depicts, rather than the enlightened social critique doubtless intended by its *auteur* director.

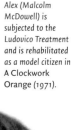

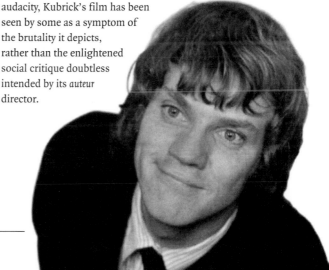

Alex (Malcolm McDowell) is subjected to the Ludovico Treatment and is rehabilitated as a model citizen in A Clockwork Orange (1971).

CHAPTER 4
SUCH STUFF AS DREAMS ARE MADE ON

A few years back, one half of a now defunct stand-up double act announced that comedy was the new rock and roll. The partnership played Wembley Arena in front of a capacity crowd to demonstrate his point.

Whatever the truth of this bold claim, there have been periods over the last few decades when, in terms of mass appeal, comedy appeared to be the new British science fiction. Both *The Hitchhiker's Guide to the Galaxy* and *Red Dwarf* began life on BBC Radio 4, ten years apart, going on from their relatively humble beginnings to become huge multi-media hits worldwide – not so much mere programmes as international merchandising franchises. A mixture of parody, satire and affectionate homage, these series at their peak followed the cardinal rule of treating their target genre with respect. As Mel Brooks so ably demonstrated, pastiche executed with a fan's enthusiasm can result in a *Young Frankenstein*, whereas dumping on the subject from a great height is more likely to produce *Spaceballs*.

The phenomenal success of the American-made *Austin Powers* films, where Mike Myers's 'shagadelic' swinging-sixties English superspy is brought out of suspended animation to face the 1990s, suggests that audiences still like their sf fantasy with a heavy dose of laughs. Revisiting James Bond and *The Avengers*, *Powers* also owes a small debt to the lesser known BBC television series *Adam Adamant Lives!* (1966), co-created and produced by Verity Lambert, where dashing Edwardian adventurer Gerald Harper is rescued from his ice tomb after 64 years in stasis, just as London is getting seriously groovy. Partnered by an exceptionally hip female sidekick, Adamant adjusts to this crazed new world with relative ease.

Unlike Austin Powers, Adam Adamant probably wouldn't have had much difficulty believing that Liberace wasn't quite the ladies' man of reputation. He'd also have done something about his teeth. The directors on the show included a young Ridley Scott, later to make his mark in decidedly joke-free science fiction. Though nominally inspired by British influences, the *Austin Powers* series – two and counting – owes just as much to the 1960s Hollywood James Bond knockoffs Derek Flint and Matt Helm, played by the impeccably cool James Coburn and Dean Martin. A big fan of the former, Powers cites the second Flint movie, *In Like Flint* (1967), as his all-time favourite (the title is a moderately bad taste homage to the phrase 'In Like Flynn', a reference to film star Errol Flynn's prosecution and acquittal on statutory rape charges). Powers certainly has as much in common with the laid-back, leering West Coast lounge lizards Flint and Helm as the true English gentlemen Bond and Steed. Character names such as Felicity Shagwell and Ivana Humpalot do not suggest a high level of wit or invention. Then again, nor does Pussy Galore. Myers is doubtless paying tribute to Matt Helm's nubile, ever obliging secretary Lovey Kravezit.

Prior to *Hitchhiker*'s debut in 1978, British comedy had sporadically veered into science fiction territory. *The Perfect Woman* (1949) features an inventor building a 'female' robot modelled on his shapely niece, who decides to take its place, the ensuing farce-style hi-jinks placing a surprising-for-the-period emphasis on fetishistic underwear. Ealing Studios' more celebrated satire *The Man in the White Suit* (1951) has the garment industry up in arms after mild mannered scientist Alec Guinness invents a super-fabric immune to both dirt and wear. Played as fairly broad comedy, *The Man in the White Suit* tackles some serious themes. Guinness's well-meant discovery threatens the capitalist bosses with commercial ruin and the workers with mass unemployment, forcing the two normally hostile factions to unite to suppress the new chemical formula. In the extended chase finale, Guinness literally has the clothes ripped from him, a harsh lesson in the necessity of 'planned obsolescence' to the existing economic order. In some ways, Guinness's naive attempt to take on vested big business interests recalls David Bowie's equally – and literally – unworldly inventor in *The Man Who Fell to Earth*. Neither has the slightest

Zaphod Beeblebrox (Mark Wing-Davey) in The Hitchhiker's Guide to the Galaxy.

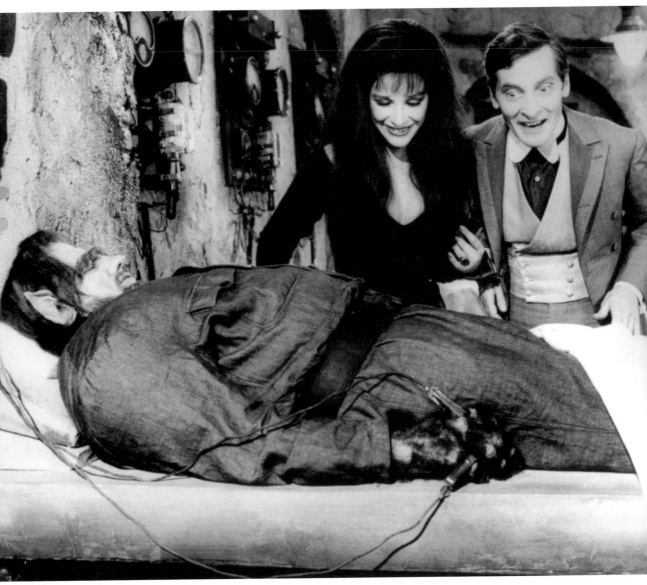

Valeria (Fenella Fielding) and Dr Watt (Kenneth Williams) revive Odbodd (Tom Clegg) in the mad scientist spoof Carry On Screaming! (1966).

appreciation of the forces lined up against them until it's too late.

In the mid-1960s, the hugely popular *Carry On* series made a couple of excursions into sf fantasy. *Carry On Spying* (1964) parodies the Bond movies circa *From Russia With Love* (1963), a team of incompetent yet determined British agents taking on the neofascist might of the Society for the Total Extinction of Non-Conforming Humans, better known as STENCH. The evil genius, Dr Crow (Judith Furse), is a hermaphrodite, the first in a projected master race. Drawing on both *The Third Man* and *The Goon Show* for additional inspiration, *Carry On Spying* certainly delivers the goods, though Kenneth Williams's snide-voiced team leader is a test of the nerves.

Carry On Screaming (1966) recreates the look and tone of the Hammer horrors with impressive fidelity (cinematographer Alan Hume had previously photographed *The Kiss of the Vampire* for the latter). This time around, Kenneth Williams is Doctor Who's disreputable nephew Doctor Watt, a reanimated corpse with an eye for niche market business ventures, kidnapping young women for transformation into uncannily life-like shop window dummies. The dirty work is left to Odbodd (Tom Clegg), a resurrected Neanderthal brute with an unfortunate tendency to leave fingers and ears at crime scenes. (Watt's electrical revivification process renders the subjects rather brittle.) In one of the best scenes, future *Doctor Who* Jon Pertwee, here playing

Professor Fettle, accidentally regenerates an entire new Odbodd from the abandoned finger. The resultant creature promptly kills its unwitting creator (Mary Shelley would probably have approved). A decade later *The Rocky Horror Picture Show* (1975), based on Richard O'Brien's cult stage hit, gave the Frankenstein saga a cross-dressing, gender bending, bi-sexual makeover. Transvestite mad scientist Dr Frank N Furter (Tim Curry), a Victor Frankenstein for the glamrock era, invites his two unwilling guests to 'come up to the lab/and see what's on the slab'. The resulting creature is Rocky Horror, a perfect man, 'with blonde hair and a tan', who probably isn't quite what either Nietzsche or the Aryan supremacists had in mind.

Three years on, with *Rocky Horror* well established as the midnight, dress-up, singalong cult movie, *The Hitchhiker's Guide to the Galaxy* hit the airwaves, less flamboyant than Richard O'Brien's determinedly naughty sf pastiche, but equally cutting in its way. Scripted by the then little known Douglas Adams, the series begins in fairly standard sit-com territory, with the timorous yet plucky EveryEnglishman Arthur Dent (Simon Jones) protesting against the destruction of his suburban home by lying down in front of the bulldozers. Unimpressed by the crying need for yet another bypass – to be built through his property – Dent makes his views on the modern age very clear: 'I've gone off progress. It's overrated.' Events take an unexpected cosmic turn when extraterrestrial demolition craft arrive, in the form of the Vogon Constructor Fleet, advising the inhabitants of Earth that the planet is in the path of a new hyperspace express route and must be destroyed. Dent's guide through this mindblowing series of events is his friend Ford Prefect, a freelance researcher for the intergalactic *Hitchhiker's Guide to the Galaxy* publication, from the planet Betelgeuse by way of Guildford.

Douglas Adams got an early break into the great British science fiction tradition, selling a handful of stories to *The Eagle* comic for ten shillings each. His subsequent career as a radio and television writer seemed destined to go nowhere much, despite an obvious talent for comedy of the offbeat kind. By his own admission, Adams's idiosyncratic, often surreal brand of humour owed a sizeable debt to *Monty Python's Flying Circus*, John Cleese being a particular favourite. After leaving Cambridge University in the early 1970s, Adams worked for a year with Python Graham Chapman, mostly on an unrealised television project. By 1977 he was in need of the elusive big break, which promptly came along. The phenomenal success of *Stars Wars* suddenly made just about any science fiction project attractive to producers, however far it strayed from the George Lucas shoot-'em-up-with-laser guns format. Having sold the idea for *Hitchhiker* to BBC Radio 4, Adams embarked on the serial without a firm story structure, not deciding upon an ending until several episodes into the story. Paid a modest £1000 fee, he claims to have worked on the first series of *Hitchhiker* for nine months from conception to broadcast, producer Geoffrey Perkins coming on board to oversee the transition.

Backed by the full resources of the BBC's radiophonic workshop, well versed in sf sound effects after *Quatermass* and *Doctor Who*, *The Hitchhiker's Guide to the Galaxy* proved an instant classic, the opening narration by The Book (Peter Jones)

from the planet Betelguese by way of Guildford

effortlessly drawing listeners into Adams's bizarre yet oddly familiar universe, sharing Arthur Dent's sense of utter disorientation. Supporting characters included the conceited, libidinous hedonist Zaphod Beeblebrox (Mark Wing-Davey), whose three arms and two heads didn't stop him from being a hit with the ladies ('The best bang since the big one') or part-time President of the Galaxy. Eddie, the relentlessly cheerful ship's computer, made HAL 9000 look a pretty good bet by comparison, while Marvin the Paranoid Android (catchphrase: 'Life? Don't talk to me about life') merely made everyone feel wretched (apart from Radiohead, who named an album after him). Even the minor supporting characters come with memorably silly names like Slartibartfast, an earnest terraform designer with a loathing of shuttlecraft. Adams didn't try so hard with Shootie and Bang-Bang, two intergalactic cops whose proclaimed liberal attitude amounts to gunning people down, then feeling bad about it. Towards the end of their trek, Dent and Prefect encounter a group of

Ford Prefect (David Dixon) in The Hitchhiker's Guide to the Galaxy.

Monty Python's Flying Circus in 1969. From left to right: John Cleese, Michael Palin, Graham Chapman, Terry Jones and Eric Idle.

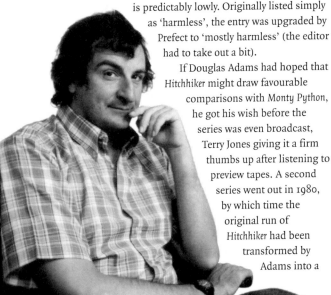

Douglas Adams – creator of The Hitchhiker's Guide to the Galaxy.

galaxy- wandering telephone sanitation specialists and like professionals, tricked into leaving their home world of Golgafrinch because the other inhabitants thought they were useless (the remaining Golgafrinchians promptly died out from a disease spread by dirty telephones).

Adams supplemented his gallery of exotic, yet petty-minded species with a range of ingenious gadgets, including the Babel Fish, which can translate any alien dialect into the user's native tongue. Plugged straight into the ear, this useful parasite makes Star Trek's piffling universal translator look pretty lame, subsequently becoming a real device in the form of a translator for an internet search engine. It's probably for the best that such potent Hitchhiker cocktails as the pan-galactic gargle blaster remain the stuff of fantasy. The now demolished Earth's status in the Hitchhiker's Guide is predictably lowly. Originally listed simply as 'harmless', the entry was upgraded by Prefect to 'mostly harmless' (the editor had to take out a bit).

If Douglas Adams had hoped that Hitchhiker might draw favourable comparisons with Monty Python, he got his wish before the series was even broadcast, Terry Jones giving it a firm thumbs up after listening to preview tapes. A second series went out in 1980, by which time the original run of Hitchhiker had been transformed by Adams into a

bestselling book. He'd also turned his attention to another British fantasy icon, then entering the twilight of its glory years. As a pupil at Brentwood Preparatory School during the early 1960s, Douglas Adams had written an end of term play called Doctor Which, based on the popular new science fiction serial. Having already penned the Doctor Who story The Pirate Planet (1978), Adams's success with the first Hitchhiker series led to his appointment as script editor for the show's seventeenth season (1979/80).

Adams seems to have accepted the Doctor Who job largely for financial reasons, feeling the BBC had been less than generous with his radio fee. The Pirate Planet, one of the better late Tom Baker stories, features the roving hollow planet Zanak, which materialises around other worlds and drains their energy and matter until nothing is left but a shrivelled, rock-sized lump. Zanak is seemingly controlled by the Captain, a half-cyborg humanoid with a robot parrot on his shoulder, his lethal pet later vanquished in a laser duel with the Doctor's mechanoid dog, K-9. This is borderline Hitchhiker territory, though played with a commendable straight face (or as straight as Tom Baker's face ever got). As script editor, Adams also reworked David Fisher's original script for what became City of Death (1979), the end result credited to departmental pseudonym 'David Agnew'. The tongue-in-cheek mix of Paris locations, Leonardo Da Vinci's 'Mona Lisa', a dogged British detective, an ancient scaly green alien called Scaroth and the creation of life on Earth showed the direction Adams wanted to take the series. Perhaps feeling that the megahit movie Star Wars had blown away all small screen science fiction competition, kindred spirits Baker and Adams decided to play the series largely for irony, which attracted protest from some purist fans but also massive viewing figures. Adams's favourite Python John Cleese made a cameo appearance in City of Death, the final episode of which drew an audience of 14.5 million, an all-time high for Doctor Who. On the downside, the approach didn't always work, as the wretched Horns of Nimon amply demonstrated, reworking the Theseus and the Minotaur legend to uninspired effect. Bull-headed aliens obliged to bend over in order to aim their laser horns lack dignity. Production on Adams's second credited Doctor Who script, Shada, was halted owing to industrial action at the BBC and the story never completed or broadcast. Featuring Cambridge University, renegade Time Lords and a prison planet where all the most evil species in the universe are represented, Shada could have been Adams's finest Who hour, though the existing footage suggests an entertaining romp rather than a provocative masterpiece.

It came as no great surprise when the BBC opted to remake *Hitchhiker* as a television serial, broadcast in 1981, using state of the art computer animation to create moving 'pages' from the book. The latter element proved to be the highlight of the show, the one instance where the visual element enhanced Adams's original ideas rather than merely copying them in perfunctory fashion. Wisely retaining key cast members from the radio series, notably Simon Jones, Peter Jones and Mark Wing-Davey, the producers recast other roles with very variable results. Adams reworked his old scripts, not always to their benefit, and made a stripping cameo appearance in episode two, but didn't rate the end result very highly. The cost of the computer effects, high enough to nearly get the show cancelled, left the rest of the television *Hitchhiker* with an inadequate budget, the production values on a par with the less impressive episodes of *Doctor Who* and *Blake's 7*.

Adams consoled himself with a run of bestselling spinoff *Hitchhiker* books (the four sequels sold fourteen million copies worldwide), a stage show, records and a computer game. Another novel, *Dirk Gently's Holistic Detective Agency* (1987), followed in the *Hitchhiker* tradition, successful enough to spawn a sequel of its own. The long gestating American film version of *The Hitchhiker's Guide to the Galaxy* seems close to getting a final greenlight after 20 years. *Austin Powers* director Jay Roach is apparently on board, though currently without a cast or approved script or final budget. Originally scheduled for a summer 2000 release, the project won't now see the light of day until 2002. Understandably, Douglas Adams is less than pleased with the situation: 'It's Hollywood doing what it does best, which is to take one step forward, two steps back.' Just how much of the original 1978 serial would remain in an Americanised feature film is open to doubt.

While *Hitchhiker*'s determinedly quirky style inspired few direct imitators, it had a natural successor in the sf comedy blockbuster stakes in the form of BBC Television's *Red Dwarf*, which also tipped its hat to John Carpenter's 1974 cult space odyssey spoof *Dark Star*. From a modest, if engaging start, *Dwarf* picked up speed and audiences, running for six seasons before terminal stagnation set in. Still an ongoing concern after eight series, the show remains a serious moneyspinner long after its creative engine burned out.

Conceived by the writing partnership of Rob Grant and Doug Naylor, the idea for *Red Dwarf*

Hologram Arnold Rimmer (Chris Barrie) in Red Dwarf.

originated in one of their sketches for the Radio 4 comedy series *Son of Cliché*. *Red Dwarf* is set approximately three million years into the future aboard a twenty-third century intergalactic mining ship, the 'Dwarf' of the title, which lost most of its crew after an unfortunate radiation leak. The last human being in the universe is insubordinate ship's technician Dave Lister (Craig Charles), a cocky but fundamentally good-natured chancer who wears his

The last human being in the universe is insubordinate ship's technician Dave Lister

underachiever status with pride. Unlike the standard last-man-alive in science fiction, notably Robert Neville in Richard Matheson's *I Am Legend*, Lister remains remarkably cheerful. This is despite the dull-witted computer's choice of holographic buddy, selected from his deceased fellow crew members. Arnold Rimmer (Chris Barrie), a chicken soup vending machine maintenance operative, carries a whole bag of chips on his shoulder, stung by the

Rimmer (Chris Barrie) with friend in the fifth series of Red Dwarf.

supposed failures of his negligible career in the space corps. Snobbish, resentful, devious and anally retentive to the point of rupture, Rimmer is without doubt the worst possible post-apocalypse companion. When the season four episode *Dimension Jump* confronts Arnold Rimmer with top space pilot Ace Rimmer, a heroic, dashing and popular version of himself from an alternative universe, the cowardly, maladroit and universally loathed Rimmer reacts with complete bitterness, unable to accept that he could have made a success of his life. The original *Red Dwarf* odd-quartet was completed by Holly (Norman Lovett), a lugubrious computer with a questionable grasp of events, and Cat (Danny John Jules), a narcissistic, self-centred humanoid creature descended via radioactive evolution from Lister's taboo feline pet, Frankenstein (Mary Shelley's artificial lifeform just won't lie down).

As the only 'true' human in the line-up, Lister drew the most audience identification, though Craig Charles appeared to worry that the character would be overshadowed by his offbeat companions in comic space odyssey, supposedly pushing the writers for more funny lines. Fixated on curries and lager, chewing his toenails and reusing soiled underwear, Dave Lister is probably no-one's idea of the ideal Everyman, yet the human race could certainly have a far worse sole-surviving representative.

Given Holly's restricted presence as a face on a screen, the introduction of a fifth main character in series three came as no great surprise. A service mechanoid in the best, or worst, tradition of Robby the Robot, Kryten is an angst-ridden android with a head variously described as 'a novelty condom' and 'an amusingly shaped ice cube'. Originally played by David Ross in a one-off season two episode, Kryten later returned as a regular in the heavily disguised form of Robert Llewellyn. Programmed with Isaac Asimov-style subservience to humans, Kryten's apparent passion for all tasks menial, especially ironing, eventually wore a little thin – how many times can a robot in an apron be funny? The writers eventually gave him more independence of mind and a bigger share of the action. One episode, *DNA*, sees Kryten achieve the classic android dream of becoming human, only to discover that he is sexually aroused by an electronic components catalogue. Having initially shunned his now redundant spare head collection, Kryten's crisis of identity can only be resolved by a return to his 'natural' state. Quoting Descartes, or possibly Popeye the Sailor Man, the ever-understanding Lister puts the issue in perspective: 'I am what I am.' Incidentally, the greaseless prosthetic base used for Llewellyn's Kryten mask is a formula devised by top American make-up artist William Tuttle, who designed the rather less lovable Morlocks for George Pal's *The Time Machine*. Kryten's debut also marked the first appearance of a female Holly (Hattie Hayridge), which dissipated the previous blokes-only atmosphere, altering the humour to a degree. Though as seemingly gormless as her male predecessor, the new Holly came out with more than one sharp putdown, utterly unimpressed by the regular bouts of macho posturing and one-upmanship. Hayridge's last appearance as Holly in the season five finale *Back to Reality* saw the computer saving the crew's lives after alien infection leads to a suicidal mass hallucination.

First shown in 1988, the original run of *Red Dwarf* was very much a situation comedy that happened to be set in outer space, rather than the lavishly produced science fiction comedy of later series. Working with a limited number of fairly basic sets, and few supporting characters, the show focused on the central Lister-Rimmer clash in time-honoured sitcom tradition, two diametrically opposed personalities trapped in a claustrophobic environment, separated by a yawning chasm of ideology, class, politics and success with girls. By series three, *Red Dwarf*'s scope and ambition had widened considerably, lending the more intimate moments a greater edge. The two-hander episode *Marooned* strands Lister and Rimmer on a freezing wasteland of a planet. Faced with almost certain death, they open up to each other with a tentative male bonding session. Rimmer's happiest moment appears to have been a psychic's revelation that he was once a eunuch in the court of Alexander the Great. Being in the presence of military genius means everything, with or without testicles. Called upon to sacrifice his beloved electric guitar for much-needed fuel, Lister does the decent thing and burns a guitar-shaped piece of Rimmer's priceless mahogany chest. In *Polymorph*, a genetically engineered, shape-shifting creature comes on board and adopts a variety of disguises to feed off the crew's plentiful negative emotions: vanity, fear, guilt. The radical character changes include Rimmer's transformation into a bearded, pipe-smoking liberal

given to T-shirt slogans such as 'Give Quiche A Chance'. Running the comedy gamut from pointed satire to vulgar farce, *Red Dwarf* sometimes featured the two simultaneously. *Backwards*, which takes place in a temporally and physically reversed universe, opts for some amusingly gross jokes, the mildest of which is drinkers in a pub apparently vomiting their beer back into the glass. The punchline has Cat realise too late that bowel movements in a backwards world will not go in the expected direction.

After three seasons, the *Red Dwarf* production left its base at BBC Manchester for the wider spaces of Shepperton Studios. The Dwarf interiors grew bigger and more intricate – the improved special effects would not have disgraced a healthily-budgeted feature film. While later instalments would swamp the admittedly faltering humour with elaborate visual trickery, the balance worked well for a time, the greater resources enabling Grant and Naylor to devise more ambitious, sometimes epic stories. A lot of the early sets looked cramped and dingy, the endless Dwarf corridors painted a monotonous shade of grey. Judicious use of Shepperton's largely abandoned backlots gave the show a refreshing sense of variety, the space hardware alternating with more natural backdrops. In order to retain the desired sitcom feel, most of the studio scenes were still recorded in front of a live audience. A number of the production team regarded this as a mistake, confining much of the show to a two-hour stage performance when it had long outgrown this format. True or not, the ideas kept coming. In *Back to Reality*, the Dwarf crew apparently wake up in a virtual reality suite, their thrilling adventures in space and time nothing more than an elaborate computer game. Moreover, they are not really the characters seen for the past five seasons, and the planet Earth, far from being destroyed, is a thriving fascist state. Lister is the Voter Colonel, a senior government figure, Rimmer his down-and-out half brother Billy Doyle.

he is sexually aroused by an electronic components catalogue

Kryten is a cop named Jake Bullet, the macho name hardly reflected by his position in the traffic division. Worst of all, Cat turns out to be ultra-geek Duane Dibbley, complete with Parka jacket, thermos flask and prominent front teeth.

Series six of *Red Dwarf* saw some major changes, most notably the loss of the actual *Red Dwarf* spacecraft and its onboard computer Holly. Grant and Naylor felt that the season five stories set on the

Left to right, the crew of Red Dwarf: Cat (Danny John Jules), Kochanski (Chloe Annett), Kryten (Robert Llewellyn), Rimmer (Chris Barrie) and Lister (Craig Charles).

scout ship *Starbug* had generated more tension and sense of danger, the smaller craft lacking the *Dwarf*'s comparatively luxurious resources. Feedback from the fans suggested that both Holly and Cat had been underused much of the time. By reducing the main cast to a tighter-knit foursome, the producers hoped to keep the format fresh, aiming for an adventure-based feature film style rather than the standard television look. In *Legion*, Rimmer gains a 'hard-light' drive mode that renders him capable of physical sensation, including repeated blows to the head. *Polymorph II: Emohawk* reintroduced popular 'guest' characters Ace Rimmer and Duane Dibbley, whose thermos flask undergoes alien duplication. *Gunmen of the Apocalypse* threw in a fistful of western clichés as the crew battled a lethal computer virus in a simulated environment. Taking their work seriously, as ever, Grant and Naylor embarked on in-depth

western research for the episode, reviewing the films of genre favourites John Wayne, Clint Eastwood, John Ford and Howard Hawks. This attention to detail extended to all production departments, the ship used by the evil, virus-spreading Simulant aliens designed to resemble the kind of cattle skull found on the desert trail, its gun turrets mounted on the 'horns'. Based largely in assorted 'Artificial Reality' settings, the story opens with a black-and-white film noir pastiche before moving to the western frontier town of 'Existence'. The chief Simulant reappears as a lean, very mean gunslinger named Death: 'Have infection will travel, that's me', accompanied by fellow apocalyptic outlaws Famine, War and Pestilence. Sheriff Kryten manages to release an antidote 'dove' programme just in time, though not before Rimmer has been beaten over the head once more with a hitching post.

While many felt that Red Dwarf had peaked with season five, the sixth series seemed well up to standard, ending with an intriguing cliffhanger as the Starbug crew prepared to do battle with their appallingly amoral future selves. By contrast, the delayed seventh season appeared appallingly stale and misconceived, for a number of reasons. Rob Grant decided to leave the series, keen to pursue non-Dwarf projects before the opportunities generated by the show's success dried up. Chris Barrie announced he would only appear in the first few episodes, claiming to be tired of the format. Keen to broaden the show's United States fanbase, still largely on the Doctor Who-style cult level, the producers attempted a degree of Americanisation (two US-shot Red Dwarf pilots, featuring Frasier co-star Jane Leeves and Star Trek: Deep Space Nine actress Terry Farrell, had failed to take off). With an eye to possible feature film development, they introduced a regular female character, Lister's former girlfriend Christine Kochanski, whose break-up with the latter led to the self-imposed period in stasis that kept him alive when the radiation leaked. Thanks to the show's spacial-temporal-dimensional hijinks, Kochanski had already appeared on several occasions, appealingly played by former Altered Images singer and Gregory's Girl co-star Claire Grogan. Despite upsetting Dwarf's carefully achieved balance of characters, this development made a degree of sense, not least because of Barrie's impending departure. As Craig Charles pointed out, Lister's sole human status would make him a seriously sex-starved man, Red Dwarf shying away from inter-species frolics (if not from masturbation). Feeling, like most of the audience, that the Grant-free scripts were not up to standard, Grogan refused to reprise her role. As portrayed by Chloe Annett, the new-look Kochanski bore precious little resemblance to the original character and stuck out like an extremely sore thumb. Season eight, with Chris Barrie back on board, returned the characters to Red Dwarf in the initial period before most of the crew were wiped out, a circular journey that smacked of desperation. (In fairness, Rob Grant's keenly anticipated sf follow-up to Red Dwarf, the alien-invasion black comedy The Strangerers, proved equally dismal, despite the best efforts of leads Jack Docherty and Mark Williams. Perhaps some partnerships just aren't meant to be split up).

Now reliant on former glories, Red Dwarf literally reworked its past to better blend in with the later house-style. The early seasons underwent extensive doctoring, remastered, re-edited and reshot, the original BBC-grade effects and models replaced with new, state of the Dwarf art footage. The overall visual style was reprocessed to substitute the standard videotape/studio look for a more filmic feel. Aside from generating extra merchandising revenue for BBC Enterprises, it's difficult to see what this elaborate, not to mention costly, makeover achieved for the series. When the BBC restored Jon Pertwee episodes of Doctor Who that existed only in black and white copies to something approaching their original colour splendour, it seemed a worthwhile exercise (though the end result was a definite compromise). Retouching Red Dwarf seems a little akin to colourising the original William Hartnell episodes of Doctor Who to enhance their youth appeal.

'I'VE SEEN THINGS YOU PEOPLE WOULDN'T BELIEVE'

Despite the best efforts of Hitchhiker, Red Dwarf and Austin Powers, the post Star Wars revival of the 'straight' science fiction genre continues at strength, though British sf has not particularly prospered in the cinema. Drawing on a wealth of British technical and acting talent, Star Wars itself sports a (mostly) Made in England stamp – yet its outlook is unquestionably American, courtesy of Californian fantasy auteur George Lucas.

Lucas opted to shoot his movie in England partly because British film technicians had a very high reputation, but also because both staff and facilities were considerably cheaper than their American counterparts. Led by respected veterans Alec Guinness and Peter Cushing, the British acting contingent for Star Wars included Anthony Daniels, cast as the neurotic yet courageous android C-3Po. Initially reluctant to be locked away inside an uncomfortable robot suit for months on end, Daniels changed his mind after seeing Ralph McQuarrie's conceptual artwork for the character. The task of transforming the original illustrations into a practical three dimensional design fell to British artist Liz Moore, whose previous science fiction credits

'People treated me like a machine and expected me to be a machine'

included the star child seen at the climax of 2001 (tragically, Moore died in a car crash before Star Wars premiered). Playing the part on location in sun-baked Tunisia proved as arduous an experience as Daniels feared, not helped by the attitude of his co-workers: 'People treated me like a machine and expected me to be a machine.'

Ridley Scott directing Alien in 1979. Scott went on to direct the science fiction classic Blade Runner (1982).

The largely British crew displayed a fairly Luddite mentality, promptly shutting down operations at six o'clock in the evening and voting against George Lucas's request for overtime. Not a big fan of Forbidden Planet's Robby the Robot, Daniels took a very different approach for C3Po, regarding the latter as a lonely character intelligent enough to recognise that he lacks true human qualities (a classic theme in robotic literature). Despite such grisly scenes as the murder of Luke Skywalker's aunt and uncle, reduced to smoking skeletons by laser fire, Stars Wars ultimately lacks what Daniels characterises as the 'stranger, darker' elements of 'true' British science fiction. The skilfully-honed fairytale narrative is firmly in the pioneering, gung ho spirit of American

sf, where good and bad are clearly defined and virtue must eventually triumph over evil whatever the apparent odds. Generating a slew of mostly dreadful imitations and rip-offs, the film also inspired the novelty British disco hit 'I Lost My Heart to a Starship Trooper', Sarah Brightman and top dance group Hot Gossip giving the nation a truly galactic thrill.

Once the initial wave of hackneyed, wannabe Stars Wars clones had passed, Battlestar Galactica prominent among them, the newly invigorated science fiction movie genre produced some quality work. Alien (1979) recreated the nasty space monster on the loose thrills of It! The Terror from Beyond Space (1958), scripted by acclaimed sf writer Jerome Bixby, and the giant-sized alien skeleton of the Italian-made Planet of the *Vampires* (1965), directed by horror maestro Mario Bava. Like Lucas's trailblazing effort, *Alien* is a Hollywood movie filmed in England with an Anglo-American cast and crew. The tone, however, is radically different, drawing on the more downbeat schools of tortuous suspense and graphic gross-out horror. Working from a script more workmanlike than inspired, British director Ridley Scott merits a large part of the credit for *Alien*'s success, his atmospheric, claustrophobic handling turning on the tension from scene one. Set aboard the *Nostromo*, a gothic interplanetary mining spaceship, the film generates mood through detail. The murky, dripping hardware and bickering, uptight crew create an environment infinitely more believable, and closer to home, than *Star Wars*' rollercoaster Death Star romp. The taut narrative and jittery, intense performances transcend the utterly formulaic *Ten Little Indians* premise, Sigourney Weaver's sole survivor earning audience sympathy and admiration despite her often dislikeable nature (considerably softened in the sequels).

Alien rang box-office bells, Ridley Scott moving out to Los Angeles on the back of its commercial and critical success. Hired to direct *Blade Runner* for Warner, he became another Englishman in Hollywood toiling away on artificial lifeforms *a la* James Whale. Rutger Hauer's murderous, yet anguished Nexus 6 replicant was clearly a descendant of Boris Karloff's monster. Loosely based on American writer Philip K Dick's 1968 novel *Do Androids Dream of Electric Sheep?*, the $28 million production deployed a predominantly Hollywood cast and crew, led by *Star Wars* veteran Harrison Ford. Dick's original book, which offered a very individual, counter-culture oriented form of science fiction, was light years away from the George Lucas formula. Despite a number of significant changes, the *Blade Runner* screenplay, co-written by Hampton Fancher and David Webb Peoples, made no concessions to popular taste. Scott's British co-producer, Michael Deeley, had previously worked on Nicholas Roeg's *The Man Who Fell To Earth*, another American-based sf allegory with a decidedly 'European' feel.

A generation earlier, a similar situation had resulted in dreary, compromised failure. Faced with an extremely unhealthy national film industry, respected British director Bryan Forbes crossed the Atlantic to helm *The Stepford Wives* (1974), a science fiction fantasy adapted from the novel by Ira Levin. Liberated photojournalist Katherine Ross moves with her husband and daughter to the seemingly idyllic

commuter village of Stepford, Connecticut, only to discover that almost all the female residents are unassertive, obedient, well-endowed slaves. Intent on achieving their ideal vision of the perfect housewife, the Stepford husbands have murdered their wives and replaced them with android doubles, a pre-emptive strike against the burgeoning feminist movement. A black satire that seems to degrade both men and women, *Stepford Wives* is not a happy blend of content and style, Forbes's po-faced, slightly leaden treatment flattening much of its potential. The incongruous presence of Nanette Newman, aka Mrs Forbes, in an otherwise American cast is proof positive that nepotism can be a bad thing. *Stepford Wives* does have a few good jokes – the robot designer is a former Disneyland employee – yet Forbes doesn't seem to have noticed. In the climactic scene, Ross confronts her own replacement, a large-breasted male fantasy dressed in a see-through nightgown. Staring at Ross through pitch-black eyeballs, the robot advances menacingly on her. As Pauline Kael, influential film critic for the *New Yorker*, put it : 'The first women's lib Gothic – hardly the landmark the world had been waiting for.'

A box-office disappointment on its original release, Ridley Scott's *Blade Runner* (1982) is probably as famous for its troubled post-production history as its storyline. Preview audiences expected Harrison Ford's licensed android slayer to be another Han Solo or Indiana Jones and made no secret of their dislike for the brooding, lonely, frequently beaten-up Deckard. Despite the tangles with scissor-happy studio personnel, Scott's film is in a different realm to Forbes's earlier effort, the director obviously in tune with his material. While it draws heavily from the quintessentially American *film noir* genre in terms of plot, tone and even visual style, there is something fundamentally un-Hollywood about *Blade Runner*'s

'The first women's lib Gothic – hardly the landmark the world had been waiting for'

take on the sf genre. Its vision of Los Angeles in 2019 is unrelentingly downbeat, cynical and melancholy, the wealthy few barricaded in their fortress-like dwellings while the impoverished multitudes roam the [acid] rain-soaked streets.

On-set strife may have helped the film, Harrison Ford's unhappiness with leading lady Sean Young giving their characters' human-android, or possibly android-android relationship a tentative, nervous quality. The shoot proved protracted and exhausting, co-star Daryl Hannah suffering major bruising during the gruelling action sequences. Ford's utterly shattered expression during the climactic rooftop scene with Hauer – the last to be filmed – called for little in the way of acting. Dismayed by poor test-screening results, Warner re-edited Scott's footage. A voiceover was added to clarify the storyline (flatly delivered by Ford in mock Chandleresque style). A short dream sequence was dropped, as it hinted at Deckard's android identity, and a fatuous 'happy' ending added where former android killer and sole surviving android drive off into the sunset together. (An approximation of Ridley Scott's original version surfaced in 1993). Even in the clumsily re-cut *Blade Runner*, there is still something poignant about dying replicant Roy Batty's final

a knight on horseback charging out of the boy's wardrobe

speech, shortened and reworked by Rutger Hauer from the original screenplay: 'I've seen things you people wouldn't believe. Attack ships on fire off the shoulder of Orion. I watched c-beams glitter in the dark near the Tanhauser Gate. All these moments will be lost in time. Like tears in the rain. Time to die.'

An appreciation for the fleeting wonders of life and a capacity for compassion are what makes a true 'human', rather than easily corrupted flesh and blood.

Despite *Blade Runner*'s eventual 'rehabilitation', truly thoughtful science fiction remains a rarity in the American cinema, any lingering ideas usually brushed aside to make way for high-tech spectacle. Notable exceptions to this rule include *Gattaca*, an intriguing if starchy excursion into *Brave New World* territory, and Terry Gilliam's *12 Monkeys* (1995), co-scripted by *Runner* veteran David Peoples. *Monkeys* is based on French film-maker Chris Marker's celebrated, if little-seen short *La Jetée*. The story involves reluctant time traveller Bruce Willis facing incomprehension and aggression over several decades, as he journeys back from the near future to determine the cause of an apocalyptic plague that drove mankind underground.

Probably still best known as the American *Monty Python* team member who did the weirdly inventive cut-out animations, Gilliam brought the same sense of surreal, flamboyant, often cruel fantasy to his early, British-made films. These included two sf themed movies far more English in feel than anything subsequently produced in this country. *Time Bandits* (1981), a dark juvenile fairytale in the very Grimm tradition, employs a uniquely theological form of time travel that would probably have infuriated the atheist H G Wells. God's overhasty creation of the universe in a mere seven days left gaping holes in the space-time fabric, through which the schoolboy hero and his dwarf companions can literally drop to encounter such historical and mythical figures as Napoleon, Agamemnon and

Former Monty Python member Terry Gilliam on the set of the nightmarish masterpiece Brazil (1985).

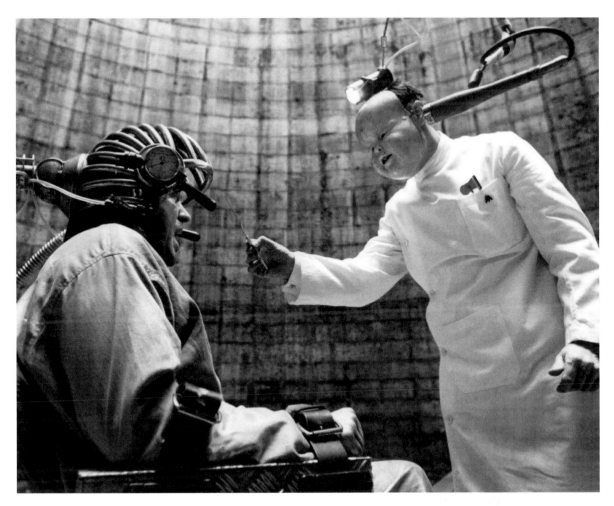

Robin Hood. John Cleese plays Robin Hood, in prime upperclass twit mode. The film also features a selection of giants, ogres, trolls, ultimate Evil and the Supreme Being himself.

The image of a knight on horseback charging out of the boy's wardrobe remains one of Gilliam's finest moments, conveying both the thrilled excitement and near terror that lie at the heart of all good fantasy. Brazil, by way of contrast, is an astonishingly confident, if overextended fusion of Walter Mitty, Franz Kafka and George Orwell, mixing 1940s-style fashions and trappings with the bleak, vicious and inefficient hardware and landscape of a futuristic dystopia. A minor clerical error leads hapless civil servant Jonathan Pryce into an inescapable, hallucinatory maze of totalitarian oppression, recurring fantasy, grotesque plastic surgery, forbidden freelance plumbing, terrorist sabotage, and the governmental torture chamber – manned by affable colleague Michael Palin. *Hitchhiker's Guide to the Galaxy* star Simon Jones turns up to issue a

wrongly arrested man's wife with a receipt as her husband is taken away for interrogation. Broken beyond repair in the final shot, Pryce is at least allowed to retreat into his dreamworld, probably permanently – which is more than Winston Smith was permitted. Gilliam's subsequent nightmarish production problems on his ultra-lavish fantasy *The Adventures of Baron Munchausen* (1988) forced him to seek gainful movie employment back in his native America, where his film career is now rooted.

Back in England, science fiction has remained a viable genre for homegrown movie talent (plus American finance), even if the end results are of varying quality. While plunges to the depths of *Fire Maidens from Outer Space* (1956) and *Saturn 3* (1980) are thankfully rare, ambition tends not to be equalled by achievement. (For the record, *Saturn 3* was scripted by novelist Martin Amis, something he should not be allowed to forget.) Director Paul Anderson aimed to create a Kubrick-inspired dystopia with *Shopping* (1994), a near-future parable of youth violence sold

Terry Gilliam's Brazil (1985) was much misunderstood and unfairly maligned on its original release. The film has since gained cult status.

Sam Neill pokes around inside the demon-haunted starship Event Horizon (1997).

as 'a *Clockwork Orange* for the 1990s'. Centring on rival gangs of shopfront ram-raiders, the film's determination to say something important in between the plate-glass demolitions worked against it. The depiction of ram-raiding as a pleasurable activity failed to provoke the hoped-for controversy and the film died at the box-office.

Shopping's most intriguing aspect is the presence of Sean Pertwee, son of Jon, as the major villain. Pertwee reappeared slightly further down the cast list in Anderson's big budget follow-up *Event Horizon* (1997). In the year 2047, the missing prototype spaceship *Event Horizon* mysteriously reappears off the planet Neptune after seven years, with no sign of the

gleaming white stasis pods and rapid-fire crew banter

crew. What the rescue team doesn't know is that the *Event Horizon* is a dimension jumping ship, capable of folding space-time with its revolutionary gravitational mechanism. A fine idea in principle, but the practice proves to be very messy. Headed by American Laurence Fishburne and New Zealander Sam Neill, the casting of *Event Horizon* is a careful *Alien*-style mix of ethnic, national and gender groups, seasoned professionals all. Fishburne's no-nonsense captain, hard but fair, clashes with Neill's uptight, secretive

scientist, who designed the lost ship and has something to hide, not least a series of unpleasantly vivid hallucinations.

There is more than a touch of Ridley Scott styling in evidence, *Event Horizon* offering the same dark, grubby, well-used space hardware, gleaming white stasis pods and rapid-fire crew banter as *Alien*. The ship itself recalls a grimed-up version of *2001*'s spaceship *Discovery*, replacing the computerised menace of HAL with a misguided dose of gothic horror. This increasingly absurd ghost-story element, dominated by Neill's visions of his dead, eyeless wife, invites unfavourable comparisons with *The Shining*, right down to the lake of blood. Homage is fine up to a point, but can only work if the movie has a discernible style and direction of its own. The dialogue, spoken with dogged professionalism rather than any real conviction, tends towards the overemphatic, notably Joely Richardson's memorable conversation killer: 'The black hole. The most destructive force in the universe. And you've created one.' The dreadful revelation is that the now sentient ship crossed over into a hellish Lovecraftian dimension of chaos and pure evil, returning to feed on the innermost fears of its new inhabitants. (Disney's 1979 sf flop *The Black Hole* also offered a metaphysical gateway to the afterlife, though at least the good guys were allowed a vaguely celestial hang-out.) The big theme is a confused retread of the old Dangerous Knowledge riff: mess with the laws of physics and it's gory splatter time. Established in the opening scenes as an intriguingly ambiguous figure, Dr Neill is reduced to nothing more than a bog-standard mad scientist, graphically eviscerating a medical colleague for no great reason. The best thing about the film is its title, named after the area of space around a black hole beyond which matter seems to disappear. Not to mention story sense.

Away from the big screen, the new generation of British science fiction novelists have wisely avoided the film industry's ragged attempts to ape Hollywood product. Ten years ago, all the innovative, vital literary science fiction seemed to originate from America, notably the 1980s 'Cyberpunk' movement established by William Gibson and Bruce Sterling, among others. Gibson's *Mona Lisa Overdrive* offered intelligent computers and cyber phantoms in conjunction with Oriental gangsters and the usual devious corporations, not to mention a Howard Hughes-style millionaire recluse. Sterling's *Schismatrix*, underpinned with a strong dose of moral philosophy, deserves cult status for its title alone.

In recent years, there has been a marked shift to the other side of the Atlantic. Malcolm Edwards, a publishing executive formerly in charge of Victor Gollancz's sf list, sees this change as little short of revolutionary: 'What's happened over the last five years has been truly amazing'. No longer looking to the US for its lead, British science fiction has found a new sense of identity, its influence spreading way beyond the country of origin. 'A whole group of writers has arrived in Britain who are taking over the sci fi world in kind of the same way as The Beatles took over the rock world.' Writers such as Iain M Banks, Steve Aylett, Roger Levy and Justina Robson have revitalised the genre. Banks's extraordinarily detailed, extremely plausible hi-tech alien cultures are widely regarded as the high watermark of current British science fiction. While the contributors to Michael Moorcock's 1960s *New Worlds* magazine often felt that the sf tag precluded recognition as a 'serious' writer, this new generation seem more or less happy with the label.

Steve Aylett, author of *Slaughtermatic*, *Bigot Hall* and *Toxicology* attaches little importance to his British roots, other than as something to react against. 'Everything that I've written... has been absolutely despite the fact that I was brought up in England.' Favouring American settings for the element of exaggeration, Aylett's sense of national identity manifests itself in fairly negative terms. 'It's just very,

very boring here... England is just so totally anti-imagination and anti-creative.' The ever-expanding information superhighway leaves him similarly unmoved: 'There's lavish access to completely useless information.' Following in the tradition of Jerry Cornelius's needle gun, Aylett's books feature a dazzling array of hand weapons, ranging from relatively self-explanatory drug-firing guns, through guns set for a particular ethnic group, to philosophy guns that enable the protagonists to deliver broadsides of existential argument. The zero approach gun requires the consent of the intended target to fire. *The Inflatable Volunteer* (1999), one of Aylett's most recent books, has something to do with a mayoral election campaign but functions largely as a relentlessly surreal jaunt through a violently hallucinatory universe. Despite the science fiction tag attached to his work, Aylett regards himself primarily as a satirist, in the tradition of Voltaire and Jonathan Swift, arguing nevertheless that 'satire has never had any effect on anything'. He views the current sf scene as fairly sterile, lacking in much needed brain protein. 'It's nice to have some ideas and some fertile stuff going on... a hundred ideas on each page.' A lot of genre output is empty and derivative: 'stillborn... dead meat... the lack of original thought is just spectacular... people are trying to suck plastic.' A truly imaginative book should explode the head of the reader in the best *Scanners* tradition (figuratively, one hopes). Feeling that the British education system is still designed to stifle true creativity and original thought, Aylett is unlikely to serve as a willing SF:UK standard bearer: 'I don't want Britain to take the credit.'

Roger Levy, whose debut novel *Reckless Sleep* deals with virtual reality and throws in a few spins on the *Blade Runner* formula, seems more optimistic about the science fiction scene. Citing the largely forgotten British author M P Shiel as an early influence, Levy sees UK sf as true speculative fiction, as opposed to the action-oriented gung ho fantasies favoured by American writers: 'Our science fiction is much more a fiction of ideas.' Four and a half years in the writing, *Reckless Sleep* underwent radical plot changes as Levy progressed. His take on VR is certainly well thought out. 'A good virtual reality is a little bit like a very, very strong cigarette': seductive, addictive and virtually impossible to give up.

Justina Robson, one of the few women writers currently involved in the British science fiction scene, made a striking debut with *Silver Screen* (1999), which deals with the ever hot topic of artificial intelligence. Having written for ten years, Robson drew rave reviews for her first published novel, not to mention a slightly ironic nomination for the high profile Arthur C Clarke Award. Robson admits to being inspired by 2001's credited co-author and his contemporaries, but in a way that probably wouldn't flatter them. 'I loved the ideas but I did not like the char-

the veteran cyberpunk couldn't make it across the Atlantic for the ceremony

acterisations in the stories.' Finding the narratives a little too slow and the protagonists superficial, she looked to the other side of the Atlantic for more dynamic sf storytelling. A big fan of the 1980s Cyberpunk movement, which she rated as 'really cool', Robson goes along with the general feeling that current American science fiction tends to be bold and forward looking. Meanwhile, the British variant prefers to explore greyer areas, usually veering into pitch blackness: 'things can go wrong and often do'. One of her favourite British practitioners is Iain M Banks, who possesses 'a wild, exciting imagination'.

Author Brian Aldiss reads from his novel Frankenstein Unbound *during a 1974 radio broadcast.*

Silver Screen is a similarly imaginative, highly inventive excursion into A-I territory, featuring a heroine, Anjuli O'Connell, whose gift of perfect recall is balanced by all-too-human frailties, her 'computer side' failing to make up for her perceived 'nerdiness'. Robson conceived the book partly as a reaction against the standard intelligent machines-revolt-against-man storyline. Much science fiction assumes that A-I lifeforms will inevitably share human traits, including the more unpleasant ones. *Silver Screen* takes a more subtle approach, one of its machines quite happy to get along with people while it pursues its own goals of self-development and survival. The mind of a machine is a closed book, completely unknowable to organic lifeforms. Identity and individuality, whether human, cyborg or a fusion of the two, are precious – if nebulous – things. As to artificial intelligence becoming a reality in the foreseeable future, Robson remains sceptical: 'I think it's possible but it's probably not very likely.'

Making a pointed distinction between 'true' science fiction, with its basis in possibility, and outright science fantasy, the judges for the 1999 Arthur C Clarke Award were full of praise for the nominated books. The chairman argued that all six shortlisted novels 'use science fiction to address complex and difficult questions that perhaps could be addressed in no other genre', a perfect fusion of medium and message. In the event, the prize went to Bruce Sterling's novel *Distraction*, though the veteran cyberpunk couldn't make it across the Atlantic for the ceremony. Justina Robson had to be content with a glowing testimony for her novel: '*Silver Screen* contemplates what it is that makes us who we are in a world where the human can meld with, and be altered by, the machine, and an artificial intelligence can lay claim to an autonomous existence.'

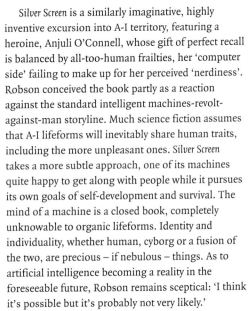

RETURN TO THE PAST

Given that Herbert George Wells touched on just about every major science fiction theme during his hugely prolific writing career, it's arguable that all subsequent sf has simply followed in his wake, updating, reworking and subverting Wells's basic themes with varying degrees of imagination and accomplishment.

The only way to beat the Wells connection is to go even further back in time to Mary Shelley's man-made creature, still a prime source for wildly divergent forms of science fiction. One of the most popular post-Karloff reworkings of the *Frankenstein* myth in America was the hit television series *The*

Six Million Dollar Man (1972-78), where plucky NASA pilot Colonel Steve Austin (Lee Majors) is critically injured when his spacecraft crashes during re-entry into the earth's atmosphere. As the narration over the opening credits puts it: 'Steve Austin ... astronaut ... man barely alive ... gentlemen, we can rebuild him ... we have the technology.'

As Stephen Jones points out, once restored to working order with a 'bionic' arm, legs and eye, this superbeing is also a troubleshooting superhero, far from the raging, patchwork creature of Mary Shelley's novel (Martin Caidin's source novel, Cyborg, is not so clear cut). Mary Shelley and her creature shared screen billing once more in the largely inconsequential Frankenstein Unbound (1990), cult schlockmeister Roger Corman's return to the director's chair after a twenty-year absence. The plot is freely adapted from British writer Brian Aldiss's 1973 novel, where former US presidential advisor Joe Bodenland is transported from 2020 'New Houston' to 1816 Geneva via a rupture in the space-time continuum, caused by bad old nuclear warfare. Frankenstein turns out to be a real person, less than delighted at Mary Shelley's PR job, and Bodenland gets to screw the budding young author (what would Percy Bysshe say?). The monster's previously frustrated primitive urges are also satisfied, with a purpose built female creature: 'It was a brief and brutal mating'. Acclaimed novelist Kingsley Amis rated the book 'a triumph', but then he also liked Michael Winner's 1983 remake of The Wicked Lady. Bridget Fonda's Mary Shelley lacks the quiet intensity of previous screen incarnations Elsa Lanchester (Bride of Frankenstein), Natasha Richardson (Gothic), Alice Krige (Haunted Summer) and Liz McInnerny (Rowing With the Wind). Roger Corman, who also co-wrote the script, fails to recapture the luridly stylish, borderline camp necrophiliac decadence of his 1960s Edgar Allan Poe series. However, for seekers of macabre novelty, the film does feature the late INXS frontman Michael Hutchence as Percy Shelley.

The British alien invasion tradition, passed down through such venerable hands as Wells, Nigel Kneale and Doctor Who, found a dubious 1990s home in the big budget sf thriller Invasion: Earth (1998), a six part series co-produced by the BBC with the Sci-Fi channel (another sign of changing times). Once again, science and the military join forces to combat an alien menace when the Earth gets caught up in an interstellar firefight. Clearly packaged with a view to overseas sales (especially over the Atlantic) the series threw in an American co-star, the normally reliable Fred Ward, who had most reviewers pining for Brian

Donlevy. Writer-producer was Jed Mercurio, previously acclaimed for the pseudonymously penned high-impact hospital drama Cardiac Arrest. Mercurio was perhaps setting himself up for a fall when he told Cult TV magazine: 'This isn't Blake's 7 – it's genuinely cinematic. We're aiming for the scope and style of the Terminator and Alien movies.' What they ended up with bore more resemblance to Independence Day and Predator, cinematic fare of a slightly different calibre.

Having made a few more pointed references to 'tea-time' British science fiction television, characterised by ropy effects and tongue-in-cheek acting, Mercurio put himself square in the line of laser fire. 'If you treat an audience with intelligence, you can make something special. With Invasion: Earth we're drawing a line under all the British science fiction that's gone before.' All Mercurio had delivered by the end of part six was a series of indifferent, if elaborate special effects, cliché dialogue and lousy acting. Hoping for an X Files-style sf hit with wide mainstream appeal, the producers of Invasion: Earth ended up with an embarrassing flop on the Space: 1999 level. Maybe British science fiction and big budgets just don't mix these days, the demands of the international marketplace largely ironing out the genre's distinctive qualities.

Speaking of teatime science fiction, Doctor Who continued for another eight years after Tom Baker's 1981 departure, albeit in slightly uncertain fashion. Having worked on the show in various capacities since the 1969 Patrick Troughton story The Space Pirates, new producer John Nathan-Turner demonstrated obvious affection for Doctor Who without appearing to understand what had made it a success. Tom Baker argues that the show isn't really science fiction at all, which contains more than an element of truth. Along with The Avengers, Doctor Who is fantasy that uses science fiction trappings, such as the central time-travel concept, often in fairly cavalier fashion. Perhaps reacting against the humorous style initiated by Douglas Adams, Nathan-Turner attempted to transform the show into pure science fiction, employing hardcore genre writers such as Steve Gallagher and Christopher H Bidmead. Bearing such self-consciously esoteric titles as Castrovalva, Kinda and Enlightenment, the resulting stories were invariably interesting, but rarely clicked as drama. Nathan-Turner didn't seem to be the best judge of casting, either, saddling Tom Baker with a job lot of rather dull companions, then hiring the decidedly non mysterious or bizarre Peter Davison to take his place. There was also a little too much trading on the show's past glories, going far beyond the accepted tradition of resurrecting old foes like the Cybermen and Daleks. The increasingly portly Brigadier Lethbridge-Stewart returned for not one but three guest appearances (*Mawdryn Undead*; *The Five Doctors*; *Battlefield*), and both Patrick Troughton and Frazer Hines rejoined the show 15 years after they quit for the 1984 Colin Baker story *The Two Doctors*.

Colin Baker, a capable actor seriously hampered by a self-consciously garish wardrobe, seemed too arrogant and egotistical for wide audience appeal, though several of his early stories were superior to

a nonsensical reference to the Master being executed on the Dalek planet of Skaro

the bulk of the Davison era. Taking a good amount of uncredited inspiration from Evelyn Waugh's 1947 novel *The Loved One*, *Revelation of the Daleks* is dark, ghoulish, blackly amusing and unashamedly violent, Davros getting half his remaining hand messily blown off in the climactic showdown.

Sylvester McCoy, Colin Baker, Peter Davison and Jon Pertwee – Doctors number seven, six, five and three – celebrating the thirtieth anniversary of Doctor Who's first transmission in 1993.

Memorable new characters included the reptilian alien Sil, a leering, legless lump of slimy green malice.

Brought to an undignified halt in 1989 during Sylvester McCoy's underappreciated tenure, *Doctor Who* has survived in various new forms, none of them terribly impressive. Jon Pertwee, Nicholas Courtney and Elizabeth Sladen reprised their 1970s characters for a pair of Radio 4 serials, scripted by ex-producer Barry Letts. The long awaited *Doctor Who: The (Made for Television) Movie* finally appeared in 1996. Paul McGann played the lead, after a flurry of casting rumours that included such varied talents as Alan Rickman, *Star Trek* veteran Leonard Nimoy and *Baywatch* star David Hasselhoff.

Having struck a co-production deal with Fox, the BBC opted to shoot their lavish tv movie in Canada, a traditional location for cost-cutting American film and television production. Sylvester McCoy agreed to a brief reprisal of Doctor number seven, brutally gunned down in front of his own TARDIS early on.

Bearing a passing resemblance to nineteenth-century renaissance man Percy Bysshe Shelley, Paul McGann scored more on earnest conviction than otherworldly charisma. The plot is fast-moving but bland, a conventional end-of-the-world science fiction adventure with an

insurmountably underwhelming finale. Moreover, the new look *Doctor Who* barely related to the original series, a nonsensical reference to the Master being executed on the Dalek planet of Skaro suggesting a cursory flick through a *Who* reference book rather than any in-depth appreciation of the show's history. While the cavernous TARDIS control room is a creation undreamed of by the BBC design department circa 1963, it counts for little when the script seems desperately anxious to go somewhere else more American-friendly. McCoy's cameo appearance is by far the best thing in the show, his poignant performance hinting at what could have been had the BBC shown more faith during his era.

Charting the slow, troubled progress of new *Doctor Who* 'movies' has become a mini-industry in itself. On past form, any new *Doctor Who* will most likely fall way short of fan expectations. As *Guardian* journalist Adam Sweeting pointed out: 'The recent Hollywoodisations of *The Saint* and *The Avengers* are two perfect specimens of the way the wit, whimsy and campness of the originals has evaporated by the time they're uncrated out on the West Coast.' Whatever becomes of further film ventures, BBC Radio 4 plans to resurrect the Doctor one more time in the shape of Sylvester McCoy, accompanied by regular companion Sophie Aldred and Stephen Fry, surely the first occasion the Time Lord has been revived in an incarnation previously riddled with bullets.

Reviving cult British sf television shows in updated, restyled and recast film versions is a perilous business at best. There is no better example of the downside than Warner Bros's *The Avengers* (1998), starring Ralph Fiennes and Uma Thurman as John Steed and Emma Peel. Directed by Jeremiah Chechik, whose previous credits included a poor American remake of Henri-Georges Clouzot's landmark thriller *Les Diaboliques*, the film is a textbook example of commercially driven bastardisation. Chechik, a declared fan of the original show, promised to stay faithful to its spirit while upping the action-adventure element, 'so kids will buy into it'. When an $80 million film intended as a major studio's big summer release runs for a scant 89 minutes, either the makers have their material pared to the bone or there was some serious post-production tinkering. With *The Avengers*, the latter quickly proved to be the case, despite fierce denials from Warner. After reputedly disastrous previews in America, the studio lost all confidence in their film and performed a radical re-edit, removing most of the opening half hour, including a lot of fairly vital background information. As one

reviewer put it: 'Where's Robert Fuest now we really need him?'

Given this track record, it's perhaps not too great a tragedy that the projected live action film version of *Thunderbirds* has yet to materialise. Put into development by Polygram and Working Title Films, the project initiated endless casting rumours – the Baldwin brothers William, Alec, Daniel and Stephen as the Tracy clan, Joanna Lumley as Lady Penelope,

Paul McGann played the eighth Doctor in an American-produced TV movie, simply titled Doctor Who, in 1996. Intended as a pilot for a new series, the film was popular in the UK but failed to find an audience in the United States.

Kristin Scott-Thomas as Lady Penelope, Bob Hoskins as Parker, Rowan Atkinson as Brains – but little of real substance. Even after the effects laden script had been scaled down to reduce the projected £55 million budget, the film stayed on the launching pad. It's worth bearing in mind that Gerry Anderson's own 1960s attempts to take *Thunderbirds* to the big screen in Technicolor and Techniscope, *Thunderbirds Are Go* (1967) and *Thunderbird Six* (1968), met with less than roaring success – despite the inclusion of Martian rock snakes, the voice of Bob Monkhouse and puppet versions of Cliff Richard and The Shadows singing the specially written 'Shooting Star'.

THE ABYSS BENEATH THE MANICURED LAWN

In science fiction fantasy, as in most other genres, cynical recycling of past successes rarely produces watchable, let alone notable, results. While many a hit film has inspired a spinoff television show, ranging in quality and longevity from *MASH* through *Alien Nation* to

John Steed (Ralph Fiennes) and Emma Peel (Uma Thurman) in the ill-fated big-screen version of The Avengers (1998).

Casablanca (with David Soul as Rick, god help us), it's fairly rare for a flop movie lacking even token cult status to inspire a small screen sequel that is not only successful but markedly superior to the original. Step forward *Buffy the Vampire Slayer*. Scripted by Joss Whedon, the original 1992 film starred Kristy Swanson as a West Coast Valley Girl forced to swap cheerleading for undead combat duties. A serious horror fan, Whedon had grown tired of seeing women depicted as helpless, expendable victims. Though no intellectual heavyweight, Buffy had one undeniable virtue: 'For once, she was stronger than the monster.' Hammer horror would meet a young, insolent All-American girl and come off worst. Buffy's tutor in slaying, the Rupert Giles prototype savant Merrick (Donald Sutherland), was clearly based on Peter Cushing's Van Helsing, impatient with his reluctant pupil's marked lack of scholarly aptitude. Unfortunately, much of Whedon's vision fell by the wayside in the finished product, which he more or less disowns. Despite the presence of co-stars Sutherland and Rutger Hauer, not to mention pin-up boy Luke Perry, the film faded from public view with barely a whimper. Five years later, Whedon persuaded original backer Twentieth Century-Fox to revive the format on the small screen. This time, the blend of supernatural menace and teen angst clicked, Buffy worrying about peer group pressure between the stakings. If only she'd listen to Whedon's sage advice: 'There is no actual normal person out there.'

In truth, *Buffy the Vampire Slayer* draws mainly on the Gothic horror tradition, though a number of episodes feature borderline science fiction elements. In one story, an unscrupulous school swimming coach subjects his champion team to a steroid treatment that turns them into vicious reptilian killers. Partial to quoting from Shakespeare's *Richard III* ('Now is the winter of our discontent...'), Joss Whedon cites Anne Rice's bestselling supernatural romance *Interview With the Vampire* as a major early influence, though some of the consequences have been less than welcome: 'People are always trying to take my picture in graveyards and things.' Partly educated at Winchester College, England, Whedon's tastes in British television tended more towards surreal comedy (*Monty Python*, *Ripping Yarns*) and historical drama (*I Claudius*) than the likes of *Doctor Who*, which he viewed only intermittently.

Despite the non-stop flow of witty adolescent quips, Whedon sees *Buffy* as a fundamentally downbeat show: 'the series is based on the premise that the entire world is horrible', evil lurking 'under the surface of every manicured lawn.... Sometimes the consequences of defeating evil can eat you up from the inside.' The monsters bite the dust but the demonic menace is never ending. 'The abyss has always got to be gazing back into you or the story doesn't really mean very much.' Mr Giles aside, the series line-up includes a strong British contingent, including the Mockney vampire couple Spike and Druscilla, described by Whedon as 'the Sid and Nancy of the vampire set'. Druscilla is a homage to his boyhood favourite *I Claudius*, named after the incestuous Emperor Caligula Caesar's sister-lover. If nothing else, the show depicts teen angst as literally a monster phase. As Stephen Jones points out, *Buffy*'s main achievement is to reinvent the old monsters for a new generation. Taken at face value, Whedon's worldview is as bleak and dystopian as anything dreamed up by Mary Shelley, H G Wells and their successors: 'I have a tendency to see life as a terrible, horrible, appalling experience'. Anyone who can survive the all-pervasive darkness is a hero.

The low-born hero of *Gattaca* (1997) is not content with mere survival, his second-class status dictating a lifetime of drab, mind-numbing menial jobs. Written and directed by Andrew Niccol, the film revisits Huxley's *Brave New World*, depicting a future society where people are rated from birth as either Valid or In-Valid according to the 'purity' of their genes. The socio-economic class divide is still alive and well, the inevitable consequence of selective genetic engineering. Only Valids can rise to the top of the social hierarchy, the Gattaca corporation. At least Huxley offered five grades of human categorisation, from Alpha to Epsilon, rather than a straight all-or-nothing. Refusing to accept his preordained lowly status, In-Valid Vincent Freeman (Ethan Hawke) illegally buys the identity of an embittered, paraplegic Valid in the form of regular supplies of the DNA perfect blood, hair and urine required to pass routine genetic check-ups. Given his fierce determination to meet the coldly clinical standards of this world, Freeman's dream of being selected for the Gattaca space travel programme does not seem so outlandish.

Intelligent and well-crafted, *Gattaca*'s determinedly muted, low key style renders the plot strangely dreamlike, intriguing rather than involving. The film opens with close-up shots of nail parings falling to the floor in slow motion as Vincent goes through his daily cleansing ritual, removing all readily detectable traces of his In-Valid self. Despite the ever-present risk of Freeman's true status being discovered, plus a sub-plot involving the brutal murder of a Gattaca

Irene Cassini (Uma Thurman) in Andrew Niccol's Brave New World thriller Gattaca (1997).

executive, there is little in the way of dramatic impetus. At one point, the chronically short-sighted Freeman, having lost a taboo contact lens, is forced to cross a busy road virtually blind, the traffic streaking by like a 2001-style light show. Niccol subsequently scripted *The Truman Show*, where affable middle-American Truman Burbank (Jim Carrey) goes through his unremarkable daily routine unaware that his entire life has been staged for a docu-soap television programme (the old Orwellian surveillance theme). Though by no means as audience-friendly, *Gattaca*'s meditation on the nature of 'true' identity is

There is no actual normal person out there

perhaps more unsettling. In both cases, Niccol gives his lead characters highly significant names – Freeman, Tru(e)man – that signify their ultimate goal in the unfolding story.

In *Gattaca* the spirit of Aldous Huxley is alive and well, though hardly playing to packed houses. But few British-made science fiction films of recent years have aspired to such intellectual heights. *Invasion*

Earth aside, home grown sf has fared rather better on the small screen, nearly fifty years after Professor Bernard Quatermass first materialised on flickering, low-tech television sets. *The Last Train* (1999), devised and scripted by Matthew Graham, is in the tradition of *Survivors* and *Threads*, well achieved apocalyptic science fiction involving a train crash, a large asteroid, suspended animation and a mysterious Government outfit known as the Ark. The central group, all passengers aboard the titular vehicle, is nothing if not mixed, including a stuffy white policeman, a cool black criminal, an Asian woman fleeing her violent, now long dead husband and a tight-lipped scientist who, initially at least, knows a lot more than she's telling. The dystopian trappings are an evocative, if familiar blend of barren landscapes, technological ruins, acid rain and savage scavenger dogs, only the mysteriously lush plant life providing any sense of renewal. Set in a very desolate Northern England, *The Last Train* was made by Carlton for the largely unadventurous ITV network, whose 1960s fantasy heyday of *The Avengers*, *Thunderbirds* and *The Prisoner* is long gone (it says something that these still-popular shows are now rerun by Channel 4 and BBC2).

Though hardly in the same league as these series, either in terms of potential icon status or popular appeal, *The Last Train* is a highly creditable effort. Graham's script follows in the H G Wells and John Wyndham tradition, using the central cataclysmic breakdown of society to explore the tensions, friendships, hostilities and moral choices within the group of survivors as they try to adjust to a perilous existence utterly different to their past life. Like

The undead are generous investors in cutting-edge medical research

Threads, *The Last Train* ends with the birth of a child, only this time around it's a sign of muted optimism amidst the general sense of resigned despair.

The previous year's *Ultraviolet* (1998) is a little more ambitious, reworking the time honoured vampire formula into a chic, twentysomething sf thriller that aims for an American-style gloss. Reminiscent of *The X Files* and *Invasion of the Body Snatchers* rather than *Buffy the Vampire Slayer*, this six-part serial was made by World Productions for Channel 4, who flogged it to (un)death without getting the desired mass audience. Producer-director Joe Ahearne had previously worked on the BBC's surprise hit drama *This Life*, an everyday saga of

backstabbing and infidelity in the legal profession that didn't need to look beyond the grave for its bloodsuckers. This time around, *Life* star Jack Davenport is cast in the lead role of a former policeman inducted into a secret society of slayers when his best friend unexpectedly turns vampire on him after an otherwise successful stag night. The vampire hunting is co-ordinated by a covert international organisation controlled from the Vatican (a premise also employed for John Carpenter's more lively *Vampires* 1998). Davenport's grimly professional colleagues are a dour former priest (Philip Quast), whose terminal illness makes the chance of eternal life a tempting proposition, and an uptight female scientist (Susannah Harker) who signed on after her husband perished at the hands, and teeth, of these stylish undead. Davenport is well tooled-up with a custom-made handgun that enables him to identify the perfectly normal looking vampires through a special viewer. However, he seems more preoccupied with his undead and gone friend's understandably puzzled fiancée, a tiresome subplot that results in a risible series finale. The background details are sometimes more interesting than the main narrative. The word 'vampire' is never used, the characters referring only to 'Code V', and only those who desire the 'gift' of vampirism will be inducted into the ranks. Stakes and oversized canines are similarly absent and the vanquished undead, reduced to powder form, are stored away in sealed metal containers, still capable of resurrection. Employing a resolutely deadpan approach, *Ultraviolet* has its share of sly humour, one character ruefully lamenting his inability to catch the undead on film or videotape: 'Surveillance is a bitch'.

Driving around in black cars with tinted windows, the vampires have no problems with daylight mobility, though direct exposure to the sun still means heavy duty frying. Aiming for world domination, the undead are generous investors in cutting edge medical research, particularly blood-related diseases such as leukemia, eager to keep their nutrition source fresh and healthy. In its determination to avoid cliché and reinvent the vampire saga for the *X-Files* generation, *Ultraviolet* seems a little uncertain where it's heading. Feeling that the standard vampire myth appealed primarily to teenage boys hungry for some hot'n'heavy sexual subtext, Ahearne attempted to work on a different level without quite achieving the desired Nigel Kneale blend of otherworldly threat, scientific probing, impending human apocalypse and veiled social commentary. Many reviewers dismissed the heavily plugged show as a derivative *X Files* clone, with portentous dialogue, low key performances, a glib sf redressing of supernatural themes and, in the Harker character, a straight copy of Gillian Anderson's moody, coldly efficient medical investigator. The slick, confident style of *Ultraviolet* couldn't quite mask the fact that its inventive, largely gripping storyline had nowhere much to go once the basic premise had been established in the early episodes. At its strongest, however, *Ultraviolet* convincingly demonstrates that British science fiction remains good for more than ironic homage or outright pastiche.

The ongoing conflict between man and socially adept vampire in *Ultraviolet* suggests that the SF:UK tradition of pessimistic, dystopian visions is alive and well, in its morbid fashion. The futuristic hardware on display is geared towards the preservation rather than the enhancement of the beleaguered human species, developed as a direct response to the ever-present undead menace. This conception of techno-magic as a defensive tool against hostile outside forces goes all the way back to *The Tempest*, where the castaway Prospero uses his Gnostic studies to become ruler of his barren island home and, in time, settle old scores. Once this is achieved, the magic is discarded with few regrets, Prospero looking forward to a quiet, stressfree retirement. Unusually for British science fiction, Shakespeare's play has an unconditionally happy ending. Even the brutish, treacherous Caliban is tamed and forgiven. Far from being a reckless over-reacher into the realm of the spirits and sorcery, the ever-pragmatic Duke of Milan knows where to draw the line. Lacking Prospero's cool objectivity, most of his successors do not – until it's far, far too late.

When Prospero destroyed his staff and book – the symbols of his learning and supernatural power – he set a precedent for future seekers after hidden knowledge. Plucked from the icy wastes of the Arctic, cursed monster-maker Victor Frankenstein begs his rescuers not to look beyond their mundane, everyday lives for elusive, danger-ridden exploration and revelation. Dr Henry Jekyll would surely have been better off if he'd left the potions alone and stayed content with the comfortable life of the wealthy Victorian hypocrite. H G Wells's chronicles of scientific investigation and alien encounters suggest that the marvels of both the universe and the human mind cannot be explored without the risk of extreme, even apocalyptic danger. This sentiment is echoed in the works of Nigel Kneale. Human curiosity and ambition will not be denied, however, whether in the realm of space exploration or artificial intelligence.

The lunar research team in *2001: A Space Odyssey* gathers around the newly-excavated four-million-year-old monolith as eagerly as their ape-like ancestors, posing for pictures before tentatively making the first hands-on contact. HAL, described by a patronising BBC interviewer as 'the latest result in machine intelligence', regards the 9000 computer series as a marked improvement on its human designers. 'We are all, by any practical definition of the words, foolproof and incapable of error.'

While the 1960s realisation of many age-old science fiction dreams did not extend to superintelligent computers, the ensuing decades have brought the concept closer to reality. In 1997, World

Kasparov promptly accused IBM of foul play

Chess Champion Gary Kasparov agreed to pit his wits against IBM's Deep Blue chess program, which proceeded to beat Kasparov over a six-game series. Not the most gracious of losers, Kasparov promptly accused IBM of foul play, claiming that Deep Blue's pre-programmed game strategy had been supplemented by illicit 'off-line' human input. While this man-versus-machine encounter was not the life-or-death struggle depicted in *2001*'s Bowman-HAL conflict, it reflects the deeply-ingrained ambivalence towards the possibility of artificial Frankenstein-style lifeforms, capable of independent reasoning, that will not only equal but surpass their masters.

Fear of the creations of human intellect lies somewhere at the heart of British sf. Prospero threatens Ariel with tree-bound imprisonment 'till thou hast howl'd away twelve winters', when the spirit shows insufficient servility, requesting his freedom two days early. Victor Frankenstein is appalled at the idea of the human race being challenged for supremacy over the earth by a new 'devil' species spawned by his creature. H G Wells famously described history as a race between education and catastrophe. Professor Quatermass's rocket succeeds only in bringing back something horrible from outer space. Stanley Kubrick went so far as to question the long-term value of intelligence to human survival. Joss Whedon talks of an abyss beneath the manicured lawn. Human intelligence and the scientific culture it has spawned bring material prosperity and mastery of the environment, but at the price of opening a Pandora's box of possibilities and dangers. This theme is the territory which British sf has always claimed as its own. It's a theme that remains potent as the twenty-first century begins to unfold.

SCIENCE FACT
TIME CHART

Year:

1543 Nicolaus Copernicus's *De Revolutionibus Orbium Coelestium*, published in the year of his death, argues that the sun, not the earth, is the centre of the solar system.

1608 The telescope.

1609 The microscope.

1620 The underwater boat.

1628 William Harvey demonstrates the circulation of the blood.

1632 Galileo Galilei publishes *Dialogues on the Two Chief Systems of the World*, which develops the case for a heliocentric solar system.

1685 Isaac Newton publishes his universal law of gravitation.

1762 Luigi Galvani discovers voltaic, or galvanic, electricity.

1783 Human flight achieved by the Montgolfier brothers in a hot-air balloon.

1790 Photograms, a forerunner of photography, reproduce images on leather sensitised with silver nitrate.

1826 The first photograph of a natural setting, using pewter plates, a *camera obscura* and a very long exposure time (eight hours).

1835 Charles Babbage conceives a mechanical computer.

1841 Fox Talbot introduces the Calotype, a multi-copy method of photography.

1846 Anaesthetic is employed for the first successful operation on an unconscious patient.

1876 Alexander Graham Bell invents the telephone.

1877 The Praxinoscope, a forerunner of the modern film projector.

1883 Francis Galton introduces the term 'eugenics', Greek for 'well-born', promoting the idea of selective breeding for both physical and mental strength.

1887 Photographic sky charts.

1888 The submersible torpedo boat, or submarine. William Friese-Green projects celluloid motion pictures. Emile Berliner invents the disc record.

1900 Planck initiates the development of Quantum Physics.

1901 Marconi oversees the successful transmission and reception of a radio broadcast.

1903 Powered flight (The Wright brothers).

1905 Corneal grafting, the first successful human transplant procedure. Einstein's Special Theory of Relativity.

1906 Transmission of primitive television pictures. Danish geneticist Wilhelm Johannsen devises the term 'gene'.

1910 Einstein's General Theory of Relativity.

1926 The liquid fuel rocket. John Logie Baird demonstrates the first practical television broadcast system. Quantum Physics: Heisenberg's Uncertainty Principle.

1930 The jet engine.

1932 The electron microscope.

1940 Research into nuclear fission for military use.

1943 The electronic computer.

1945 The atom bomb is used in warfare.

1947 The term 'flying saucer' is coined.

1948 Supersonic flight.

1952 The first hydrogen bomb is detonated.

1954 The nuclear-powered submarine.

1957 The space satellite (*Sputnik 1*).

1960 Oral contraceptive pill introduced to UK.

1961 Manned spaceflight (*Vostok 1*). The *Telstar* communications satellite transmits a live television picture between the United States and Europe. Watson, Crick and Wilkins receive Nobel Prize for discovery of DNA genetic code. The *Venera 3* space probe crashlands on Venus, the first man-made object to reach another planet. *Intelligent Life in the Universe* (IS Shklovskii and Carl Sagan).

1967 The human heart transplant.

1969 The moon-landing and moon-walk (*Apollo II*).

1971 The orbital space station (*Salyut 1*).

1972 The first voyage beyond the solar system (*Pioneer 10*).

1975 The microcomputer. The *Viking 1* probe lands on Mars.

1980s Chaos Theory developed by Lorenz, Feigenbaum and others. The IBM Personal Computer. HIV virus identified.

1985 Powerful computer software fully reveals the Mandelbrot Set. *A Brief History of Time* (Stephen Hawking). *Voyager 2* reaches Neptune.

1990 A new, genetically engineered strain of mouse is patented in the United States.

1990s Exponential growth of the Internet. Beginnings of Nanotechnology. Evidence of Global Warming discussed and debated internationally.

2000 Cloning of human embryos for research purposes legalised in UK.

SF:UK
TIME CHART

Year	Literature	Film	TV/Stage/Radio/Comics/Albums
c 1611	The Tempest		
1726	Gulliver's Travels		
1818	Frankenstein		
1823			Presumption; or, The Fate of Frankenstein (S)
1886	The Strange Case of Dr Jekyll and Mr Hyde		
1895	The Time Machine		
1896	The Island of Dr Moreau		
1897	The Invisible Man		
1898	The War of the Worlds		
1901	The First Men in the Moon		
1920		Dr Jekyll and Mr Hyde	
1923			R.U.R. (S)
1930	Last and First Men		
1931		Frankenstein	
1932	Brave New World	Dr Jekyll and Mr Hyde Island of Lost Souls	
1933	The Shape of Things to Come	The Invisible Man	
1935	Odd John	Bride of Frankenstein	
1936		Things to Come	
1937	Star Maker		
1938			The War of the Worlds (R)

R.U.R.

Frankenstein

Dan Dare

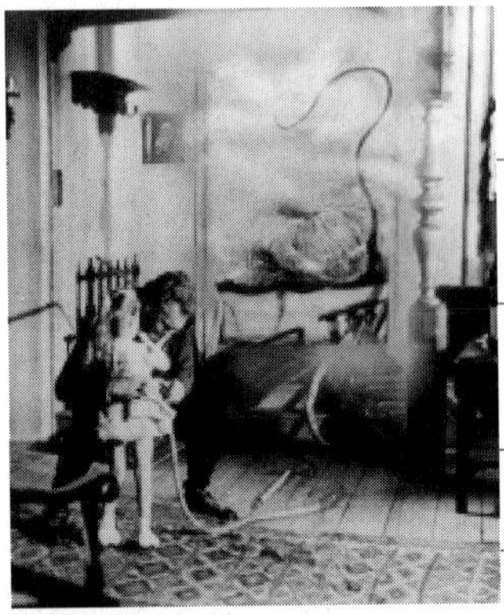

The Trollenberg Terror

The Day the Earth Caught Fire

Dr. Strangelove

Year	Literature	Film	TV/Stage/Radio/Comics/Albums
1941		Dr Jekyll and Mr Hyde	
1949	1984	The Perfect Woman	
1950	'The Sentinel'		Dan Dare, The Eagle (C)
1951	The Day of the Triffids	The Man in the White Suit	
1953	The City and the Stars	The War of the Worlds Spaceways Four Sided Triangle	The Quatermass Experiment (TV)
1954	Childhood's End		1984 (TV) Journey into Space (R)
1955	Moonraker The Lord of the Rings	The Quatermass Xperiment	Quatermass II (TV)
1956	The Death of Grass	Forbidden Planet	
1957	The Midwich Cuckoos	The Curse of Frankenstein Quatermass 2	
1958		The Revenge of Frankenstein X the Unknown The Trollenberg Terror	Quatermass and the Pit (TV)
1960		The Time Machine The Two Faces of Dr Jekyll	
1961		The Day the Earth Caught Fire	Supercar (TV) The Avengers (TV)
1962	A Clockwork Orange The Drowned World Hothouse	The Day of the Triffids	
1963		The Damned	Doctor Who (TV) Fireball XL5 (TV)
1964	Michael Moorcock takes New Worlds editorial chair	First Men in the Moon The Evil of Frankenstein Dr. Strangelove, or: How I Learned to Stop Worrying and Love the Bomb Goldfinger Carry On Spying	Stingray (TV)
1965		Thunderball	Thunderbirds (TV) The War Game (TV)

Year	Literature	Film	TV/Stage/Radio/Comics/Albums
1966	The Crystal World	Carry On Screaming	Adam Adamant Lives! (TV)
1967		Frankenstein Created Woman Quatermass and the Pit You Only Live Twice Thunderbirds Are Go!	The Prisoner (TV)
1968	Stand on Zanzibar	2001: A Space Odyssey	Captain Scarlet and the Mysterons (TV) Joe 90 (TV)
1969	The Final Programme Behold the Man Barefoot in the Head	Doppelganger Moon Zero Two Frankenstein Must Be Destroyed On Her Majesty's Secret Service	Eagle cancelled (C) Year of the Sex Olympics (TV) UFO (TV)
1970	The Atrocity Exhibition Indoctrinaire	I, Monster THX 1138	
1971		Diamonds Are Forever Dr Jekyll and Sister Hyde	
1972	Fugue for a Darkening Island	A Clockwork Orange	The Stone Tape (TV) The Six Million Dollar Man (TV)
1973	Crash Rendezvous with Rama	Frankenstein: The True Story Flesh for Frankenstein The Final Programme Zardoz Sleeper Live and Let Die	The Rocky Horror Show (S)
1974	The Inverted World	Frankenstein and the Monster From Hell	Space: 1999 (TV)
1975		Tommy The Rocky Horror Picture Show	Survivors (TV) The Night That Panicked America (TV)
1976		The Man Who Fell to Earth	Into Infinity (TV) Action (C)
1977	The Condition of Muzak	Victor Frankenstein The Spy Who Loved Me Star Wars The Island of Dr Moreau	2000AD (C)

Joe 90

Zardoz

Year	Literature	Film	TV/Stage/Radio/Comics/Albums
1978	Gloriana	Jubilee	Blake's 7 (TV) Hitchhiker's Guide to the Galaxy (R) War of the Worlds (A)
1979	God's World	Time After Time Moonraker Alien	Quatermass (TV)
1980	The Gardens of Delight Moreau's Other Island		Brave New World (TV)
1981		Time Bandits	
1982	2010: Odyssey Two Chekhov's Journey	Blade Runner Halloween III: Season of the Witch	V for Vendetta (C) Threads (TV)
1984	The Wasp Factory	1984 The Terminator	
1985	Walking On Glass	Brazil	Edge of Darkness (TV)
1986		Gothic	Watchmen (C)
1987	The Handmaid's tale	Prince of Darkness	
1988		Haunted Summer	Red Dwarf (TV)
1989	Unquenchable Fire	Rowing With the Wind	
1982	The Child Garden The Course of the Heart	Frankenstein Unbound	
1993	Body of Glass		
1994	Vurt The Crime Studio	Mary Shelley's Frankenstein Judge Dredd Shopping	
1996	The Calcutta Chromosome Slaughtermatic	The Island of Dr Moreau Mars Attacks! Crash Event Horizon Gattaca	Doctor Who – The Movie (TV) The Quatermass Memoirs (R)
1998		Gods and Monsters The Avengers	Ultraviolet (TV) Invasion: Earth (TV)
1999	Silver Screen The Inflatable Volunteer		The Last Train (TV)

Blake's 7

Mary Shelley's Frankenstein

INDEX